Intersectional Feminist Readings of Comics

Intersectional Feminist Readings of Comics collects theoretically informed close readings of comics and graphic literature that apply an intersectional feminist lens to the interpretation of multiple contemporary North American graphic narratives.

The essays use a range of interpretive lenses drawn from theoretical models in contemporary aesthetics, media studies, and literary criticism to analyze mainstream figures like DC's Catwoman and Marvel's Miss America and Doctor Strange, to contextualize historical and speculative comics by Indigenous American illustrators, and to explicate autography by critically lauded Jewish, queer, and female cartoonists. In the first half of the book, the chapters examine ways in which superhero comics, and the cinematic and televisual adaptations thereof, reify, revise, and reject gender parity, systemic misogyny, and heteropatriarchy through visual and textual rhetorics of representation. In the second part of the volume, the chapters look at the ways that feminist interpretive practices illuminate the radical work undertaken by cartoonists from historically marginalized communities in the US and Canada. Across both halves, readers will find applications of longstanding feminist critical traditions, like ecofeminism, as well as new intersectional extrapolations of narratology, autobiographical studies, and visual rhetoric, which have been applied to the selected comics in insightful and innovative ways.

This is a lively and varied collection suitable for students and scholars in gender studies, cultural studies, media studies, and literary studies.

Sandra Cox is Assistant Professor of English at Southeast Missouri State University, where she teaches courses in American literature by writers from historically marginalized communities. She holds a doctorate in literary studies from the University of Kansas (2011). Her first monograph, entitled *An Ethics of Reading*, was published in 2015. Dr. Cox has written articles on comics published in *The Journal of Comics and Graphic Novels* and twice in *Watchung Review*, and articles on feminist literary criticism published in the journals *Assuming Gender*, *Postcolonial Interventions*, *Parlour*, *Red Feather*, and *[Inter]sections*. She has also contributed chapters on visual media and/or gender studies to edited collections that include *Bodies and Culture: Discourses, Communities, Representations* (2012), *Weaving the Legacy: Remembering Paula Gunn Allen* (2017), and *Where Is Adaptation* (2018).

Interdisciplinary Research in Gender

Classical Hollywood Cinema, Sexuality, and the Politics of the Face
Paul Morrison

Representing Abortion
Edited by Rachel Alpha Johnston Hurst

Dismantling Rape Culture
The Peacebuilding Power of 'Me Too'
Tracey Nicholls

Freewomen, Patriarchal Authority and the Accusation of Prostitution
Stephanie Lynn Budin

Spatialities in Italian American Women's Literature
Beyond the Mean Streets
Eva Pelayo Sañudo

Women's Suffrage in Word, Image, Music, Stage and Screen
The Making of a Movement
Edited by Christopher Wiley and Lucy Ella Rose

Intersectional Feminist Readings of Comics
Interpreting Gender in Graphic Narratives
Edited by Sandra Cox

Caffie Greene and Black Women Activists
Unsung Women of the Black Liberation Movement
Kofi Charu Nat Turner

Forced Migration in the Feminist Imagination
Transcultural Movements
Anna Ball

https://www.routledge.com/Interdisciplinary-Research-in-Gender/book-series/IRG

Intersectional Feminist Readings of Comics

Interpreting Gender in Graphic Narratives

Edited by Sandra Cox

Routledge
Taylor & Francis Group
LONDON AND NEW YORK

First published 2022
by Routledge
2 Park Square, Milton Park, Abingdon, Oxon OX14 4RN

and by Routledge
605 Third Avenue, New York, NY 10158

Routledge is an imprint of the Taylor & Francis Group, an informa business

British Library Cataloguing-in-Publication Data
A catalogue record for this book is available from the British Library

Library of Congress Cataloging-in-Publication Data
Names: Cox, Sandra, Ph.D., editor.
Title: Intersectional feminist readings of comics: interpreting gender in graphic narratives / edited by Sandra Cox.
Description: Abingdon, Oxon; New York, NY: Routledge, 2022. | Series: Interdisciplinary research in gender | Includes bibliographical references and index. |
Identifiers: LCCN 2021012606 (print) | LCCN 2021012607 (ebook) | ISBN 9780367704728 (paperback) | ISBN 9780367704711 (hardback) | ISBN 9781003146520 (ebook)
Subjects: LCSH: Comic books, strips, etc.--United States--History and criticism. | Motion pictures and comic books. | Superhero films--United States--History and criticism. | Women in literature. | Sex role in literature. | Women in motion pictures. | Sex role in motion pictures. | Feminist theory. | LCGFT: Literary criticism.
Classification: LCC PN6725 .I58 2022 (print) | LCC PN6725 (ebook) | DDC 741.5/973082–dc23
LC record available at https://lccn.loc.gov/2021012606
LC ebook record available at https://lccn.loc.gov/2021012607

ISBN: 978-0-367-70471-1 (hbk)
ISBN: 978-0-367-70472-8 (pbk)
ISBN: 978-1-003-14652-0 (ebk)

DOI: 10.4324/9781003146520

Typeset in Sabon
by MPS Limited, Dehradun

Contents

Figures

Contributors

Sandra Cox is Assistant Professor of English at Southeast Missouri State University, where she teaches courses in American literature by writers from historically marginalized communities. She holds a doctorate in literary studies from the University of Kansas (2011). Her first monograph, entitled *An Ethics of Reading*, was published in 2015. Dr. Cox has written articles on comics published in *The Journal of Comics and Graphic Novels* and twice in *Watchung Review*, and articles on feminist literary criticism published in the journals *Assuming Gender*, *Postcolonial Interventions*, *Parlour*, *Red Feather*, and *[Inter]sections.* She has also contributed chapters on visual media and/or gender studies to the following edited collections, including *Bodies and Culture: Discourses, Communities, Representations* (2012), *Weaving the Legacy: Remembering Paula Gunn Allen* (2017), and *Where Is Adaptation* (2018).

Ande Davis conducted his doctoral studies at the University of Missouri-Kansas City and holds an MFA in creative writing from Minnesota State University-Mankato. His scholarship on race and popular culture has previously appeared as a chapter contributed to the anthology *Netflix Nostalgia: Streaming the Past on Demand* (2019) and an article published in *Chiricú Journal* (2019). He is currently studying law at Washburn University School of Law.

Nicole Dib is Assistant Professor of English at Southern Utah University. She completed her PhD in contemporary multiethnic American literature at UC Santa Barbara in 2020, where she wrote her dissertation on road-trip narratives by US writers of color. Her scholarly work appears or is forthcoming in *MELUS: Multiethnic Literature of the United States*, *The Routledge Companion to Critical Masculinity Studies*, and *Teaching the Classics in the U.S. Prison System*, among other journals and edited collections. She has presented her research on Native American and First Nations comics writers at the International Conference on Narrative as well.

Shane Gomes is Assistant Professor of English at Tennessee State University, where he currently teaches courses in composition and world literature. He earned his doctorate in Rhetoric, Writing, and Culture from North Dakota State University in 2020 and his MA in English from the University of Northern Colorado in 2015. His research focuses on the areas of comics, comics pedagogy, and usability/user experience, all with an emphasis on issues of accessibility and equity in the classroom. This is his first scholarly publication.

Alex Link is Associate Professor in the School of Critical and Creative Studies at Alberta University of the Arts, where he is also the Associate Vice President of Academic Affairs. He teaches courses in comics and popular genres such as the Gothic and has co-created two comics series with Riley Rossmo for Image. His publications can be found in such journals as *European Comic Art*; *The Journal of Popular Culture*; *Contemporary Literature*; *Gothic Studies;* and *CLUES: A Journal of Detection* and as book chapters in *Animal Comics*, *Representing Multiculturalism in Comics and Graphic Novels, Contexts of Violence in Comics,* and *The Streaming of Hill House.*

A. Luxx Mishou is a queer femme Victorianist and gender studies scholar researching cosplay, comics, fashion, and the gothic. She holds a doctorate in Victorian literature and gender studies from Old Dominion University, where she defended her dissertation, *Holy Stitches Batman: Performative Villainy in Gothiclam,* in 2020. She earned an MA in English literature and language from the University of Maryland College Park (2007) and a BA in English from Washington College (2005). She has recently contributed chapters to *Fan Phenomena: Rocky Horror Picture Show* (2015); *Fashion and Material Culture in Victorian Popular Fiction and Periodicals* (2019); and *Sartorial Fandom: Fashion, Beauty Culture, and Identity (forthcoming).* Dr. Mishou has presented her research on masculinity in comics at the Comics and Popular Arts Conference (2018), on Alison Bechdel at MLA (2018), and on cosplay at NeMLA (2015) and SCMS (2017, 2019). Her first scholarly monograph, *Cosplayers: Gender and Identity,* was published in 2021.

Michael Reinhard is a PhD candidate in Cinema and Media Studies at the University of California, Los Angeles. He earned his MA in the Humanities with a film concentration and a BA in English Language and Literature from the University of Chicago in 2014, where his graduate thesis focused on the co-option of camp aesthetics by girly films in the 1990s. His work has appeared in *Feminist Media Studies* and *Transformative Works and Cultures.* Additionally, he has presented at the yearly Society for Cinema and Media Studies and Screen Studies conferences. His research interrogates the brand aspects of diversity rhetoric in the cultural industries.

Monica Roxanne Sandler is a PhD candidate in Cinema and Media Studies at the University of California, Los Angeles. Her research focuses on historical and contemporary issues in American film industry labor, policy, and economics. Her recent studies have turned to franchising copyright in Marvel Cinematic Universe adaptations and public relations output within Hollywood institutions. She is currently editing an interview series on the careers of the comic writers Walter and Louise Simonson.

Cody Shrum is currently an instructor of English and Discourse at The University of Missouri-Kansas City. He received an MFA in Creative Writing and Media Arts from UMKC in 2020 and a MA in Creative Writing from Pittsburg State University in 2015. His fiction and poetry have appeared in or are forthcoming in such journals as *Prime Number Magazine*, *The Midwest Quarterly*, and *Harbor Review*. His areas of scholarly expertise are in American comics, Alison Bechdel's works in particular, and contemporary American short fiction.

Acknowledgements

Every editor of an anthology of essays begins her acknowledgements by noting that the genre of the edited collection is, by its very nature, a collaborative effort. I have three groups of people who must be thanked and without whom the book would not exist in its current form.

First and foremost, I must acknowledge that this book was written by A. Luxx Mishou, Ande Davis, Michael Reinhard, Monica Sandler, Shane Gomes, Nicole Dib, Cody Shrum, and Alex Link. I had the good fortune to be in a position to recognize the significance of the work they were already doing, and the benefit of their patience in finding a home for it in print. If this book fulfills any of the critical aims I set out for it, then that is because of their expertise, talents, and diligence, by which I am humbled and for which I am very grateful.

Secondly, I would be remiss if I did not thank four of my colleagues for their help with manuscript preparation. Chanda Williams-Doles and Joshua Horton provided invaluable assistance with copy-editing, and without their efforts, I might still be sifting through drafts looking for errant punctuation and re-re-reconsulting the *Chicago Manual of Style*. Missy Nieveen Phegley started the conversation that became the call for submissions, and she gave some of the contributors helpful guidance as they developed early drafts of three of the seven chapters collected here. Susan Kendrick read innumerable early drafts of both the prospectus and introduction and provided generous feedback and careful surface-level editing for the first complete draft of the book; she also provided invaluable moral support during the challenges that working on this volume during a global pandemic inevitably produced.

Finally, I would like to thank Alex McGregor and Eleanor Catchpole-Simmons and the rest of the editorial team at Routledge for believing in this project from the jump and for being so helpful as we worked to complete it.

Introduction

Drawn to and from gender: some of what it means to critique comics through intersectional feminist theory

Sandra Cox

What is this collection of essays trying to accomplish?

Intersectional Feminist Readings of Comics collects seven chapters that each undertake a cultural contextualization and theoretically informed close reading of comics using methods gleaned from trafeminist interpretive practices. In the first half of the book, the chapters examine ways in which superhero comics and the cinematic and televisual adaptations thereof reify, revise, and reject gender parity, systemic misogyny, and heteropatriarchy. This analysis strives to be inclusive of a diverse range of gender identities and to consider how feminist reading intersects with critical race and queer theory in application to the study of popular culture. In the second part of the volume, the chapters apply feminist interpretive lenses in order to illuminate the radical work undertaken by cartoonists from historically marginalized communities in the US and Canada. The collection aims to illuminate the visual and textual representations of sex, gender, and sexuality in contemporary North American comics and graphic novels as a means of extending and responding to an exciting moment occurring within Comics Studies as a field, which, like the comics industry, is finally taking up the work of becoming more equitable and inclusive.

The exigent impulse that led to this volume was twofold. First, although there has been no small amount of print committed to feminist readings of comics in monographs or special issues or individual journal articles, a collection of essays that situated the praxis of gender theory as a singular means by which to interpret the genre of graphic narrative seemed to be a relevant contribution to a spate of recent scholarly discourse about intersectional feminist reading practices. Although that is obviously an aggrandizing thing for an editor to write, books like this one are the way a field might be grounded more firmly in previous scholarly discourses that are not siloed by discipline. Some of the scholars whose work is collected here have expertise in film studies, or literature, or creative writing, or women's studies, and, to wit, each of them brings a specific perspective to the application of feminist theory to comics. The integration of those perspectives together, I argue, serves the field at large, and I hope other critics

DOI: 10.4324/9781003146520-101

agree. In a roundtable on "Comics and Methodology," published in *Inks* in 2017, media studies scholar Henry Jenkins argued that one of the hallmarks of a burgeoning field is the emergence of "a series of monographs [that] demonstrate the value of a particular approach, a particular author, a particular genre" (62); those kinds of books are the means by which a critical field is established outside disciplinary boundaries.

Jenkins also notes, in that same panel discussion, that comics studies in the present is shaped by critics who understand "comics as an art form" and scholars who were persuaded by "McCloud's advocacy for comics as a medium" (63). The chapters in this book offer no clear consensus about concrete definition of comics as either a form of visual narrative art or a medium through which ideas are communicated by juxtaposing images. However, whether one adopts the Eisnerian definition of "sequential art" or accepts the designation given by literary critics and rhetoricians of comics as "pictorial narrative," gender is quite literally rendered in graphic novels and comics which merits interpretation. To wit, collected here are chapters where the so-called "literary turn" in comics studies, which Bart Beatty rejects in the same roundtable from the inaugural issue of *Inks* (73–74), is the foundational premise of the close-reading of comics and graphic novels as narrative objects that might be read as historiography, memoir, or fiction. For instance, Cody Shrum situates Bechdel's graphic memoirs in conversation with critics who see narratological implications for the crafting of nonfiction, and Shane Gomez posits an ecofeminist analysis of folkloric allusions in *Beautiful Darkness*. Those chapters work to make a critical reading of representations of gender and sex relevant to that formal interpretive praxis. *Intersectional Feminist Readings of Comics* builds out from the foundation laid by feminist literary critics and media scholars already working in comics studies, but this volume also contains chapters in which the formal analysis of comics, as a mode of visual storytelling, is central to claims about the rhetorical capacity of comics as a medium rather than an aesthetic, literary or historical object. In particular, Ande Davis and A. Luxx Mishou present their readings of superhero comics as historical artifacts and aesthetic objects that reflect the demands of a changing audience rather than leave the sediment of misogyny, racism, ableism, and homophobia undisturbed as they interpret longstanding tropes within the genre. Davis's engagement with culturally specific modes of analysis and Mishou's insistence on centering the extratextual consequences of the representations of sex workers both serve to show how popular imaginings are correlated with public discourse about human rights.

Regardless of the disciplinary grounding of the analytical claims presented, the hope was that by inviting readers of mass market comics (and the prolific and interwoven transmedial adaptations thereof) to join readers of "canonical" or "literary" graphic novels (and participants in the critical systems that brand those comics as such) for the purpose of considering how representations of and discourse about gendered identity might be explicated through interrogating assumptions about gender, sex, and sexuality evoked within graphic narratives. This book is not the first one to undertake such an extension of the field using identity and hegemony as the organizing principle. The last decade in particular has seen the field of Comics Studies grapple with the kyriarchical contexts from which comics and graphic novels made in the global North during the twentieth and twenty-first centuries necessarily emerge. Volumes like Frances Gateward and John Jennings' (2015) Eisner Award-winning anthology *The Blacker the Ink: Constructions of Black Identity in Comics and Sequential Art* worked to centralize an approach to Comics Studies that centralized the perspectives of Black cartoonists and auteurs but also insisted on the critical attention to the ways that visual tropes and normative narrative devices might be used to both reify and resist the implicit narrative of white supremacy that undergirds the comics and graphic novels examined therein. Building on her contributions to that work, Rebecca Wanzo's (2020) very recent but clearly very important collection *The Content of Our Caricature: African American Comic Art and Political Belonging* takes a historiographic look at the reclamation of comics by Black artists, writers, and cartoonists responding to a legacy of mediated representation meant to communicate the limits of access available to African American subjects. Similarly, last year's *Graphic Indigeneity: Comics in the Americas and Australasia* considered how transnational conceptions of ethnicity and race may be meaningfully manifested in comics by and about Indigenous identity, in which editor Frederick Luis Aldama (2020) notes that representations of "Indigenous identities, histories and experiences circulate far and wide" in a medium that is as immediate as comics; however, Aldama also argues that not every representation serves to "enrich an understanding of the complexity of Indigenous subjectivities" (v) and points out that critical interventions in those narratives is essential to the project of coalition building for Indigenous peoples.

Race and ethnicity are not, of course, the only identities with which gender, sex, and sexuality meaningfully intersect. Esther De Dauw and Daniel Connell's (2020) collection *Toxic Masculinity: Mapping the Monstrous in Our Heroes* shows that even the centering of white, cisgendered, heterosexual men in superhero comics has implications for understanding the uncanny as something embodied and displayed through the mechanics of comics to such an extent that readers are obligated to contend with the physical as narrative object. Likewise, Jose Alaniz and Scott T. Smith's (2020) edited collection *Uncanny Bodies: Superhero Comics and Disability* begins by arguing compellingly that this very feature of putting the characters on view is one of the reasons that comics are "open to innovation and capable of speaking to diverse audiences" (ix). Because the sort of scholarship done in those collections has shown that claim to be incontrovertibly true, the contribution these chapters make is to further exemplify the fruitfulness of explicating identity and systemic oppression in ways that are simultaneously accessible and complex, rather like comics and feminism.

What doesn't the collection do, then?

Although plenty of edited collections focus specifically on the work of well-known, critically and commercially successful women cartoonists already occupy the intersection of Comics Studies and Feminist Theory, this volume seeks to broaden the scope by undertaking the consideration of comics that may not seem, on-face, to be explicitly feminist works of visual narrative. The outgrowth of perspicuous expressions of intersectional feminist themes within comics over the last decade would make such a volume possible, certainly. Many of the cartoonists working on those titles (of which Okorafor's *Shuri,* De Connick's *Bitch Planet,* Liu's *Monstress*, Beaton's *Hark! A Vagrant!,* and Stevenson's *Lumberjanes* come to mind quickest for your editor, dear reader) are writers and artists from historically under-represented groups within the comics industry whose work entirely is deserving of exactly that sort of critical attention. Rather than ground this collection in analyses of comics that would flag their feminist didactic purposes for readers as condition of the premise of the world built by the cartoonist, I've chosen chapters that compellingly explicate the ways that each of these comics treats the subjects of feminist analysis through the mediated formal structures that make sequential narrative art a compelling mode for interrogating the abstract.

As the chapters individually and collectively demonstrate, most any comics depicting gendered characters in relation to one another might become an informative example of how ideologies of gender are reflected in and perpetuated by a medium that unifies the linguistic and fine arts. Through examining mainstream figures (like DC's Catwoman and Marvel's Miss America and Doctor Strange) alongside heroines in historical and speculative comics by Indigenous American illustrators, the chapters work in tandem to support similar claims about how nationalizing narratives work to situate gender and desire in particular social and historical contexts. The same is true for the chapters that examine graphic memoirs and romans á clef by critically lauded cartoonists. Likewise, varied genres of comics—from graphic historiographies about land theft to adaptations of the generic conventions of fairy tales in graphic novels—are considered through a range of interpretive lenses drawn from theoretical models used in contemporary intersectional feminist aesthetic and literary criticism. Some of the critical methods—like narratology and ecofeminism—are well established in critical conversations about graphic literature, which have been expanded to make space for the analytical possibilities offered by comics studies' interdisciplinary orientation. Other chapters seek to create and apply mechanisms for better understanding those possibilities in praxis. For example, the third chapter by Michael Reinhard and Monica Sandler argue that Marvel's

Cinematic Universe adapts and permutes the comics to create what they call a "diversity aesthetic," which demonstrates how identity-bending enables narrative suture with multiple points of possible audience-identification. By considering how the transmediation of the convention of gender-swapping in Marvel comics lives outside the medium, Sandler and Reinhard are able to clearly situate the intersectional nature of representational justice as originating within comics, rather than being imposed by the medial features of film.

What's with the two parts?

The bipartite structure of the volume sets those comics (and the adaptations thereof) whose cartoonists made use of the conventions of world-building to craft allegories of gender-, sex-, and sexuality-based oppression in the extratextual world. By considering how DC's Gotham, the Marvel Cinematic Universe, and European fairy tales as microcosms through which corporeal ephemera accumulates cultural significance, the critics collected in the first part of the volume unpack how gender and desire intersects with class, race, and national origin in each of those imagined worlds. The second half of the book works to examine how fictionalized narratives might function as autobiographical or autoethnographic testimonies about the ways that gender, sex, and sexuality constrain or inform agency for characters who have faced personal or cultural trauma that shapes their gendered and sexual identities. By considering how the claiming of lesbian identity, Jewish identity, and Indigenous identity within those narrative structures bear witness to trauma, the critics whose work is collected in the final section of the volume suggest that feminist readings of comics might help to better understand how the traumatic past can be interpolated into a more hopeful present.

Because another aim was to create a collection that illustrated the breadth of feminist reading methodologies available for applying to comics with varied didactic purposes, the selected chapters that make use of well-established cultural, aesthetic, and literary modes of interrogating gender, sex, and sexuality in visual and textual narratives. While most of the methods drawn from feminist theory in the following chapters are well established in broader scholarly conversation, the contribution of this volume is that it builds upon other previously published critical works that enact feminist interpretation of comics. Chute's (2010) groundbreaking *Graphic Women* was certainly central to framing a call for papers and in conceiving of how authorial intention might function at the intersection of comics and gender studies. This book is also indebted to previous collections edited by comics critics like Janine Utell (2019), whose *The Comics of Alison Bechdel* figures so prominently in the research for the penultimate chapter here. Several chapters bear out the enduring truth of Tensuan's (2007) claim that female cartoonists are in "the vanguard of artists who are exploring the forms and conventions associated with comics as a means of revisiting and revising the conventional narratives that inscribe one's political, social, and gendered roles" (951). Other chapters consider how depictions of women and femmes in works within the medium fit into larger cultural and critical discourses about identity, representation, and narrative. As stated, the scope of this volume is not anchored to exploring only those comics written by women or noncishet creators but also to considering the form and content of comics written for and about women and noncishet people. There have already been many broad considerations of the ways in which graphic storytelling can be used in the service of movements to end sexism and misogyny and to destabilize heteropatriarchy.

Mihaela Precup and Rebecca Scherr's guest co-edited double special issue in 2018 and 2019 on sexual violence in *The Journal of Comics and Graphic Novels* brought up concerns about the ethics of rendering sexualized bodies in comics that were by men and women. Those articles were also about how feminist reading practices may be grounded in the formal analysis of visual grammars at work in the medium. Rebecca Wanzo's 2009 article "The Superhero: Mediations on Surveillance, Salvation and Desire" was essential to the framing of part one; her argument that "revisions of superhero mythos are often interrogations of what kinds of identities and ideologies are cast as ideal in US culture and, as such, are useful springboards for discussion ideological mainstays informing narratives of good citizenship" (93) came to be the through-line that tied Mishou's work to Davis's to Reinhard and Sandler's. After considering how the archetypes work as vessels of ideology, Gomes's work on fairy tale archetypes and the revision of the dark pastoral seemed an appropriate bridge between the focus on medium as both mode and message to a consideration of textual records of cultural history and personal accountings of lives along the intersection of gender with race, ethnicity, spirituality and sexuality.

After moving into that mode of analysis it felt important to also consider how existing conversations about race, ethnicity, spirituality and sexuality were working for say, Indigenous peoples, in the case of Nicole Dib's analysis of the first two volumes of *Moonshot: The Indigenous Comics Collection* (2015 and 2017), alongside *Deer Woman: An Anthology* (2017) and *Sovereign Traces: Volume 1* (2018). The centering of culturally specific practices in both the visual and historiographic narratives in each anthology calls readers to consider whether or not the broad demography of comics readers framed in part one is always part and parcel of the act of graphic record-keeping and testimony-sharing. The same holds true for Alex Link's examination of the complex intersection of Jewish identity and sexuality in Leela Corman's *Unterzakhn* and for Shrum's reading of Alison Bechdel's graphic translation of the confessional mode in her corpus of nonfiction. With those commonalities of didactic purpose, if not subject matter, in mind, the exigent purpose of the second part of the book is to better understand how the medium of graphic storytelling can be or might have been used to reify, reflect, interrogate, and disrupt the social construction of gender as a tool of systemic oppression, and any attempt at fulfilling that second purpose would have to consider the tropes of comics outside the superhero genre to supplement the focus of much of the first part. The two parts together demonstrate the breadth of expository and critical focus that is possible within intersectional feminist reading methods, which helps to fill in some of the terrain left for exploration in the field.

What are intersectional feminist reading methods exactly?

Because the organizing principle of this volume has been the collecting of intersectional analyses of gender, as presented in and reflected by graphic narratives, one might ask whether or not all analyses of gender, sex, and sexuality "count" as feminist reading practices. What, exactly, is meant by "feminist readings" here? How might the distinctions between the praxis employed by literary critics and media critics complicate the project? While Chute, Utell, Tensuan, and other literary critics certainly shaped some of the answers to those questions that readers can infer from reading this collection, it is also true that the volume seeks to broaden the limited scope of that single-discipline's lens. When giving the keynote address at the International Comics Arts Forum in 2014, film scholar Bart Beaty paraphrased Fredric Jameson's

> famous dictum that it is easier to imagine the end of the world than the end of capitalism, [quipping] that it was easier to imagine the end of the world than the end of the dominance of literary methods in comics studies. (Jenkins 2016)

One volume does not, of course, singularly undo any of these disciplinary divide; by choosing to organize around a subject of analysis rather than a singular methodology, the editorial sequencing of chapters here illustrates the ways in which the medium stretches to accommodate many different feminist lens, all of which are contextualized by situating gender as star in a constellation of complex identities rendered both visually and textually.

Regardless of the methodological grounding of the feminist analysis presented, the chapters that follow this introduction all pose a consideration of the theoretical grounding of feminist reading practices, even if the theory used to support those practices differs from chapter to chapter. Sarah Ahmed, in her article "Whose Counting?," published in 2000 in the inaugural issue of the journal *Feminist Theory,* argued that categorical definitions of feminism as a unified theory are perhaps of less utility than a clear concept of how the act of interrogating the intersections of structural inequity with cultural notions about gendered identity works in the service of social change. For this reason, Ahmed "prefer[s] to use the verb 'feminist theorizing' as it makes clear that there is a process involved that does not necessarily lead to an object 'feminist theory,' [which] involves more than the local sites of contestation around gender norms" (99). Because this turn toward the act of interpreting gender as the locus of analysis allows for a broader intersectional approach to understanding literature and other media, feminist readings of comics would always already work in the service of an ongoing theoretical intervention to promote a more nuanced understanding of structural inequity.

Ahmed (2000) explains that "theorizing involves a set of techniques for moving beyond local sites of resistance, and indeed, of linking the local to other locals, or broader social processes" and that feminist reading is a scholarly extension of feminist activism because it is "after all, something feminists do in order to explain why gender norms are so difficult to contest in the first place" (100). In an effort to theorize feminism through the comics analyzed in this collection, which can be seen as visual and textual localities wherein feminism might be put into interpretive practice, editorial decisions have been made in order to encourage a multiplicity of viewpoints on structural inequity as they relate to the comics' depictions of gendered subject. Some chapters are interested in costuming and the materiality of the gendered body as drawn in the comics and represented in the diegetic discourse of the text. Others are interested in the way that ethnic, racial, and national identities are also inscribed and described within or against gendered representations. All of the chapters explore the aesthetic values and socio-political messages implicit in comics.

There has been a great deal of ink and paper committed to the work of providing feminist readings of textual literary narratives as part and parcel of that examination, and in much of that work there has been a tacit debate about the relative value of feminist aesthetics and the praxis of close-reading as a means of interpreting narrative text. In 1989 (which is, coincidentally, the same year that Kimberlé Crenshaw coined the phrase "intersectional feminism" and that the last iteration of the General Standards were revised by the Comics Code Authority before its formal abolition in 2011), Rita Felksi's monograph *Beyond Feminist Aesthetics* definitively explicated how the disconnect between high theory and popular culture shape understandings of what "feminist reading," as an interpretive praxis, means:

> [T]here exists a symptomatic tension in feminist literary theory between a pragmatic position, which seeks to repoliticize the literary text by reinserting it into the sphere of everyday communicative practices, and a simultaneous awareness of the potential limitations of a purely functionalist aesthetic, which stresses immediate political effects and is unable to address the specificity of literature as a site of plural signification and aesthetic pleasure which may resist as well as transmit dominant ideological positions. (175)

In the years since Felksi's book, proponents of close reading took aim at the ways that any mode of feminist discourse in the humanities and behavioral sciences seems to be at odds with the aesthetic interventions that both comics and feminist political activism make out in the extratextual world. Yung-Hsing Wu explains Felski's claims about the oppositions between what "functionalist aesthetics" that overtly and explicitly defy the sort of "everyday communicative practices" in which patriarchy is so often firmly ensconced as a kind of "common wisdom" among feminist critics, who generally acknowledge "that close reading and the political sensibilities of contemporary criticism could not be more different" Yung-Hsing 2016 (87). Rather than accept this dialectic between politics and aesthetics, Wu argues for greater attention to so-called "popular texts" through the formalist analysis of close reading as a means of decoupling the interpretive praxis from that appreciative expression. Wu explains that "close reading is doubly alienated from the intellectual practices of feminism, ethnic studies, gay and lesbian studies, queer theory" and that "a feminist belief in the *closeness* of reading, locating it in the theory and politics of consciousness-raising, signifies the feeling of closeness with identification" (87). Like Ahmed, the volume asks readers to willingly see feminist theory as an elastic category of methodological approaches, and, like Wu, the contributors and I have imagined "reading" to be a process of assigning meaning to the visual and textual forms through which that narrative is conveyed through the medium of comics.

Each chapter in this volume enacts a feminist theorization of the practice of reading closely in both senses of the phrase. The scholars whose work is collected here attend carefully to the formal and narratological interventions of comics that make use of visual rhetoric as well as textual signification; in investigating the often intimate relationships between reader and comic, between critic and cartoonist, and between image and text, the chapters theorize gender and the cultural construction thereof as a means of understanding how and why sexism seems so clearly anchored to other vectors of oppression as exemplified by a selection of comics. All seven chapters model some ways that one might be reading comics and "doing" feminism at the same time, and though those practices are anchored to specific texts, the utility of the methods proposed, demonstrated and examined is far broader.

The first half of the book is concerned with the ways in which "popular" is less a statement against merit for privileged appreciation and more a qualifier for producing the second sort of closeness Wu describes. In the first four chapters, this is accomplished while also attending to the fantastic or uncanny elements of comics, which seem ideal for explicating some core theoretical concepts associated with feminist theory, like ecofeminism and intersectionality. The deep histories of characterization that mark mainstream characters in mass market comics or feminine archetypal heroines and victims in fairytales provide fertile ground for growing an increasingly radical visual rhetoric about gender and sexuality contained in the larger meta-discourse about expression, representation, and adaptation. The first chapter considers the ethos of adaptation and the aesthetic values of difference in the pages of Marvel comics and the cinematic universe derived from them. By exploring how race, ethnicity, gender, and sexuality work to reveal and permute American Orientalism in material culture, Sandler and Reinhard ask, and answer, some important questions about why casting and criticism matter with regard to blockbuster film franchises and best-selling serial comics. In the second chapter the explication of the development of DC's hypersexualized supervillain Catwoman is plotted alongside the movement for sex-workers' rights and the historiographic dimensions of self-censorship in the comics industry. Both the political movement outside the comics and the evolution of the character within them show the growing socio-cultural disdain for sexual agency that is not securely controlled by heteropatriarchy. Mishou's analysis of contemporary legislation that situates itself as protectionist, while reinforcing some toxic power dynamics, is compelling evidence for Wu's claims.

The third chapter extends the analysis of a single female character by undertaking a close reading of the re-launch of Marvel's transdimensional heroine, Miss America, who is newly imagined as America Chavez, an openly queer Latina heroine written by Gabby Rivera. Using Gloria Anzaldúa's groundbreaking work on border-spaces and identities as a guide to tracking America's unfolding characterization, Davis presents Miss America as an exemplar of the concept of naplanta, a transformative locus of intersecting identities and ideologies that Anzaldua speculated would be especially useful in conceptualizing power and status for marginalized peoples. In the fourth chapter, Gomes rereads the architextual features of fairy tales as a means of considering how environmental devastation and the exploitation of women are rooted, quite literally, in the forest of cartoonist Fabien Vehlmann's imagination, as well as in the commoditization of the women's bodies and the natural world. Gomes' analysis also has clear ramifications for the practice of ecofeminism as a mode of resistance as well as a theoretical engagement with kyriarchical structures both in graphic narrative and in the extratextual world.

In the second half of the volume, the chapters do the work of bridging practice and theory by considering how historically marginalized voices are amplified in comics that narrativize and speculate about means by which direct action might address inequity outside the worlds built within the comics. Ahmed (1998), in her book *Differences that Matter*, points out that claims about the "inherent contradictions between the demands of feminist practice (as struggle) and feminist theory (as engagement)" seem to suggest that theory informs the "contingencies of practical politics" (24). This is perhaps most obvious in the fifth chapter of the book where Indigenous history, speculative fiction, and visual rhetoric work in tandem to produce a sovereign feminist politics that addresses a longstanding legacy of land theft and genocide. By relying upon Indigenous cartoonists and scholars to explicate the relationship between the current political situations in North

America, that chapter does the feminist work of amplifying the voices of Indigenous activists and historians while also making a contribution to current understanding of how visual narratives fit into Indigenous storytelling traditions. The work the second, third, and fifth chapters accomplish together illustrates how comics may be used as a vessel for feminist theorizing rather than a genre that is always already operating to destabilize patriarchal and colonialist structures. Similarly, the sixth and seventh chapters work in tandem to consider lesbian and Jewish women's identities as means of revealing the implicit challenges contained in comics by Alison Bechdel and Leela Corman, respectively. In chapter six, the ways in which the confessional impulses in memoir collide with the testimonial functions of recording lesbian, gay, and bisexual history make for a productive intervention in understanding the formal gestures made in graphic nonfiction. In chapter seven, the work begun in chapter one on sex work and archetypes of femme identity is extended to interrogate the other half of the mother/slut dichotomy as claims about the liminal space between maternal objects and sex objects is filled in by feminist theorizing about the narrative functions of comics. In both of those chapters, the relationship of verisimilitude, memoir, and autoethnography (as well as the hazy boundaries between family and geographic and religious communities) are renegotiated using the same kind of consciousness-raising implicit in aestheticizing the personal as Felski called for in her foundational treatise.

Taken together, the chapters in the volume highlight the feminist theorizing already taking place in the main and subtexts of these comics. In her coda to *Disaster Drawn* (2016), Hillary Chute argues that "the comics medium has evolved as an instrument for commenting on and re-visioning experience and history" (265). These intersectional feminist readings of comics attempt to bear out the truth of that observation by highlighting how graphic narrative can "enter the public sphere as a form of witness" (265) because "lines of the page, how they juxtapose time and space, convey the simultaneity of experience—the different competing registers" can be a powerful means by which a discursive intervention becomes the impetus and theoretical guide by which reading leads to social and ideological shifts. If feminism is a verb, then making and reading comics are certainly an important and useful way "to feminist," as it is my dearest hope that this volume will show.

References

Ahmed, Sarah. 1998. *Differences that Matter: Feminist Theory and Postmodernism.* London: Cambridge University Press.

Ahmed, Sarah. 2000. "Whose Counting?" *Feminist Theory* 1 (1): 97–103. doi:10.1177/14647000022229083.

Aldama, Frederick Luis, ed. 2020. *Graphic Indigeneity: Comics in the Americas and Australasia.* Oxford: University Press of Mississippi.

Chute, Hillary. 2010. *Graphic Women: Life Narrative and Contemporary Comics.* New York: Columbia University Press.

Chute, Hillary. *Disaster Drawn: Visual Witness, Comics, and Documentary Form.* London: Harvard University Press, 2016.

Crenshaw, Kimberle. 1989. "Demarginalizing the Intersection of Race and Sex: A Black Feminist Critique of Antidiscrimination Doctrine, Feminist Theory and Antiracist Politics," *University of Chicago Legal Forum* 1 (Article 8): 139–67.

Davis, Blair, Bart Beaty, Scott Bukatman, Henry Jenkins, and Benjamin Woo. 2017. "Roundtable: Comics and Methodology." *Inks: The Journal of the Comics Studies Society* 1 (1): 56–74. doi:10.1353/ink.2017.0004.

De Dauw, Esther, and Daniel J. Connell, eds. 2020. *Toxic Masculinity: Mapping the Monstrous in Our Heroes.* Oxford: University of Mississippi Press.

Felski, Rita. 1989. *Beyond Feminist Aesthetics: Feminist Literature and Social Change.* New York: Harvard University Press.

Gateward, Frances, and John Jennings, eds. 2015. *The Blacker the Ink: Constructions of Black Identity in Comics and Sequential Art.* New York: Rutgers University Press.

Jenkins, Henry. "Comics and Canons: An Interview with Bart Beaty." *Confessions of an ACA Fan*, October 18, 2016, http://henryjenkins.org/blog/2016/10/comics-and-canons-an-interview-with-bart-beaty-part-one.html.

Nyberg, Amy Kriste. 1998. *Seal of Approval: The History of the Comics Code.* Jackson: University of Mississippi Press.

Precup, Mihaela, and Rebecca Scherr, eds. 2018. "Sexual Violence in Comics." Special issue, *Journal of Graphic Novels and Comics* 8(3-4). doi:10.1080/21504857.2017.1329981.

Sergi, Joe. 2012. "Tales from the Code: How Much Did Things Change After the Enactment of the Comics Code of 1954?" *Comic Books Legal Defense Fund.* cbldf.org/2012/08/tales-from-the-code-how-much-did-things-change-after-the-enactment-of-the-comics-code-of-1954/.

Smith, Scott T., and José Alaniz, eds. 2020. *Uncanny Bodies: Superhero Comics and Disability.* College Station: Pennsylvania State University Press.

Tensuan, Theresa. 2007. "Comic Visions and Revisions in the Work of Lynda Barry and Marjane Satrapi." *Modern Fiction Studies* 52 (4): 947–64.

Utell, Janine. *The Comics of Alison Bechdel: From the Outside In.* Jackson: University of Mississippi Press, 2019.

Wanzo, Rebecca. 2009. "The Superhero: Meditations on Surveillance, Salvation and Desire." *Communication and Critical/Cultural Studies* 6 (1): 93–97. doi:10.1080/14714208026663694.

Wanzo, Rebecca, ed. 2020. *The Content of Our Caricature: African American Comic Art and Political Belonging.* New York: New York University Press.

Wu, Yung-Hsing. 2016. "Closely, Consciously Reading Feminism." In *This Book is an Action: Feminist Print Culture and Activist Aesthetics*, edited by Jaime Harker and Cecilia Konchar Farr, 87–110. Chicago: University of Chicago Press.

Part I

Racialized heroes and sexualized villains

1 Contested adaptations: legacies of orientalism, the she-hero, and Hollywood's diversity aesthetic in Marvel's *Doctor Strange* (2016)

Michael Reinhard and
Monica Roxanne Sandler

In an episode of the podcast *TigerBelly* from 16 December 2016, comedian Margaret Cho discussed an email chain with actress Tilda Swinton about her casting as the Ancient One in Marvel's *Doctor Strange* (2016). Swinton contacted Cho after a controversy had broken out connected to the creative decision to feature a Celtic woman in a part traditionally depicted as a Tibetan male. This role is especially significant because the character's guidance leads the protagonist, Stephen Strange, to access magical powers through Asian "mysticism." The outrage over Swinton's casting crystallized when the Media Action Network for Asian Americans (MANAA) made a public statement condemning the use of whitewashing in the newly released Marvel film. Their president, Rob Chan, criticized the decision: "Given the dearth of Asian roles, there was no reason a monk in Nepal could not be Asian. Had [writer/director Scott] Derrickson cast an Asian as the revered leader who guides the main character to become a better human being and to develop his sorcery powers, it would've given a big boost to that actor's career" (Yee 2016). Swinton's casting joined a larger wave of controversies over the recent use of white actresses to play characters of Asian descent, which has included Emma Stone's casting in *Aloha* (2015) and Scarlett Johansson portrayal of "Major" in *Ghost in the Shell* (2017).

On the podcast, Cho described her interactions with Swinton as deeply troubling, explaining that being asked to untangle the white actress's confusion over the controversy due to her Asian descent made her feel subservient. She commented: "It was weird because I felt like a house Asian, like I'm her servant. Like the ones when they have in the [British] Raj, they would have the house servant who was your confidante ... I had a weird feeling about the entire exchange" (TigerBelly 2016). Soon after, however, Swinton's agent Brian Swardstrom released the email communications to the online media outlet *Jezebel* (Juzwiak 2016). Amidst the exchange, Swinton makes a point that condenses many of the recent changes taking place in Marvel's cinematic and comic book multiverses. She notes, "the biggest irony about this righteous protest targeting this *particular* film is the pains the makers went to avoid it." Swinton's framing argued that the

DOI: 10.4324/9781003146520-1

production was concerned about stereotyping characters of Asian descent through orientalizing tropes. Marvel had resolved to sidestep these concerns by redefining or "re-storying" the character into a Celtic woman, ultimately bending the race and gender of the canonical character to avoid controversy in both the United States and China. In doing so, *Doctor Strange* offers a case study about how industrial considerations and cultural politics work as evolutionary pressures on the adaptation of Marvel's comic books.

While Swinton's comments did not clear up the controversy of whitewashing in the Marvel Cinematic Universe (MCU), the incident reveals two competing visions of ethical social representation: MANAA's condemnation of white-washing in Hollywood vs. Swinton's claim that Marvel's internal discussions were premised on how best to adapt a character with a problematic history from the original canon. These dueling perspectives on the ethics of re-presentation showcase how issues of diversity are produced in the MCU. At the time of the scandal, Marvel had already faced wider problems with diversity and representation in its films. As Ariana Quinonez (2015) wrote for *Hypable*,

> The Marvel Cinematic Universe has a diversity problem. There's no way to really skirt around this issue politely: it's a fact. Five out of the six Avengers that make up the largest movie franchise in the world are straight, white, conventionally-beautiful males. That's over 83% of the Avengers franchise headlined by people born of systematic privilege.

At the time of *Doctor Strange*'s release in 2016, there had yet to be a woman or a person of color in the leading role of a Marvel film. Swinton's casting, however, showcased an attempt to bring greater representation of onscreen diversity to a character associated with a problematic past. Swinton, known for her androgynous persona in films like *Orlando* (1992), was seen by Marvel as a progressive choice to take on the role. Her casting, paradoxically enough, was their attempt to keep up with the times, adapting the original comics to contemporary national and geopolitical contexts.

In this way, Marvel turned to the white female body as an opportunity for marketing feminism and avoiding ethnic tensions in the Chinese film market. *Doctor Strange* demonstrates what Sarah Banet-Weiser (2015) has termed the "economies of visibility" to refer to the ways in which political categories like gender and race have been transformed into everyday cultural and economic practices like film attendance and spectatorship. In our analysis, these textual alterations to the comic book text through contemporary logics of gender and race have aimed to cultivate what we term a "diversity aesthetic" across Marvel's myriad film franchises, an aesthetic that illustrates the evolutionary models of textual adaptation at work in the MCU. Through this aesthetic, goals of diversity have produced not only the transformation of marginal characters like the Ancient One in the Marvel canon but also yielded large-scale productions like *Black Panther* (2018) and the upcoming *Shang-Chi and the Legend of the Ten Rings* (2021) that challenge and respond to numerous fan criticisms about the gender and racial exclusivity of the MCU. Marvel's recent approach to negotiating the gender and racial divides of the 2010s have sought to pursue a cinematic universe that undercuts charges of racism and sexism in its original comic books by incorporating elements of gender and race-bending. These instances of "bending" speak to an array of fan desires and practices that change the gender or racial identities of core characters to yield new personal, romantic, and sexual possibilities for fans and the original canon. At the same time, this bending reflects how comic book texts have been adapted into global blockbusters with distinct cultural and political "evolutionary" pressures at work for each domestic box office, thus reflecting the existing field of tensions in the global film marketplace.

Our essay covers the relationship of the comic books to identity-bending by putting *Doctor Strange*'s issues of gender and race in its adaptation to the screen into dialogue with Marvel's history of gender-swapping. We trace the development of this practice by looking at the history of the "she-hero" figure, a principal way that Marvel has introduced female superheroes since the 1940s. Rather than launch new and original superheroines, characters like Miss America, Namora, and She-Hulk were created as female versions of well-established male figures: Captain America, Namor, and Hulk, respectively. We focus on the invention and phenomenon of the "she-hero" as the clear precedent for not only the Ancient One but the recent *Captain Marvel* film as the necessary industrial contexts for understanding these changes in Marvel's content strategies. Our essay argues that this "diversity aesthetic" can be studied for how it demonstrates the role of identity-bending to sustain multiple points of identification for a global audience by triangulating original texts, domestic audiences, and international geopolitics. Yet beyond this scope, we also assert that this diversity aesthetic—largely cultivated through recourse to publicity and marketing language—has often worked to domesticate desires for a more inclusive canon by flattening gender and race into equally considered but nonetheless aestheticized commodities. In this way, decisions like Tilda Swinton in *Doctor Strange* appear to refer back to the legacy of the she-hero tradition. We argue that Marvel's management of multiple national audiences presents competing visions of social change in how the comic book canon is adapted for the big screen. In making this argument, our work seeks to examine the industrial considerations and their evolutionary pressures on the process of film adaptation at work in contemporary Hollywood.

Forget everything you think you know: re-storying the Ancient One

Marvel's film publicity reveals how the diversity aesthetic is connected to the relationship between Hollywood and the global film market. At the same time, there are important lessons for scholars of adaptation when thinking about how industrial considerations shape and impact Marvel's original comic books for the big screen. As Robert Stam (2000) observes, the discussion of film adaptation has traditionally re-inscribed "the axiomatic superiority of literary art to film" (58) by privileging issues of fidelity to the original work. Undergirding these attempts, the novel is believed to have an "extractable essence" that is translated into other forms of adapted media. Stam questions the efficacy of fidelity as a critical tool precisely by asking "Fidelity to what?" (57). Instead, he positions us to think beyond a merely strictly textual approach, inviting us to reconsider adaptation as a form of historical translation. Stam writes: "our statements about films based on novels or other sources need to be less moralistic, less panicked, less implicated in unacknowledged hierarchies, more rooted in contextual and intertextual history. Above all, we need to be less concerned with inchoate notions of fidelity" (75–76).

Following in this direction, Bortolotti and Hutcheon (2007) combine their expertise as a biologist and literary scholar to argue biological evolution and cultural adaptation as homological to one another. In their words, "Stories, in a manner parallel to genes, replicate; the adaptations of both evolve with changing environment" (444). In evoking this homology, Bortolotti and Hutcheon, too, unsettle the fidelity discourse in adaptation studies by introducing how texts undergo types of evolutionary pressures as they are adapted across historical periods, audience constructions, and different forms of media. For this reason, Bortolotti and Hutcheon's conception of adaptation as a homology to evolution positions us to understand the historical lineage of texts as they are adapted through new temporal and spatial contexts. The materiality of the written text as an adapted and therefore re-presented work is filtered through not only a range of decisions to increase the perceived quality of the new text but also questions of cultural ideology, as well. *Doctor Strange,* moving in this direction, offers a compelling case study on how global geopolitics exerts its own types of evolutionary pressures on how source material is adapted to the screen for the global marketplace. By studying *Doctor Strange*'s tensions around racial representation and casting, we understand how Marvel's delineation of a socially conscious diversity aesthetic for its filmic works reflects how disparate racial geographies and imaginations shape original source material in Hollywood's system of global production.

In *Doctor Strange*, as Dr. Stephen Strange nears the doorway of the Ancient One's spiritual sanctuary in Nepal, he is told to forget everything he thinks he knows. Those words address both the diegetic and meta-reality of the comic book's filmic adaptation. Entering the doorway, Dr. Strange offers up clumsily: "The Ancient One? What's his real name? Right. Forget everything I think I know"—a statement that functions ironically as the audience's introduction to the gender-bending of Tilda Swinton's portrayal. This spirit of forgetfulness is called forth in other moments of the film, particularly in one scene where Mordo, another student of the magic arts, describes the Ancient One's origins: "No one knows the age of the Sorcerer Supreme. Only that she is Celtic and never talks about her past." When the Ancient One first appeared in the Marvel comic books in *Strange Tales #110* (1963), Stan Lee and Steve Ditko characterized his origin within this same fictional setting of Kamar-Taj in the Himalayas. The Ancient One is developed in greater detail over *Strange Tales #148* (Lee and Ditko 1966), wherein the reader learns that his magical powers are the consequence of his friend, Kaluu, discovering the secrets of the mystic arts and sharing them with him. They soon disagree over the proper use of these powers. The Ancient One suggests they use their new magic to make their small village a utopia, while Kaluu is tempted by the conquest of nearby towns. Not long after, Kaluu succeeds in placing a mind-control spell over Kamar-Taj as they crown him their king. As the Ancient One attempts to rid his home of this new corrupt monarchy, he succeeds in banishing Kaluu to an alternate dimension at the cost of his village. Within the cinematic *Doctor Strange*, however, Mordo refuses to deliver this backstory long associated with the character. Instead, the scene works to re-story the original comic book continuity, in which key elements like the location of the Ancient One's sanctuary are preserved while other components, like a clear backstory, are elided.

For this reason, Swinton's gender-bending functions as a narrative placeholder for the Tibetan Ancient One, a character with a problematic portrayal in the comics. In a video interview with *Double Toasted,* C. Robert Cargill, the film's lead writer, spoke at length about the production decisions in the film. He describes the Ancient One as a cultural landmine, stating "I could tell you why every single decision that involves the Ancient One is a bad one, and just like the Kobayashi Maru, it all comes down onto which way you're willing to lose" (*Double Toasted* 2016). The Ancient One's origin story mobilizes longstanding tropes about mysticism and the Orient. In *Strange Tales* #148, Lee and Ditko (1966) described the inhabitants of Kamar-Taj as "a race of people who, though not outwardly advanced, had developed the arts of joyous living to a degree undreamed of by more complex civilizations!" Furthermore, the comics present the Ancient One as a vehicle for the white male protagonist, Dr. Strange, to acquire his superhero status, suggesting clear racial hierarchies from the Tibetan sorcerer's secondary supportive role. Within the film, however, the character's re-storying is marked by this diversity aesthetic by translating the racial underpinnings of *Doctor Strange*'s source material in order to avoid controversy in the film's reception.

The need to re-story the character's link to the Far East through ancient, mystical secrets was further echoed within the marketing of the film. In a press stop in Hong Kong, Director Scott Derrickson discussed the motivations for changing the original canon, describing the Ancient One as simply too risky for the contemporary media environment: "The Ancient

One in the comics is a very old American stereotype of what Eastern characters and people are like, and I felt very strongly that we need to avoid those stereotypes at all costs" (Chu 2016). Derrickson later explains that the character's identity-swap emerged out of an attempt to minimize orientalist depictions of Eastern identities. He continues: "The first decision that I made was to make it a woman ... but when I envisioned that character being played by an Asian actress, it was a straight-up Dragon Lady" (Lawler 2016). Derrickson's remarks show an awareness of Hollywood's historical production of these stereotypes, directly referring to the figure of the dragon lady, a character archetype popularized by Anna May Wong in *The Thief of Baghdad* (1924) and *Daughter of the Dragon* (1931).

The "dragon lady" figure has long been associated with wider depictions of Asian representation in American film and literature often known as the "yellow peril." The origins of this trope can be first observed in the period after the abolition of slavery in the US when immigrant labor from Asia increased in supply. In this period, suspicions and conspiracies about the threat of Chinese laborers to native-born citizens and workers surged. Gina Marchetti (1994) contends that the representation and image of the yellow peril "combines racist terror of alien cultures, sexual anxieties, and the belief that the West will be overpowered and enveloped by the irresistible, dark, occult forces of the East" (2). In Marchetti's view, these political tropes, partially rooted in a fear of primitive masses, do much to legitimize the historical period of Western colonialism by working to rationalize European and American territorial expansion as a legitimate reaction to a militarily powerful Asia that threatened Christian life (2).

Between the 1870s and 1940s, an array of political and cultural texts point to how the yellow peril became a global staple of narratives under Western colonialism. These works included H.J. West's *The Chinese Invasion* (1873), Atwell Whitney's *Almond Eyes* (1878), and Pierton W. Dooner's *Last Days of the Republic* (1880), which dramatized the state of California as the frontlines against a Chinese horde (Lyman 2000, 690). In these books, the representation of Asian characters frequently relied on presenting these figures in terms of mystical and exotic elements. Of note, especially in the context of Marvel's problematic history of Asian representation, was the development of the yellow peril villain as an archetype for the adventure novel. The British writer Sax Rohmer (1913) synthesized these cultural fears into commercial success with Dr. Fu Manchu in his novels between 1913 and 1959. The early narratives of Fu Manchu rely on serialized narratives of an evil Chinese doctor who infiltrates London with plans to take over the Western world. Rohmer's novels fixated on hidden conspiracies from the Orient, wherein Asian exoticism and peoples become antagonists for racial and global domination against the Western world. In *The Insidious Dr. Fu Manchu* (1913), the character is depicted as a purveyor of exotic animals and earthly agents whose scorpions, pythons, fungi, and bacilli are all elements in his arsenal of murder (Rohmer 1913, 171). Manchu's use of gangs and dacoits (an Indian term for bandits) recalls the yellow peril's repositioning of the yellow horde as a distinct threat to the white race. Indeed, Sir Denis Nayland, the colonial commissioner in the novel, labels Dr. Manchu's "existence ... a danger to the entire white race which, now, we are powerless to avert" (as quoted in Rohmer 1913, 172). As Seshagiri (2010) notes, these narratives were largely responsible for "inverting the British Empire's racial and political hierarchies to imagine a dystopian civilization dominated by evil Orientals" (53).

The yellow peril threat, the literary tropes of which spanned across the Euro-American cultural field, force us to contend with the ways that colonialism's lingering history makes race legible globally by imprinting exotic and mystical characteristics onto the literary and filmic representations of Eastern peoples. Moreover, the Fu Manchu character became an example of the strength of intellectual property even in the early cultural industries of Britain and the United States. Rohmer's original novels were first translated to the screen with the arrival of the Stoll Production Company's film *The Mystery of Fu-Manchu* (1923). By the end of the decade, Hollywood studios, like Paramount Pictures, gained control of these productions with the arrival of Warner Oland playing the part in *The Mysterious Dr. Fu Manchu* (1929). This history of Dr. Fu Manchu as an adapted character points to the salience of this Asian villain archetype in genres as far-ranging as not only the British spy novel but also American comic books with *Detective Comics #1* (1937), which featured the debut of the character Ching Lung as a Fu-Manchu-style villain.

Positioned within this global production of the yellow peril trope, Marvel's adaptation of *Doctor Strange* has forced the company to contend with its own difficult history of Fu Manchu as a recurring reference point for its racial representation into the 1970s. Atlas Comics published *Yellow Claw #1* (1956), in which the titular character poses as a Fu-Manchu-style villain with a Cold War twist, as the series draws upon Yellow Claw's Chinese background with anti-communist attitudes familiar to popular narratives about American national identity. Later, Marvel introduced the Mandarin in *Tales of Suspense #50* (1964). Characterized as power-hungry in his quest for world domination, Mandarin's backstory, too, portrays the anti-communist attitudes of the Cold War. Introduced on the cover as "The Awesome Power He Possesses Matches The Evil In His Heart!" Mandarin's origin story features his birth to a rich Chinese father and a mother of English noble roots. A descendent of Genghis Khan, his family's fortune was exhausted by paying for the Mandarin's training. No longer able to afford the taxes of Communist China, the Mandarin is exiled, and he swears to avenge himself against the communist government. Thereafter, the character of Fu Manchu himself appeared later as a supervillain nemesis in *Special Marvel Edition #15* (1973). In this way, the process of bending the Ancient One embodied, in some sense, a reflexive recognition of the outdated political and racial themes of its earlier comic book series.

Marvel, to be fair, has not always viewed exotic imaginings of the Orient as simply about manufacturing a racial imagination rooted in fears of cultural difference. The popularity of kung fu titles like *The Green Hornet* (1966-67) and *Enter the Dragon* (1973) allowed for other distillations of racial tropes through kung fu as a martial arts practice. Daniel Martin (2018) directly examines the introduction and appropriation of the kung fu hero by companies like Marvel to chart the ways in which these new literary texts "occurred at an intersection of the cultural values of Hong Kong cinema and American comics" (1522). This process of Americanizing the genre led to new networks of circulation for kung fu film titles, as they migrated from diasporic audiences in Chinatown theaters to more native-born audiences across the American city. Moreover, these new circulations created aesthetic shifts, forms of evolutions and adaptations themselves, and, therefore, new derivations from the original film text, as English-dubbing became a strategy used to overcome potential objections by audiences to consume subtitled foreign films. These successes subsequently produced titles at Marvel that featured kung-fu-inspired characters, including the villain Shang-Chi, "Master of Kung Fu" who was introduced to readers as the unknown son of Dr. Fu Manchu in *Special Marvel Edition #15* (1973).

As Marvel facilitated stereotypes in its representations of heroes of Asian descent, they also presented images of American superheroes who mastered and appropriated secrets of the Orient as the foundation of their power. In *Marvel Premiere #15 (*1974), Danny Rand was introduced as Iron Fist, famed for his use of martial arts and his ability to use his chi, an ability credited to the mystical lost city of K'un-Lun. Contrasted against Shang-Chi, Danny Rand was notable for how he presented a "more" American hero to Marvel's readers. Shang-Chi, trained to be a killing machine who believed his evil father was a moral man, existed in the world of London with its associations to the British spy novel. Danny Rand, a white character, recalled the glory of the American superhero rooted in the metropolitan city, as Danny lives in New York seeking vengeance on his father's murderer. Within Rand's storyline, echoes of the mournful stories of orphans and outcasts that comprise much of the Marvel and Detective Comics (DC) canon are observable. The two comics themselves also embody the ideological needs of American culture of the period, as the language of the yellow peril adapted to the rise of Chinese Communism as a potential ally of the Soviets. For Shang-Chi, this meant returning to the motifs of the yellow supervillain as an antagonist of the colonial global order ruled by the West.

In the contemporary moment, activist groups like MANAA have fought to eliminate these images of stereotyping and cultural appropriation within popular entertainment, a dynamic that should be recognized as not only media criticism but also forms of evolutionary pressures on the process of adapting Marvel's comic books into film. The issue, however, has remained a constant blind spot for both Hollywood and Marvel productions alike, highlighting the ignorance or perhaps indifference of industry executives. With the release of the Netflix television adaptation of *Iron Fist* (2017–2019), Marvel was heavily criticized for continuing its tradition of showcasing white male heroes training under characters of the Orient only to become the "ultimate masters" of Asian martial arts. This backlash over cultural appropriation was further propelled when it was revealed that Lewis Tan, an Asian American actor who appeared in *Iron Fist* as a villain, had originally auditioned for the part of Danny Rand. The show runners instead chose to go with the English Finn Jones (Jung 2017). When confronted on this issue in an interview with *Inverse*, the series co-creator Roy Thomas, tone-deafly declared:

> I just think some people have too much time on their hands, I guess. They have an infinite capacity for righteous indignation. By and large, that tends to be misplaced quite often because if you're becoming all upset over things that are just stories, and if you don't like it, instead of trying to change somebody else's story, go out and make up your own character and do a good job of it. That's just fine, but why waste time trying to run down other people's characters simply because they weren't created with your standards in mind? Now if something is really racist or degrading to a sex or race, an ethnic group or something like that, that's something else, but Iron Fist isn't that and never has been. It's all about a fictitious race, a fictitious place like a Shangri-La, and one person who happens to be its emissary. There's no reason why he can't be Caucasian (Busch 2017).

Thomas's statement minimized the racial history of filmic representation and its number of harmful stereotypes by framing such concerns as misplaced righteous indignation. The backlash surrounding *Iron Fist* was especially notable coming not long after Marvel's controversy over the Ancient One in *Doctor Strange*. Subsequently, the series was canceled by Netflix following its second season premiere after being panned by critics and becoming a source of activist media criticism in its first season.

For how ambivalent Thomas's response was to this *Iron Fist* backlash, individuals associated with *Doctor Strange* instead seemed to have viewed Swinton's casting as a way to sidestep earlier forms of cultural othering signaled by the yellow peril threat. The stereotype's influence across a swath of texts led the Marvel production team to draw on the potential of gender-bending. The choice of Tilda Swinton as the face of this casting decision, however, suggests the ways in which Hollywood's avoidance of racial controversy has drawn recourse to the white female body as capable of providing a respectable image to its desire for cultural diversity. In so doing, *Doctor Strange* illustrates the binding tensions between race and gender that are developing in the representational discourse of Hollywood. Responding to the controversy, Marvel released a statement to Mashable:

> Marvel has a very strong record of diversity in its casting of films and regularly departs from stereotypes and source material to bring its MCU to life. The Ancient One is a title that is not exclusively held by any one character, but rather a moniker passed down through time, and in this particular film the embodiment is Celtic. We are very proud to have the enormously talented Tilda Swinton portray this unique and complex character alongside our richly diverse cast. (Rosenberg 2016)

At first glance the comment that the title "is not exclusively held by any one character" echoes Thomas's thoughts on the cultural mistranslations of the recent *Iron Fist* TV series. Yet, here, Marvel's public relations team uses language that re-stories the original canon, contextualizing the "Ancient One" title as simply a type of moniker in order to represent the character as Celtic with the fair-skinned Swinton. The actress, additionally, is described to embody this unique and complex character alongside a richly diverse cast. In acknowledging the potential of Swinton's casting as a net positive for diversity, MANAA countered that "While actresses deserve the kinds of bold roles usually reserved for men, white actresses are seen on-screen more than Asians of any gender" (Yee 2016). Their response underscored Marvel's ill-preparedness to acknowledge the conditions of the entertainment industry that have made whitewashing an attractive possibility for major backing studios like Disney. Marvel's attempts to re-center Swinton as an embodiment of a rich diversity leveled gender and race as equal categories of analysis in the fight for cultural representation. This rhetorical move demonstrates the ways that cultural discourses around representation taking place in the public sphere have impacted the types of production considerations in Hollywood films. Moreover, Marvel's publicity language illustrates how this diversity aesthetic attempts to frame the public reception of the film. It works to augment the audience's investment in these production decisions by contextualizing the inclusion of stars like Swinton as representative avatars of a new spirit of inclusion in Hollywood.

This diversity aesthetic, moreover, masks other ideological frameworks as evolutionary pressures that come to bear on Hollywood's global system of production. As the controversy played out, the film's creators demonstrated how these story changes were not generated out of a spirit for social justice alone. C. Robert Cargill, during his interview with *Double Toasted,* further identified that the delicate geopolitical conditions of the Asiatic region, in part, created structural conditions for representing the original Marvel canon:

> The Ancient One ... originates from Tibet, so if you acknowledge that Tibet is a place and that he's Tibetan, you risk alienating one billion people who think that that's bullshit and risk the Chinese government going, 'Hey, you know one of the biggest film-watching countries in the world? We're not going to show your movie because you decided to get

> political.' If we decide to go the other way and cater to China in particular and have him be in Tibet... if you think it's a good idea to cast a Chinese actress as a Tibetan character, you are out of your damn fool mind and have no idea what the fuck you're talking about (*Double Toasted* 2016).

Here, Cargill aggressively alludes to wider economic problems connected to film distribution in China. The Chinese government maintains very strict censorship laws designed to limit unfavorable presentation of the country and the law to its public. Qiuqing Tai (2016) refers to China's media censorship guidelines as an authoritarian practice where the state seeks to limit any discussion of subject matter that makes it look unfavorable. She writes that the party serves "to monitor and control the content of news through its propaganda apparatus at all levels" and notes that "common taboo topics include Tibetan and Uighur separationist movements, political reform and democracy, labor protests, individual human rights activists, and so forth" (190). Managing the politics of modern China has long posed an issue for Hollywood companies seeking to adapt intellectual properties that feature Tibet as part of their subject. In the year 1997 alone, two controversies over the representation of Tibet and the Dalai Lama prevented *Seven Years in Tibet* (1997) and Martin Scorsese's *Kundun* (1997) from being released in the country. More recently, the remake of *Red Dawn* (2012) was edited after its production, following fears that it might not receive international distribution in China for the depiction of its government as an invading force in the United States. Metro-Goldwyn-Mayer (MGM), the production company, eventually hired special effects companies to remove all Chinese flags and insignia and replace them with North Korean ones in order to avoid censorship concerns abroad. In this way, Swinton's casting served to side-step the potential distribution conflicts with China by correcting potentially problematic dimensions of Hollywood's reliance on processes of adaptation for its formulated successes.

Moreover, Cargill's remarks embody claims by scholar Edward Said (1979) that orientalism "puts the Westerner in a whole series of possible relationships with the Orient without ever losing him the relative upper hand" (7). Cargill removed his own culpability in Marvel's whitewashing by displacing his responsibility onto the Chinese government's inability to handle the representation of a Tibetan character. Here, Hollywood's version of global capitalism positions China as the culpable party for its failure to sensitively include characters of Asian descent. Here, the diversity aesthetic manifests as a discourse that legitimizes Hollywood's own failings around diversity. It is this moment where Swinton as an avatar for the greater inclusion of women in Hollywood, thus, breaks down in its ideological coherence. The geopolitical and economic factors of distribution created a production environment in which the exchange of gender and racial identities were coequal to one another. In doing so, this circumstance displaces the painful history of Orientalizing stereotypes onto the erasure of Asian identities through the celebration of (white) women's inclusion in the MCU. Moreover, it also illustrates the ways in which the visible representation of identity groups has become increasingly viewed by Hollywood as an aesthetic commodity in and of itself.

This instance in *Doctor Strange*, however, highlights Marvel Studios' wider economic approach to the Chinese market. MCU commodities have achieved huge box office gains in China. *Avengers: Endgame* (2019) is the fourth highest grossing film of all time in the country, and *Avengers: Infinity Wars* (2018) is in the top 20 on a list predominantly featuring nationally created films (Mendelson 2019). The Chinese government, however, only allows 34 foreign films to be released within the country each year as a way of maintaining their national film industry. As Jennifer Bisset (2019) comments, "movie studios will go to major lengths to make the cut." *Iron Man 3* (2013) is one of the most notable examples of Marvel tailoring productions to the Chinese market. After the investment from the Chinese film group DMG Entertainment, an alternative version of the film was released for mainland audiences (Brzeski 2012). While most of the differences were minor, the addition of a new scene featuring Chinese film star Fan Bingbing was notable. The scene shows Bingbing in the role of a surgeon, speaking in Chinese to another doctor before a medical procedure on Tony Stark. The surgery itself is recut to connect footage of Robert Downey Jr., Gwyneth Paltrow, and Don Cheadle from the original film with shots of Bingbing and the other medical team to make it appear as though they are in a Chinese hospital. Bingbing's appearance, however, was marketed heavily in China at the film's release, yet ultimately amounted to little more than a tiny cameo near the end of the movie.

Beyond the alternative version of the film, *Iron Man 3*'s casting reflected the curation of a diversity aesthetic for the Chinese government. Ben Kingsley, a British born actor of Indian descent, played the role of the Mandarin, the perceived villain of the movie. Kingsley's performance can be seen as another attempt by Marvel to sidestep issues with a character's problematic history by "bending" the racial identities of characters in its canon and avoiding the casting of a Chinese-born or Chinese American actor that might cause censorship issues in the foreign market. Kingsley's depiction of the Mandarin is ultimately revealed to be an imposter, merely a front for the real white and male villain of the movie. In 2019, however, it was revealed that the *actual* Mandarin would serve as the primary villain in *Shang-Chi: Legend of the Ten Rings*. Tony Leung, a Hong Kong film star, was announced to play the part. The decision was immediately met with concern over the problematic history of the character in the comics (Stone 2019). The casting in China also raised some regionally specific issues over the choice to feature someone with Leung's ethnicity as an actor from Hong Kong in the villain role instead of someone from the mainland. Media scholar Chris Berry at the time explained:

> It would be more risky if he was a mainland star. Casting a Hong Kong star — even someone as beloved as Tony Leung — in this orientalist villain role is safer. That's especially true now that everyone in [China] is looking quite negatively at Hong Kong. (Bisset 2019)

This dynamic highlights yet another way in which diversity in Marvel's film properties is aestheticized to manage perceptions of racial and cultural hierarchies in the film industry, reflecting how the ideologies of branding can work to adapt texts through the evolutionary pressures of the marketplace. It is our argument that this cultivation of a sensitive diversity aesthetic has been one way that Marvel's film properties have allowed themselves to find global success by working through industrial processes of adaptation to translate the original comic book canon to a variety of national film markets.

Her character, his name—the history of the she-hero

When Dr. Strange misidentifies the man in the sanctuary as the Ancient One, the film's creative team plays upon the audience's similarly gendered expectations. As the camera turns on the former surgeon's face in confusion, Swinton's character pours him a cup of tea as she claims her presence as the Ancient One in the narrative. This moment marked the first explicit example of gender-bending in the MCU, a practice with its own very rich tradition in comics and fandom. Gender-bending, also known by the variants gender-swapping or gender-switching, is a commonly seen practice in comics and other mediums where a character of a different sex or identity assumes a role traditionally known to be a straight white male. Long associated with fan fiction and slash's textual poaching, the term has been described as a form of cultural production whose main trope provides the possibility for the canon to take on renewed significance to female fans. As Kristina Busse (2017) writes: "gender-switching stories thematize a variety of negative experiences often particular to women, such as greater objectification, concern with body image, and a sexual vulnerability including the larger emphasis on virginity, the risk of pregnancy, and the greater danger of sexual violence" (53). These gender changes typically raise textual questions about the social vs. biological experience of gender. In doing so, they deconstruct the relationship of the canon to social identity by working to re-story key elements and provide the greater possibility for women's inclusion in public life.

These questions posed by gender-bending are similar but not coequal to the issue of race-bending in which the race of a character is changed. Each tradition interrogates the canon's common assumptions about inclusivity. Since Swinton's introduction in *Doctor Strange* (2016), Marvel-related productions have featured other characters like Carol Danvers, Monica Rambeau, and Miles Morales, whose origins each emerged in the comics from racial or gendered transformations of original characters. These changes follow our conception of the diversity aesthetic in large part because of Marvel's longer history of creating female characters cultivated specifically for the purposes of broadening market appeal. Here, the use of "aesthetic" appeals to the word's meaning as "a pleasing appearance or effect" (Merriam-Webster). We argue that the term captures the company's efforts to make women's inclusion in the comics a source of ideological investment for fans without providing any meaningful intervention in the genre's masculine hierarchies. At the same time, this adaptation of male characters marks out, in the canon's evolutionary terms, the success of pressure from media activists and international government censors alike.

The history of identity-bending in the comics illustrates how attempts to increase women's visibility in the superhero genre has often reflected cultural ambivalence. Superheroes, since their emergence as a popular genre in the 1930s and 1940s, have long rested on specific gendered and nationalist assumptions about their characters. Bradford W. Wright (2001) has written at length on the ways that the comic books themselves presaged the emergence of the US into World War II, especially as they linked masculinity with American ideals (30). A specific identifying example can be seen in the first cover *Captain America #1* from 1940, which featured the patriotic young Steve Rogers punching Adolf Hitler a year prior to the US' declaration of war against any Axis power. Scholars like Jason Dittmer (2013) have also argued that Marvel's Captain America explicitly provided the archetype of the nationalist superhero through Rogers, the ultra-masculine super soldier saving the United States of America in its darkest hours (38). This early example showcases how superheroes have historically embodied masculine ideals. Robert Genter (2007) has considered the connections between masculinity and the cultural moment of the 1950s and 1960s. He explains that Marvel's core characters spoke to the political conditions of young Americans of the era by taking up "meditations on the organization man, the scientific-military establishment, and the dangers of conformity echoed a burgeoning critique of America by radicals such as Tom Hayden and Paul Goodman" (974). Yet, in so doing, they reflected an imagination about the masculine perspective of not only their protagonists but their readers, too. These series spoke not just to the conflicts of American masculinity between the 1940s and 1960s, as their framing of the male superhero frequently invoked individual men as the ideological units and leaders of society.

Within comics, this view of masculinity, however, was further realized through consistent heterosexual and gendered metaphors that showed the hero's parallel calls to protect both society and his female romantic interest. Narrative tropes have long featured an imperiled female subject endangered by male villainy, requiring the superhero's male intervention to save the day. At the same time, the history of female superheroes frequently paralleled the company's efforts to differentiate their comic book offerings rather than reflect ideological cohesion. With the arrival of Wonder Woman in *All*

Star Comics #8 (1941), readers saw one of the first prominent representations of a superheroine ever seen in comics. As young Americans were learning the news of the Japanese attack on Pearl Harbor, they, too, were greeted with Diana of Paradise Island's brave decision to take up her golden lasso to support the American fight against Nazism. DC, its publisher, had launched the serial to almost instant success for the attention of male and female readers alike. Not long after, competitors like Timely Comics (later renamed to Marvel Comics in 1961) created their own female leads, responding to what they identified as clear market needs. Their production of female superheroes toggled between two approaches. Between 1941 and 1947, the company introduced original characters like Blonde Phantom, Nellie the Nurse, and Patsy Walker, none of whom were a breakout success like Wonder Woman. Timely's second approach consisted of the development of the "she-hero," characters that serve as female sidekicks for original male heroes. This term uniquely captures the derivative nature of these attempts to create and include female characters like Namora and Miss America into the original Marvel canon. These two characters seized on the already developed audiences for male superheroes like Namor, the underwater crime fighter, and Captain America, Timely's biggest commodity during World War II.

When Namora first appeared in *Marvel Mystery Comics* No. 82 in 1947, she was introduced as an ancillary female character to the male Namor. Namora meets her male counterpart while living under the sea after her family was killed by a group of mainland monsters. Her quest is to seek vengeance. When Namor obliges her company, he asks her name to which she replies: "Aquaria Nautica Neptunia! But since I will be your partner why not call me Namora?" (Lee and Powell, 1947, 5). Here, the near reproduction of Namor's name illustrates how the she-hero characterization tended to reduce issues of gender down to aesthetically drawn and visible forms of characterization. Namora's naming, thus, reflected Marvel's assumption of how male characters could be simply redrawn as female for new readerships. She is soon after revealed to have roughly the same powers as Namor, both of whom possess the ability to be healed by water, and takes up a romantic relationship with her male counterpart. In this way, Namora's position in the comics ultimately functioned to support the central premise of the main character's heterosexual masculinity, yielding little intervention in how representations of women might transform the characterizations of the male superhero. Namora, as a case study, gestures how the cultivation of a diversity aesthetic in the comics allowed for women's inclusion in Marvel's multiverse as superheroes while their presence was domesticated through their deference as supporting roles to titled male characters.

The place of the she-hero was neither exclusive to the period of the 1940s nor did it prove unaffected by the font of social criticism posed by second wave feminism. In the decade following the public protest over the Miss America pageant in 1968, Marvel launched new female versions of their characters in the form of Jennifer Waters' She-Hulk and Carol Danvers' Ms. Marvel. A response to the feminist movements of the era, these new she-heroes developed a greater level of agency. Danvers, the subject of the recent *Captain Marvel* (2019) MCU production, emerged as one of the most successful instances of a she-hero in the comics. Her identity developed directly from the original male version of Captain Marvel, who was helmed by the character Mar-Vell, an alien who came to earth with superhuman strength and the ability to teleport and fly. Ms. Marvel first appeared in *March Super-Heroes* #13 in 1968, before serving as Mar-Vell's longtime military leader and eventually gaining his same superpowers. In *Ms. Marvel* #1, when asked for a name, Danvers proclaims: "You can call me Ms. Marvel. My costume ties me to Captain Marvel, in a way I don't yet understand. Till I do understand, I'll need a name — and Ms. Marvel is as good as any" (Conway and Buscema 1977, 15). Melanie Gibson (2016) notes the significance of the name Ms. Marvel within Danvers's superhero identity. *Ms. Magazine,* published since 1972, is largely credited with the popularization of the term "Ms." as a form of address for women. *Ms. Marvel* became one of Marvel's most popular series as a textual nod to the growing fight by women for greater legal and economic independence (Gibson). For this reason, the she-hero represents the by-product of a business strategy; it adapted the traditional male superhero by using gender as the frame of its diversity aesthetic in order to expand the brand's commodity offerings for female fans. This reflects the myriad ways cultural producers manage the perception of social identities represented onscreen and through publicity material as part of larger efforts to court new audiences and demographic groups. Such brand extensions rightfully need to be understood through evolutionary processes of adaptation as industrial texts navigate shifting terrains of cultural ideologies and audience formations.

Like the characterization of Namora, however, Danvers eventually develops a romantic relationship with her male counterpart, thus illustrating the heterosexual underpinnings of the she-hero. Danvers' role as Mar-vell's subordinate female counterpart and girlfriend highlights some of the inherent limitations of the sexist structures of the comic book industry. In the 1970s, though still true today, comics were both predominantly created by male writers and artists and read by a majority male fanbase. Gibson notes,

> In analysing these comics, the dominance of male comic creators and audiences in relation to the superhero genre is significant. Female characters appeared infrequently and it became a truism… that these were inherently sexist figures who were created solely for the pleasure of a heterosexual male audience. (136)

She argues that due to the gender makeup of comics, looking at both its creators and fans alike, the success of female superheroes was intricately bound up in issues of masculine desire.

These stories about women were, thus, shaped by their appeal to likely male readers. Comics writer Kelly Sue DeConnick echoed this critique over the limitations of Marvel's she-heroes:

> When so many of our female heroes were conceived as boobed versions of their male counterparts — Ms. Marvel, She-Hulk, Spider-Woman — it's a tough sell. They're, like, the side dishes, supplements — something you might want to get in addition to your main course, but they're not the reason you picked that restaurant in the first place. They're not the meat and potatoes. They weren't conceived of as meat and potatoes and we don't package them that way. (Hudson 2012)

DeConnick was the writer of the *Captain Marvel* series in 2012, a series which saw Danvers assume the role of a previously male superhero. Here, Deconnick explains that her goal with Danvers as Captain Marvel was to finally allow her an escape from her she-hero past. Danvers's transformation from Ms. Marvel to Captain Marvel in 2012 was a starting point for a new movement amongst rising Marvel heroines that would eventually translate into the MCU. This goal was to draw on the precedent of Ms. Marvel in the 1970s to present female characters who claimed greater possession over their superhero identities and storylines. To this point, the comics have featured the launch of Jane Foster in the role of Thor, an African American woman as Iron Man, and Jennifer Walters who drops the pronoun in "She-Hulk" to claim greater ownership of the Hulk title. This history, thus, captures both how the she-hero reified the textual marginalization of women previously intimated by their absence as heroes, as well as the intervention of various feminisms on Marvel's forms of female representation.

These changes around diversity reflect a new reconsideration of gender in the Marvel canon. In *Understanding Comics*, Scott McCloud (1993) highlights the role of identity in comics by examining the issue of form. He notes that the incorporation of simplified images works to place cartoons in a world of generalized concepts (41). For this reason, McCloud argues that the heroes of these comics often signify less the actions of a concrete person and more heroes as representative icons of larger political and social ideologies. Thus, the hero identity takes on a special significance in depictions of the moral fight for good that expands much further than the storylines of men (or women) with special abilities. McCloud's work on the semiotics of comic books, thus, raises questions about the significance of the character name behind the mask. To this point, Peter Coogan (2011) takes up the issue of title in his definition of the superhero: "These minimal connections between heroic codename and character are not foregrounded in the hero's adventures, but those adventures did serve as models for the creators of superheroes in their portrayals of their heroes' foppish alter egos" (79). Moral character is thought to be understood in terms of the debates over representation that mark any given historical reality. These very debates work to mobilize the attention of industry executives that place critical pressures on the processes of adaptation that are a hallmark of film production.

These questions have been raised as the subject of recent comics and Marvel Studios' film productions. When African and Latin American Miles Morales officially assumes the title of Spider-Man in *Spider-Man: Into the Spider-verse* (2018), he concludes, "Anyone can wear the mask. You could wear the mask. If you didn't know that before, I hope you know that now." The film uniquely featured both gender and race-bending to not only showcase Miles Morales but also embrace depictions of Spider-Gwen, Gwen Stacy's female version of Spider-Man, and Penny Parker, who is of Asian descent, in the superhero's title. These representations work to delink canonical assumptions about the categories of race and gender that mark superhero identities. Significantly, this delinking of character and hero predates these transformations in Marvel's cinematic universe. Indeed, Carol Danvers expressed a similar notion in the comics to Morales's statement when she took on the title of Captain Marvel in 2012. When Danvers speaks to Captain America in *Captain Marvel #1*, she raises the explicit significance of superhero titles: "Captain Marvel wasn't his name. It was his mantle. Now, it's his legacy. And he wanted you to have it." The issue concludes as Danvers gloriously declares: "I'm taking the damn name" (2012, 15).

In that moment, Danvers assumed a title that she has now been canonized as owning in the MCU. It is this same spirit that has impacted Marvel's recent changes to the gender and race identities of its characters, allowing actresses like Brie Larson and Tilda Swinton to metaphorically "take the damn name" while providing, at least initially, limited interventions in the continuity for their characters and their origins to support these changes. As the publicity discourse of these casting decisions play out, Swinton and Larson represent articulations of aesthetic choices that center diversity and inclusion within Hollywood's global production culture. This circumstance not only speaks to the influence of the millennial generation but also the enlistment of this same generation as unpaid marketers on social media. It is precisely here that the "diversity aesthetic" takes up specific resonance, as it centers feelings of inclusion and diversity amongst its fans that work to market the cultural and ideological framing of the film's reception. In this corporate calculus, the company has demonstrated a rethinking of its relationship to the issue of gender and race within its canon of intellectual property, an observable dynamic in the practices of adaptation that mark its translation of comic book properties into the global film marketplace.

Danvers' depiction on screen is especially notable for its departures from the original canon. In *Captain Marvel* (2019), Danvers appears with no reference to her she-hero past as Ms. Marvel. In fact, the film toys with her problematic legacy in its depiction of one of the film's primary male characters. Jude Law's character, Yon-Rogg, serves as a Kree warrior who guides Danvers. Pompous and arrogant, he performs in the likeness of Mar-vell in the comics, acting as though he is Carol's only teacher and guide. The film later features Danvers fighting Yon-Rogg after it is revealed that the Kree were villainously attempting to annihilate an entire species. While this fight would give voice to a rewriting of the gender hierarchy between Ms. Marvel and Mar-Vell, it is the film's ultimate twist that withholds this promise. Law's character is revealed not to be Mar-vell at all. Rather, it is Annette Benning's role who had served as Danvers' military mentor in the time before she had powers. Thus, this moment provides another example of gender-swapping in the film as Danvers assumes the title of Captain Marvel in her honor. Additional nods to gender-bending are further incorporated by the introduction of Monica Rambeau, who also held the title of Captain Marvel in the 1980s after Mar-Vell died in combat. As *Captain Marvel* was framed publicly as the MCU's feminist title, it returned to the legacies of gender-bending in its comics in order to give nod to their aesthetic and narrative history.

This celebration of gender-bending within *Captain Marvel* links the cinematic universe with the comic books through its acknowledgement of the role that the she-hero played in increasing female representation. As ideas about inclusivity circulate in the political debates of the era, we now observe how they have initially been refracted in Hollywood's systems of adaptation. This is seen partly in the spectacular demise of long-awaited productions like *The Lone Ranger* (2013) and *Ghost in the Shell* (2017) that struggled domestically in the United States, due, in part, to the perception of their insensitive racial casting of Johnny Depp and Scarlett Johansson in non-white roles. These debates have connected to other cultural concerns in banner entertainment properties helmed by Marvel Studios, thus explaining the mutual fear of Marvel's team in both avoiding the exotic orientalism of the Ancient One and Tibetan identity as a source of geopolitical tension. Their attempts to unsettle the original material of the comic book canon has illustrated how Marvel's global productions have sought to adapt the representations of various cultural identities across a number of different national audience constructions. This aesthetic management of their diversity on-screen has resulted in putting issues of gender and race into tension with one another, thus creating two conflicting rubrics of how to visualize social change on screen.

I'm taking the damn name: concluding points on the diversity aesthetic

As Albert S. Fu (2015) has suggested, continuity and canon are vital forces in the maintenance of fandom (279). Canon designates what textual material is considered official, and it reflects the ideological coherence of the serialized comic books. Moreover, canon also takes on the resonance of religious scripture for certain fans, and this ideological coherence impacts and shapes their forms of personal investment in these stories. Unsurprisingly, fans have challenged the idea of official canon by their efforts to re-story the original material through fan fiction. These practices like gender-bending allow for new articulations of social identities in Marvel's traditionally male universe. These fan practices are both predated and continuous with the company's history of translating its male characters into female counterparts. Yet more than this, changes to Marvel's official continuity presented in their comic series and movies reflect how the diversity aesthetic translates the needs of certain audience constituencies to feel represented by the canon. The resulting efforts to re-story this body of work, while not always successful, speak to the clear issues of cultural belonging that are raised by the centrality of the canon within fandom.

The recent developments in the MCU illustrate the commitment to challenging the identity characteristics of core canon characters. At the San Diego Comic-Con in 2019, Marvel Studios announced that they would center the upcoming *Thor: Love and Thunder* around Jane Foster's assumption of the superhero role. This decision came on the heels of changes to the underlying comic in November 2014. The first issue of the new *Thor* book, written by Jason Aaron, featured a mysterious woman wielding Mjölnir, Thor's iconic hammer. This gender-swap thus confirmed the famous words of the series: "Whosoever holds this hammer, if he be worthy, shall possess the power of Thor." By issue *Thor* volume 4, #8 (2015), it was revealed that Jane Foster, Thor Odinson's longtime love interest, was the new hero. The storyline, in fact, harkened to a title from the 1970s—the second era of she-hero prominence—entitled "What if Jane Foster had found the Hammer of Thor?" which considers an alternative timeline in which Foster, not Thor's comics alter ego Don Blake, had lifted the hammer to fight injustice. Events presented in *What If* were always intended as alternative histories and not part of the main Marvel 616 timeline. Aaron's contemporary comic, however, served to redefine this story as a part of Marvel continuity.

This Thor arc had massive significance for many female readers, highlighting some of the key distinctions between gender-swaps and she-heroes within fan communities. In *Thor* #1, one fan, Sarah Jean Maefs, writing to the Marvel editorial staff noted the significance of seeing a female version of Thor:

> Thor was my hero. He was noble and strong. He was smarter than people ever gave him credit for. He was full of joy and duty. He was a champion, a leader, an example that even when we are low we are redeemable... Thor was both perfect and flawed at the same time. I often fell into day dreams where I found the hammer, that I picked it up. That I was worthy and was granted the power of Thor... I wanted

> to be Thor, but I didn't want to crossplay. I didn't want to be a She-Thor. I hated being called Lady-Thor or ThorGirl... I wanted to be Thor if Thor were a Woman. I wanted to be as though I as a woman picked up the hammer and I was granted the power of storms. (Aaron 26)

On this point, the notion of canon slips easily into political parallels around citizenship, as fan activism mirrors desires for the inclusion of new social identities within the writing of the nation. Maef describes some of the most key distinctions between the new age of gender-swapping and the previous era of she-heroes: women now hold the title rather than operating as female versions of the male superhero. Writing before the first issue was published, Maef concludes: "In October, I will see what I always dreamed of. I will see what -- in my mind -- is a comic book starring me. A woman who raised the hammer" (26). Maef also alludes to the wider gender-swapping practice and how the new version of Thor fits alongside characters like Carol Danvers:

> like Carol Danvers before her, she took on the legacy of a man before her. Took his title, his mantel, and punches a hole in the sky. Like Carol she isn't Lady-Marvel, she is Captain Marvel. This new Thor, she is her own woman, taking on the position of this realm's protector, she will be the Thor the world needs. (5)

Maef notes the significance of female representation in the comics and the ways that the inclusion of women in the superhero canon capture intimate feelings of belonging for fans. For them, the canon in the comics comes to function as a metaphor for public life.

This analysis has shown that Marvel Studios' bid for greater inclusivity in its cinematic universe features a return to their strategy of gender-bending from the 1940s and 1970s, when the concept of the "she-hero" was first pioneered. As we identified, the practice of gender-bending its male heroes into women was viewed as an economically valuable way of integrating female protagonists into the canon. Of course, these changes required efforts to re-story the original canon for this strategy of social integration. The resulting history included examples of Namora and Miss America who took on the identities of their male counterparts, as they solidified the centrality of the male superhero. They, at the same time, fought for the inclusion of women within Marvel's official comic book universe. As we identified, this iteration of the "she-hero" maintained the subordination of women but was not without historical interventions in its cultural imagination around issues of diversity. In the 1950s through 1970s when social movements centered the politics of identity in the fight for civil rights, the she-hero experienced similar innovations that produced the more independent Ms. Marvel who seized on the feminist-oriented honorific to assert a greater role from her supporting position to Mar-vell. It is this same character history that Marvel would seize upon for its cinematic universe as it produced *Captain Marvel* to give greater voice to feminist discourse that had renewed popularity throughout the 2010s.

By returning to the "she-hero," Marvel's content strategy has placed continuity and canon in direct contention with one another, as was the case with their decision to change the Ancient One to a moniker given to Swinton's portrayal of the now-Celtic monk. Moreover, economic considerations also placed unique burdens on the historical continuity of Marvel's comic books, requiring revisions not only for domestic, social, and political reasons but geopolitical ones, too. Fears of an absent Chinese market over the inclusion of the Tibetan character challenged Marvel's cinematic universe to embody the individual's fight for social harmony that is a feature of their early comics. The company's hailing of a rhetoric around diversity and inclusion for their slate of production works to embody a vision of social integration, while at the same time it domesticates similar desires that are not economically valuable. The idea that Asian American representation must be subjected to the geopolitical conditions of a commercial industry is, to be sure, a more complex debate, but it illustrates how Disney and Marvel have approached adapting the original Marvel canon to negotiate the social politics of its intellectual properties for the modern day. These transformations thus must be viewed through the prism of how national divisions over race and gender, among other cultural categories, create evolutionary pressures on the adaptation of original intellectual property into globally distributed Hollywood films.

For this reason, we argue that the diversity aesthetic informs Marvel's process of adapting the original comic book canon and that it can be observed as producing a publicity discourse that aims to link film's commodity culture with desires for social change. We have organized these efforts under the rubric of the diversity aesthetic to distill the ways in which Marvel has endeavored to bring the feeling of greater social representation to its filmic canon, around constructions of racial and gender identity. These efforts have found recourse to the history of bending in the comic books as one strategy among others to bring core properties into the MCU with a more equitable and inclusive face. Moreover, the desire to brand the MCU as consistent with modern feminist conversations has been used to negotiate the economic fears of non-white, racial casting in films like *Doctor Strange*. While some fans did support and were intrigued by the idea of a female as the Ancient One, its racial insensitivity became apparent through its centering of white women's representation as a vision of cultural diversity. With this feeling of social inclusion, the company worked to deflect interrogation into the systemic ways in which race and gender hierarchies are produced through Hollywood casting. On the surface, this discourse may appear to corroborate narratives of the changing face of Hollywood; however, it also conceals the systematic ways in which

Hollywood continues to regulate a very specific racial economy of its casting that embodies the industry's imagination about its geopolitical and economic conditions.

In so doing, an analysis of the company's re-working of gender in its canon illustrates the domestication of fan and social criticism about the masculinist underpinnings of the superhero film while working to contain this same criticism against the MCU's racial hierarchies. Marvel's cultivation of publicity language around this social criticism suggests how this diversity aesthetic reflects Marvel's use of representation as an aesthetic commodity and less about the arduous work of creating a more inclusive canon of core film properties. Here, we point to the celebration of Swinton as a net benefit for female representation in Hollywood *and* as a blunting force against the charges of whitewashing and potential orientalism, despite the script's hesitance to reimagine the character within the film's universe. This friction between gender and race is of significance not only for what it reveals about current debates around inclusive casting but for how it showcases the continued state of Hollywood's star-focused mode of production. As Hollywood responds to these calls, one of the remaining challenges for advocates will be to navigate the role of this "diversity aesthetic" to mask the hardening of social hierarchies in the guise of inclusive rhetoric. Given the criticisms from online commentators, other celebrities, and media activist groups like MANAA, individuals, indeed, are paying attention to the continued state of diversity in Hollywood. It is our hope that we, as scholars, lend our historical research to these efforts.

References

Aaron, Jason. 2014. *Thor Vol. 1: The Goddess of Thunder (2014-2015)*. New York City: Marvel Comics, October.

"Aesthetic". 2019. *Merriam-Webster.com*. Merriam Webster. Web. 27 July 2019.

Banet-Weiser, Sarah. 2015. "Keynote Address: Media, Markets, Gender: Economies of Visibility in a Neoliberal Moment." *The Communication Review* 18 (1): 53–70.

Bisset, Jennifer. 2019. "Marvel is censoring films for China, and you probably didn't even notice." *Cnet*, November 1: https://www.cnet.com/features/marvel-is-censoring-films-for-china-and-you-probably-didnt-even-notice.

Bortolotti, Gary R., and Linda Hutcheon. 2007. "On the Origin of Adaptations: Rethinking Fidelity Discourse and "Success"—Biologically." *New Literary History* 38 (3): 443–58.

Brzeski, Patrick. 2012. "Disney's Marvel to Co-Produce 'Iron Man 3' in China." *The Hollywood Reporter*, 16 April , https://www.hollywoodreporter.com/news/disney-marvel-iron-man-3-china-co-production-dmg-312323.

Busch, Caitlin. 2017. "'Iron Fish' Creator: Whitewashing Controversy "Righteous Indignation." *Inverse*, March 17, https://www.inverse.com/article/29155-iron-fist-marvel-comics-whitewashing-roy-thomas.

Busse, Kristina. 2017. *Framing Fan Fiction: Literary and Social Practices in Fan Fiction Communities*. Iowa City: The University of Iowa Press.

Chu, Karen. 2016. "Doctor Strange Director Addresses Whitewashing Controversy." *The Hollywood Reporter*, October 13, : https://hollywoodreporter.com/heat-vision/doctor-strange-director-whitewashing-controversy-938051.

Conway, Gerry and John Buscema. 1977. *Ms. Marvel* 1, no. 1. New York: Marvel Comics, January .

Coogan, Peter. 2011. "The Definition of the Superhero." *A Comic Studies Reader*. Edited by Jeet Heer and Kent Worcester, 77–93. Jackson: University Press of Mississippi, .

DeConnick, Kelly Sue. 2012. *Captain Marvel* 1. New York: Marvel Comics. July

Dittmer, Jason. 2013. *Captain America and the Nationalist Superhero: Metaphors, Narratives, and Geopolitics*. Philadelphia: Temple University Press,

Doctor Strange. 2016. Directed by Scott Derrickson. Marvel Studios.

Double Toasted. 2016. "EXCLUSIVE! DOCTOR STRANGE WRITER "C. ROBERT CARGILL" - Double Toasted Interview." *YouTube*, April 22 , https://www.youtube.com/watch?v=eEpbUf8dGq0&t=17m54s.

Fleming, Jr., Mike. 2019. "Destin Daniel Cretton Marvel's Choice to Direct "Shang-Chi." *Deadline*, March 13, https://deadline.com/2019/03/destin-creston-shang-chi-marvel-choice-1202575136.

Fu, Albert S. 2015. "Fear of a Black Spider-Man: Racebending and the Colour-Line in Superhero (Re)casting." *Journal of Graphic Novels and Comics* 3 (3) (December): 269–83. doi: 10.1080/21504857.2014.994647

Genter, Robert. 2007. "With Great Power Comes Great Responsibility: Cold War Culture and the Birth of Marvel Comics." *The Journal of Popular Culture* 40 (6) (November): 953–78. doi: 10.1111/j.1540-5931.2007.00480.x.

Gibson, Mel. 2016. "Who does she think she is? Female comic-book characters, second-wave feminism and feminist film theory." *Superheroes and Identities*. Edited by Mel Gibson, David Huxley, Joan Ormrod, 135–46. Routledge.

Hudson, Laura. 2012. "Kelly Sue DeConnick on the Evolution of Carol Danvers to Captain Marvel [Interview]." *Comics Alliance*, March 19, comicsalliance.com/kelly-sue-deconnick-captain-marvel.

Jewett, Robert, and John Shelton Lawrence. 1977. *The American Monomyth*. New York: Doubleday.

Jung, E. Alex. 2017. "Meet Lewis Tan, the Asian-American Actor Who Could Have Been Iron Fist." *Vulture*, March 20, https://www.vulture.com/2017/03/lewis-tan-marvel-iron-fist-interview.html.

Juzwiak, Rich. 2016. "Tilda Swinton Sent Us Her Email Exchange with Margaret Cho about Doctor Strange, Diversity, and Whitewashing." *Jezebel*, December 16, http://jezebel.com/tilda-swinton-sent-us-her-email-exchange-with-margaret-1790203875.

Lawler, Kelly. 2016. "Whitewashing Controversy Still Haunts 'Doctor Strange.'" *USA Today*, November 7, https://www.usatoday.com/story/life/entertainthis/2016/11/07/doctor-strange-whitewashing-ancient-one-tilda-swinton-fan-critical-reaction/93416130/

Lee, Stan, and Bob Powell. 1947. *Marvel Mystery Comics,* No. 82, Marvel Comics, May.

Lee, Stan, and Jack Kirby. 1964. "The Hands of the Mandarin." *Tales of Suspense* 1(50), Marvel Comics.

Lee, Stan, and Steve Ditko. 1963. "Doctor Strange Master of Black Magic!" *Strange Tales* 1 (110) Marvel Comics.

Lee, Stan, and Steve Ditko. 1966. "The Origin of the Ancient One!" *Strange Tales* 1 (148). New York: Marvel Comics.

Lyman, Stanford M. 2000. "The "Yellow Peril" Mystique: Origins and Vicissitudes of a Racist Discourse." *International Journal of Politics, Culture and Society* 13 (4) (Summer): 683–747. doi: 10.1023/A:1022931309651.

Marchetti, Gina. 1994. *Romance and the Yellow Peril: Race, Sex, and Discursive Strategies in Hollywood Fiction.* Berkeley: University of California Press.

Martin, Daniel. 2018. "The Americanization of the Hong Kong Kung Fu Hero: Orientalism and Social Class in Marvel Comics' *Iron Fist.*" *The Journal of Popular Culture* 51(6) (December) 1521–39.

McCloud, Scott. 1993. *Understanding Comics: The Invisible Art.* New York: Harper Perennial.

Mendelson, Scott. 2019. "Box Office: 'Avengers: Endgame' Topped 'Avatar' Thanks To China, Not America." *Forbes*, August 8, https://www.forbes.com/sites/scottmendelson/2019/08/08/avengers-endgame-infinity-war-avatar-marvel-iron-man-black-panther-last-jedi-star-wars-spider-man-pikachu-mulan-china-box-disney-office/#6855f25b7943.

Quinonez, Ariana. 2015. "Marvel's cinematic diversity problem." *Hypable*, April 30, https://www.hypable.com/marvels-cinematic-diversity-problem.

Rohmer, Sax. 1913. *The Insidious Dr. Fu-Manchu: Being a Somewhat Detailed Account of the Amazing Adventures of Nayland Smith in His Trailing the Sinister Chinaman.* New York: McBride, Nast & Company.

Rosenberg, Adam. 2016. "Marvel Defends 'Doctor Strange' Casting With New Character Info." *Mashable*, April 26, https://mashable.com/2016/04/26/doctor-strange-ancient-one-celtic/#mFXjZ2wtUSqD.

Said, Edward. 1979. *Orientalism.* New York: Vintage Books.

Salkowitz, Rob. 2016. "Is China Why Hollywood Movies Are So White? Not So Fast (And Furious)." *Forbes*, February 24, https://www.forbes.com/sites/robsalkowitz/2016/02/24/is-china-why-oscarssowhite-not-so-fast-and-furious/#7b2af7a1c2c0.

Seshagiri, Urmila. 2010. *Race and the Modernist Imagination.* Ithaca and London: Cornell University Press.

Spider-Man: Into the Spider-Verse. Directed by Peter Ramsey, Bob Persichetti, and Rodney Rothman, Marvel Studios, 2018.

Stam, Robert. 2000. "Beyond Fidelity: The Dialogics of Adaptation." *Film Adaptation*, edited by James Naremore, 54–76. New Brunswick: Rutgers University Press.

Stone, Sam. 2019. "Shang-Chi: Why Some Chinese Fans Aren't Happy About the MCU Film." *Comic Book Resources*, July 25, https://www.cbr.com/shang-chi-movie-chinese-social-meida-concerns.

Tai, Qiuqing. 2016. "China's Media Censorship: A Dynamic and Diversified Regime." *Journal of East Asian Studies* 14 (2): 85–209. doi:10.1017/S1598240800008900.

TigerBelly. 2016. "Margaret Cho and the Yellow Telephone." *YouTube*, December 16. https://www.youtube.com/watch?v=ZNkT9CJclD4.

Weinraub, Bernard. 1996. "Disney Will Defy China on Its Dalai Lama Film," *The New York Times.* November 27. https://www.nytimes.com/1996/11/27/movies/disney-will-defy-china-on-its-dalai-lama-film.html.

Wright, Bradford W. 2001. *Comic Book Nation: The Transformation of Youth Culture in America*. Baltimore and London: The Johnsons Hopkins University Press.

Yee, Lawrence. 2016. "Asian American Media Group Blasts Tilda Swinton Casting in Doctor Strange." *Variety*, November 3, https://variety.com/2016/film/news/doctor-strange-whitewashing-ancient-one-tilda-swinton-manaa-1201908555.

2 On the fringes and tassels of respectability: Catwoman and censoring the femme form

A. Luxx Mishou

Introduction

In the 1940 *Batman No. 1* "the Cat," a villainess who will later be known as Catwoman is introduced as a jewel thief planning to relieve the wealthy Mrs. John Travers of her extraordinarily expensive necklace. Caught in her escape by an observant Batman, the Cat's first introduction to comics readers is deceptively two-dimensional. She is a pinup figure of feminine deviance, capturing the appreciative eye of the Caped Crusader and tantalizing readers with the image of a woman available for punishment: "a beautiful young woman!" the comic proclaims (*Catwoman: A Celebration of 75 Years,* 2014, 21). In her reveal, the Cat is given a portrait panel to herself, her dark hair perfectly coiffed, her breasts pointed and perky, and her waist slim in a fashionable green dress. When Batman searches her person for the missing necklace, she coolly offers him a slender ankle, flashing a shapely calf and white high heel and saying, "What's the use – I know when I'm licked!" (21). The exchange is the picture of gender normativity, as an authoritative masculine Batman brings a pouty femme fatale to heel, physically overpowering her as he violently grabs both of her wrists and growls, "we work on different sides of the *law!*" (22).

Though her professional villainous colleagues include mass-murdering clowns, psychopaths, and gangsters, Catwoman faces pointed attacks by mid-century American moral crusaders as a particularly grievous threat to the moral sensibilities of young readers. But why? In this chapter, I argue that Catwoman is regarded as dangerous for her artistic representation as a consistently attractive and autonomous femme, who visually embodies expectations of femininity, while violating codes of behavior in her very strength, independence, and rejection of subservient domesticity: a feline fatale.[1] Catwoman is the archetype of the conniving, manipulative beauty, and she's good at it. However, Catwoman's publication history demonstrates the consequences for femmes who exercise such agency and America's cultural rejection of the example of the empowered figure. After commanding the audience's attention—and Bat's interest—from *Batman #1*, Catwoman is mercilessly thwarted by the Comics Code Authority

DOI: 10.4324/9781003146520-2

(CCA), a self-regulatory (read: censoring) body established to police content in comics from 1954. As a "sympathetic criminal," Catwoman violates no fewer than thirteen CCA sanctions, and the mid-century verdict is strict: 12 years of figurative solitary confinement, forcing the character into unceremonious retirement. According to the CCA, Catwoman is far too dangerous for the reading public. Her censorship sets a dangerous precedent, and this chapter examines how the same sensibilities used to kick Catwoman out of comics in 1954 motivate the 2018 implementation of SESTA-FOSTA, a system of censorship used to impose restrictive legislature on art and suppress the cultural representation of femme bodies today.

My subject in this chapter is censorship and how the historical example of comics controversy is again revisited in contemporary legislation that seeks to censor the femme in public forums, arts, and entertainment. American culture continues to regulate the representation of the femme form, applying similar tactics of shame, and likewise introducing restrictive measures intended to limit representations of femme autonomy. Just as mid-century Catwoman falls under the restriction of the CCA, modern femme artists and performers such as burlesque dancers are policed by social media and online forums who censor their voices and art under the guise of the protection of victims of child exploitation. As Jack Butler writes in *Gaga Feminism*, "the child has all too often served as a justification for the most wretched forms of social and political conservatism in the US since at least the mid-nineteenth century" (Halberstam 2012, 15), and today that conservatism presents itself as strict laws governing online speech, the ramifications of which impact not just Internet forums used by performers for networking and exposure but the actual lived experiences of already-vulnerable populations.

The modern social panic over representations of the femme body in digital spaces is not unlike previous censorship efforts directed at popular media. Respectability politics have governed popular cultural production since their introduction by the Victorians, forwarding arguments of morality, taste, and class to control the public sphere. For Victorians, and in time moving forward, respectability is defined by heteronormative, white, middle-class standards of sexual repression, industrial production, and a system of social hierarchy which enforces shame and ignorance in minority and high-risk populations for the express purpose of maintaining political and domestic power systems. Often, these politics have gendered motivations and consequences, calling for the regulation of bodies and stories in order to maintain a narrative of patriarchal superiority. The ramifications are far reaching, as professionals in even presently legal fields of sex work and popular entertainment find their networks clipped and their content threatened by legislation such as SESTA-FOSTA.

Contemporary burlesque performers are familiar with the cultural restrictions of the femme form and the laws and regulations which govern its artistic exposure. As striptease artists, burlesque performers of all gender expressions reveal their bodies to audiences in a mutually consensual performance, but the extent of the reveal is controlled by localized laws rather than creative choice. Local legislations called Blue Laws have historically forbid specified secular activities on Sundays, such as whether or not bars may operate or if a grocery store may sell wine. Today, Blue Laws impact social activities and local commerce at the hands of Alcoholic Beverage Commissions or Committees (ABCs), who are empowered to enforce puritanical morality through the granting and revoking of alcohol licenses. Local ABCs determine which activities may be hosted in venues that serve alcohol, with particular regard for "adult" entertainment, and *if* an ABC allows bars and restaurants to host burlesque shows the regulations often dictate the level of exposure allowed within venues.[2] These restrictions speak directly to the regulation of the adult femme body, even within consenting spaces, as evidenced by the femme-focused regulation of a performer's top, requiring one wear "an underbra," to cover the swell of the breasts, as the state of Tennessee requires. The burden of upholding patriarchal notions of morality is projected onto femme's bodies, defined by this system as originally deviant and requiring strict policing, less a femme performer make a creative decision to display her body in a way that legislative leaders have determined is detrimental to the moral fabric of a community. The respectability politics of Blue Laws are so long invested in policing the femme body that they are directly responsible for the history of the burlesque costume itself, as the invention of g-strings and pasties—iconic costume pieces—is originally developed specifically for legal adherence to morality policing. The success of the system is judged by the success of this policing—how rigidly controlled the body remains.

SESTA-FOSTA takes this regulation further, encouraging social media platforms to read the femme body as inherently sexual and thus reflective of a new dichotomy of trafficking victim/illicit law breaker. As a consequence of the false binary of Madonna/whore, the femme form is historically marked as a site of inherent licentiousness, and the artistic display of the femme body thus morally disruptive and even dangerous; female bodies are regulated to the domestic sphere, where they are controlled by and for the pleasure of husbands and fathers. This poor and lamentable example is the driving force behind Dr. Frederic Wertham's infamous cultural charge, *Seduction of the Innocent* (1954).

Catwoman and censoring the femme form

Dr. Fredric Wertham's seminal work is, frankly, seductive. Affectively persuasive and built on a heady blend of ethos and pathos, the voice of Dr. Wertham's text is one of compassionate intelligence and honest concern for the young people who serve as his primary focus. He progressively lambasts juvenile reformatories for their restriction and inability to *help* youths who are not, Wertham asserts, intrinsically bad (2), but "seduced" into delinquent behavior through the negligence of a society that callously permits the unchecked proliferation of dangerous and filthy popular media (12). In 1954, Wertham challenges the unchecked comic book industry when he publishes *Seduction of the Innocent*, laying at comics' feet a charge of seducing juvenile readers to unethical and immoral behavior. Seemingly foregoing the understanding that correlation does not equal causation, Wertham interviews "delinquent" children and finds a common element upon which he gleefully lays all the blame: comics. When spoken by such an authority—an educated and professional 59-year-old German American lauded for his progressive work on mental illness, specifically in his efforts to treat underserved populations—these conclusions are accepted by the public at face value. Though some scholars deride Wertham's assertions and methods (Tilley 2012), some seek to restore his academic reputation (Nyberg 1998), and some remark on his influence as a historical instance (Hajdu 2008), I take Wertham at his words; specifically, the critical language he used in *Seduction* as a call to action, the code the comics industry wrote in response, and the consequences felt by a particular demographic vilified by both: femme-bodied figures.

Comic historians David Hajdu, Hillary Chute, and Amy Nyberg observe that the 1954 Comics Code is a direct response to Wertham's call to action, reading the language of Wertham's assault on the media in the language of the Code itself (Chute 2017). The Comics Code is neither a self-reflective consideration of the cultural responsibilities of comics publishers nor a thoughtful analysis of the psychology of its largest market but a pacifier offered to a public alarmed by the charges extended in Wertham's attack. In his introduction, Wertham marks an increase in the severity of juvenile crimes and the unpreparedness of juvenile courts to respond accordingly. He suggests a correlation between the audacity of violent youth committing these crimes with a sense of hubris learned of comic books, writing that,

> Comic books point that [the unpreparedness of juvenile courts] out even to children. One of them shows a pretty young girl who has herself picked up by men in cars and then robs them, after threatening them with a gun. She calls herself a "hellcat" and the men "suckers." Finally she shoots and kills a man. When brought before the judge she says defiantly: "You can't pin a murder rap on me! I'm only seventeen! That lets me out in this state!" (Wertham 1954, 4)

Wertham asserts that comics are to blame for both the girl's criminal inspiration, and her brazen and misinformed understanding of the consequences—that comics teach her to commit crimes and assure her that she can get away with this. That the Comics Code then asserts that "In every instance good shall triumph over evil and the criminal punished for his misdeeds" is a logical extension from an industry fearful of the external editorializing and censorship encouraged by Wertham (15). Publishers see it as in their best interest to regulate themselves in accordance with Wertham's conclusions, supporting a cultural space defined by the psychiatrist as best supporting morally and ethically developing youth. Yet to a modern reader, Wertham's conclusions and assertions are suspect, poorly supported by cherry-picked anecdotes and offering sweeping and sensational conclusions (not unlike comics!) rather than scientifically sound psychological studies.

In his analysis of sex in comics, Wertham projects onto the femme body the fears of patriarchal "morality," offering excerpts of comics that purportedly demonstrate BDSM tropes, physical and sexual violence, gender deviance, and homosexuality. *Seduction* as a text is a cultural artifact reflective of the mores and expectations of respectability in mid-century America. It communicates both the instructive desire for nuclear families operating in strict gender spheres and the depth of horror for material that violates social codes of conduct. Wertham's text publicly enforces respectability politics through the pathetic (pathos) trope of paternalistic concern for minors and children. Significantly, Wertham is silent on questions of domestic abuse and violence children may witness at home, fixating on comics alone as detrimental influences on the behaviors and development of children rather than social and domestic culture. Of the unregulated comics industry, Wertham laments that "children are left entirely unprotected. They are shown crime, delinquency and sexual abnormality" (13). This is a freedom he argues he does not find in adult publications:

> Newspaper comic strips function under a severe censorship exercised by some 1,500 newspaper editors of the country who sometimes reject details or even whole sequences of comic strips. For comic books there exists no such censorship by an outside agency which has the authority to reject. (Wertham 14–15)

Although Wertham argues that the content of comics is extraordinary and unique to the genre, at least three of his specific examples are readily found in nineteenth-century literature. He writes with shock of a comics story which includes "Running over a young girl on the sidewalk," not unlike the opening of *Jekyll and Hyde* (Wertham 1954, 179). Wertham latter asserts that "[threatening to break his sister's arms] is not the kind of thing that boys used to tell their little sisters. To break people's arms, or to threaten to do so, is one of the comic-book devices," demonstrating his ignorance of Le Fanu's Victorian classic *Uncle Silas* (180). Of Wertham's many criticisms, violence and pornography are the most repeatedly cited and remain subjects of concern in contemporary spaces. Wertham argues that "[o]nly a decent sexual orientation can lead to a decent sex life, for practically all psychological sex problems are ethical problems" and that "[c]omic books stimulate children sexually. That is an elementary fact of my research. In comic books over and over again, in pictures and text, and in the advertisements as well, attention is drawn to sexual characteristics and to sexual actions," indicating that the lessons learned of comics are formative yet detrimental sexual orientations (175). For the sake of the present analysis, his descriptions of comics illustrations of femme bodies are poignant. Wertham goes on at length describing the ways comics actively work to seduce children, suggesting that,

> One of the stock mental aphrodisiacs in comic books is to draw girls' breasts in such a way that they are sexually exciting. Wherever possible they protrude and obtrude. Or girls are shown in slacks and negligees with their pubic regions indicated with special care and attention. Many children miss that, but very many do not. In other run-of-the-mill comic books, as was first pointed out to me by adolescents who collected them, special emphasis is given in whole series of illustrations to girls' buttocks. This is a kind of fetichism and in some individuals leads to rigid fetichistic tendencies either in fantasy or in actual life later. Such preoccupations, as we know from psychoanalytic and Rorschach studies, may have a relationship also to early homosexual attitudes. (Wertham 1954, 178)

Attention to women's breasts, "pubic regions," and buttocks are heralded as deviant illustrations that may either lead young male readers to deviant sexuality, or fetishistic fixations that will lead them to homosexuality. Curiously, the text lacks a level of analysis that explains either of these suppositions, offering descriptions as clear indicators that comics include illustrations of femme bodies but without explaining logically how such illustrations harm the sexual orientation of readers; that biologically realistic representations are present is enough to raise Wertham's alarm. This contrasts with Wertham's later reading of *Batman*, which he specifically argues incites homosexual tendencies by romanticizing the relationship between Batman and Robin (189–90).

The point of contention regarding the objectification of the femme body is a bit at odds with Wertham's anxiety over the femme's social representation, which Wertham fears will leads boys into homosexuality. I say at odds because Wertham is deeply concerned that the sexualized representation of women's bodies will encourage a fetish that leads to homosexuality but also laments an absence of attractive women who will encourage heteronormative relationships. Like illustrations of women's buttocks, "[a] homoerotic attitude is also suggested by the presentation of masculine, bad, witchlike, or violent women. In such comics women are depicted in a definitely antierotic light" in contrast to the desirable masculine heroes (Wertham 1954, 188). Wertham even names Catwoman as a prime example of the detrimental representations being offered to young readers, complaining that "[i]n these stories there are practically no decent, attractive, successful women. A typical female character is the Catwoman, who is vicious and uses a whip. The atmosphere is homosexual and anti-feminine. If the girl is good-looking she is undoubtedly the villainess" (191). Conveniently ignoring the representation of Julie, Batman's attractive fiancé, and other damsels in distress, Wertham's analysis highlights the magnetism of Catwoman's portrayal. She *is* a seductive figure, and one who demands space and independence in a cultural narrative that labels such demands as morally reprehensible.

Batman himself has no compunctions over lusting after Catwoman, frequently positioning himself as her moral savior and attempting to bring the deviant femme figure back to the peaceful domesticity of law-abiding heteronormativity. As described in the introduction of this chapter, Catwoman first appeared in the 1940s *Batman #1*, the same issue that introduced the Joker (*Catwoman: A Celebration of 75 Years* 2014). In her first caper, the Cat nearly absconds with a necklace worth half a million dollars, cleverly disguised as an old woman with a sprained ankle. But, having deduced her identity and captured her midflight, the Dynamic Duo expresses excitement to finally see the face of the infamous burglar, who is immediately described as "a beautiful young woman!" by the narrator and "a pretty girl" by her own admission. Ten panels later, Batman purposefully allows her to escape, responding to Robin's alarm with "[f]ancy that," and closes the comic by daydreaming of the "lovely girl!" and her "lovely eyes!" and hoping he will "bump into her again sometime." In these early narratives Batman has to remind himself, as he does here, of his girlfriend Julie (*Catwoman* 2014, 22). Julie, as a contrast to Catwoman, is a figure of normativity—a promise of a nuclear family. Though Wertham and his contemporaries seem eager to "ship" Batman and Robin (as many continue to do today), the comics authors are equally eager to frame Bruce Wayne and Dick Grayson in the context of suburban normality with the promise of a future partner and influential maternal figure. She is the calming influence on Batman's passion for Catwoman.

Catwoman herself consistently rejects these domestic narratives. From the first, she tempts Batman to join her criminal efforts and scoffs at his offer of redemption. Catwoman is undoubtably attracted to Batman, but she is unique in that she privileges her independence, desires, and profession over a romantic relationship that comes with so many qualifiers. Catwoman is both attractive and successful, but she is not the "decent" woman that Wertham desires for the very independence that leads to an empowered personal life and a successful criminal career. At times she does reform, only to continually return to her Catwoman identity and independent agency. The final scene of "The Cat" from *Batman No. 1* serves as a perfect illustration of the danger of the comic femme: an intelligent, attractive, and successful woman flees the company of the masculine authority figure to maintain her independence from domestic and patriarchal institutions. Though she's drawn for a normative reproductive domestic role, in being beautiful and feminine, she's *characterized* by her investment in autonomy. Although Mary Ann Doane compellingly argues that "the femme fatale 'is not a subject of feminism, but a symptom of male fears about feminism'" (quoted in Hanley 2017, 15), I argue that Catwoman is in fact both—scripted as an illustration of patriarchal fears of the inversion of gendered power and sexual agency, she becomes an alluring suggestion of possibility. And, according to the feminist work of Joanna Frueh and Maria Elena Buszek, there's cause to celebrate and emulate the autonomous, embodied femme.

Bombshells: the threat of pin-up girls

It is significant that the Code developed in response to Wertham's attacks addresses the behavior of all characters and the appearance of femmes.[3] In a section titled "Costumes," the code bans not just "suggestive and salacious illustration" but also clothing that is not "reasonably acceptable to society," stating specifically that "Females shall be drawn realistically without exaggeration of any physical qualities" ("The Comics Code of 1954"). Both regulations seek to control and confine the femme body specifically. By issuing that "females shall be drawn realistically without exaggeration," the code is not only controlling comics illustrations but also is enforcing a system of normativity that defines "good" femme bodies over "bad" femme bodies, forwarding classist, racist, and sexist ideals. Similarly, the code seeks to enforce conservative dress in an age when strip-teasers continue to perform in burlesque halls and artists like Gil Elvgren (1914–1980) make a living painting scantily clad pin-ups from live models. These women, models, performers, and cat burglars alike, are soundly defined by the code's regulations as uniformly deviant and inappropriate for comics content.

Wertham's critique of Catwoman specifically, but comics more generally, leads to severe consequences for the representation of the character. In response to *Seduction,* whole comics lines are threatened, and Batman villains as a body are either given social makeovers or expurgated (Madrid 2009, 58). Mike Madrid (2009) recalls that

> with the Code's clean up, women had to be drawn 'realistically,' and as a result, many simply disappeared from comic books. Batman's sexy foe Catwoman was deemed too racy for the new world of the Comics Code. She was gone by 1955. (58)

The character of Catwoman is irreconcilable with the values espoused by the Comics Code, and its authors' expectations of gender, agency, and autonomy. Without supernatural strength or chemical motivations, Catwoman is a physically capable character who directly uses both her exercised athleticism and her physical attraction to secure her wealth and comfort. Her 1940 introduction tells readers that the Cat is already established as a successful cat burglar, and she achieves that success through creative intelligence, gymnastic performance, bravery, and her manipulation of performative beauty. Were Catwoman as a character less normatively attractive, or more traditionally subservient, she may have been granted a reprieve; ultimately, it is the union of her successful femininity and successful criminality that condemns her, as it will continue to do so once the character is again given a public stage. As a criminal, the bodily work in which she engages challenges her femininity, and her independent motivation for wealth and success over marriage and reproduction marks her bodily use as wrong.

To offer her body publicly, be it as an actress, model, or sex worker, is to be immoral and unfeminine, displaying not the piety and reserve expected of women, but the crass commercialism and vanity reserved for men: a moral judgment bequeathed by Victorian predecessors. Says feminist author Maria Elena Buszek (2006), "So suspicious was the public woman of the period [nineteenth-century America] that it was argued that a woman simply presenting herself in a public forum like the meetinghouse or polling booth would compromise her femininity" (38). Wertham's critique of femme representation in comics is centered on both illustration and action—the *seductive* figures and malignant motivations of characters like Catwoman. In this, perhaps he is right. Unlike her Golden Age colleagues, the Joker and Two-Face, Catwoman is distinctly bodily. Throughout their representations, the Joker and Two-Face are illustrated in consistent sartorial constructions: one in a purple suit, the other in a bifurcated suit. Their villainous identities are signaled by their clothing, and though their unusual faces serve as dehumanizing markers, their bodies are not, in Golden Age comics, offered to comics readers for consumption. But Catwoman is not so consistently fashionably represented, and her identity is instead projected onto her body, as she is represented both masked and bare-faced, often with her physics-defying skirts riding up to reveal her garters and pointed heels. Such a tableau is shameful and disgraceful to Wertham and conservative audiences, but feminist scholarship has reclaimed the performative femme in recognition of her potential to challenge patriarchal systems of power.

In *Pin-Up Grrrls*, Maria Elena Buszek extends Joanna Frueh's (2001) theory of the monster/beauty, "of aesthetic/erotic self-creation by developing beauty as showiness that emerges from intimacy with one's aesthetic/erotic capacity rather than as the hopeless pursuit of perfect appearance," to consider the representations of women and sexuality in popular culture (11). Like Frueh, Buszek pushes back against critical notions of beauty that necessarily represent women as victims to standards of beauty and considers the potential agency of monster/beauty and the "awarishness" she finds in pin-ups and femme performers. Buszek (2006) writes that,

> [nineteenth-century burlesque performers] were unsettling not simply because they were on stage, but also because of their conscious

> contemporaneity and sexual self-awareness. Worse yet was the face of their willingness to exploit both to advance their careers … as for many social critics of the late nineteenth century, women's ability to provoke sexual desire was an unfortunate fact of their existence inevitably hindering women's ability to function in the public sphere. However, for women to actually invite, control, and relish the same was another, more dangerous issue entirely … modern women very much aware of their "own awarishness." (42–43)

Buszek identifies this awarishness in the proliferation of performer's photographs, which individuals circulate for self-promotion and sell to fans. These images represent the "exploitation" of women's "sexual desire," but also their own ownership of their gender performativity and stylized aesthetics and their awareness of the commercial and professional value of offering such artifacts. In short, these women understand the practical value of their sexuality, and the performers of Buszek's history do not hesitate to use that sexuality to their professional benefit.

This is also the threat of the Cat, from her first introduction—a femme fatale not for physical violence against men, but for her awareness of her beauty, her awareness of the effects of that beauty, and her willingness to use that beauty to her individual, independent benefit. Catwoman is a monster/beauty in the same way as Buszek's pin-up: she is a monster/beauty for her awarishness and her active weaponization of her own physical appearance. In every iteration, Catwoman is a normatively but excessively beautiful young woman with dark hair and pointedly femme proportions emphasized by her athleticism. But more than her figuring, she is written with an *awareness* of her own beauty and the potential it holds in society. This awareness allows Catwoman as a character to use her beauty as a tool to achieve her goals, from infiltrating fashion events to steal products (*Batman No. 3*) to engineering her escape from the Caped Crusader himself. Her first issue illustrates both her awarishness and its useful application, without the crutch of an anonymous cape and cowl—the beauty of her face influences Batman's decision to allow the Cat's escape, even going so far as to thwart his sidekick's efforts to pursue her. Once her identity is revealed, the Cat exercises the power still afforded to her by her normative physique, flirting her way to freedom. The same superhero who sends a man falling into a vat of acid to die (*Detective Comics No. 27*), strangles henchman (*Detective Comics No. 29, No. 34*), shoots a vampire woman with a silver bullet (*Detective Comics No. 31),* and hangs a man who was the victim of Dr. Strange's experimentation (*Batman No. 1)* lets a jewel thief escape while complimenting her appearance. Simply, Batman lets the Cat go because she's pretty. Wertham and his supporters fear others will similarly accept the autonomously motivated machinations of femmes who disrupt power systems and so work to vilify the representation of Catwoman and remove her influence from popular media. This, too, is the threat of the femme who utilizes their representation for artistic and professional gains: for burlesque performers advertising shows and festivals and sex workers who seek safe spaces and community support. In the wake of the legalization of Internet censorship, the restriction and regulation of the femme form is again proven material, as sex workers and stage performers face the consequences of legislative action.

On fringes and tassels: burlesque, old ideas, and SESTA-FOSTA

On 11 April 2018, President Trump signed into law the bi-partisan supported "Allow States and Victims to Fight Online Sex Trafficking Act of 2017," better known as SESTA-FOSTA, denying companies protections from user-generated content, as previously extended by Section 230 (Levy 2017, "How Section 230 Helps Sex Trafficking Victims…"). While Section 230 explicitly states that the publisher of third-party online content (i.e., *YouTube*) is not the author of the content (videos) and is therefore not liable for the content, SESTA-FOSTA reverses the 1996 provision of the "Communications Decency Act" to hold publishers legally liable for the content published on their platforms. Effectively, this act is intended to target sites used to advertise sex work, making companies legally liable for sex work advertisements posted by users; this is the kind of censorship effort Wertham seeks in his publication of *Seduction* and the sort avoided by the self-regulatory development of the CCA. Supporters of SESTA-FOSTA argue that forums such as *Craigslist* and *Backpage* have been complicit in human trafficking, and they wish to hold the companies legally and financially responsible (Jackman 2018). Detractors counter that the very visibility of these sites aids advocates and law enforcement professionals in the identification and recovery of sex trafficking victims and the apprehension of perpetrators (Levy 2017, "Virtue of Unvirtuous Spaces"; Miller, Mazzucchelli, and Lewis 2005).

The language of the bill, as presented and signed, calls into question the intentions and motivations of its authors and supporters. The vitriol directed at *Backpage* is clear; its use by sex workers and potential clients alike have earned the site a black mark from conservative quarters and moral crusaders who seek to regulate social and sexual behavior in accordance with their own specific, albeit not necessarily universal, moral codes. Despite its sensational title, the bill is written so as to conflate human trafficking with consensual sex work. Under the mantle of saviors of the exploited, SESTA-FOSTA effectively targets sex workers as a whole by denying them the safeguards of modern practice and communication and seeks to silence and dehumanize professionals by forcing them to the more dangerous working conditions of street work.

The reach of the bill extends beyond *Backpage,* as other social media platforms find themselves similarly responsible for user content and similarly motivated to target particular users. Like the regulations of the CCA, which define how women can be illustrated in comics, SESTA-FOSTA disproportionately targets the representation of femmes across social media platforms. Femmes are labeled by SESTA-FOSTA as both victims and perpetrators, and they, regardless of their occupations, are being targeted for content removal and user sequestering as company owners argue that the visual representation of scantily clad or highly performative femme bodies threatens the public good. The result is a widespread wave of censorship that removes images of femme bodies and punishes users—typically femmes themselves—who create and distribute digital content representing their femme bodies. This censorship is akin to the cultural censorship born of mid-century, post-WWII respectability politics, as women and other femme bodies are forced from the public sphere they gained during the war back into the sheltered and shuttered domestic sphere. As Catwoman is retired from comics representation for being too sympathetic and attractive, so now are living women being vilified for their bodily autonomy.

Comics narratives exploring Selina Kyle's own history as a sex worker demonstrate contemporary cultural taboo and the narratives of victimization that continue to define sex work in majority culture: before she is Catwoman, Selina Kyle is introduced as a sex worker left beaten and bleeding in an alley, where she is rescued by a nun and taken to a hospital. At the hospital, a masculine detective gives her the contact information for a "guy who can teach you how to take care of yourself" (*Catwoman* 2014, 228–32). With seemingly few options, Selina returns to the man who beat her, only to be asked to meet a client on her first night home. She resists but agrees. Perhaps unintentionally, these narratives also illustrate an actual problem of sex work identified by sex workers: the pimp. In the absence of virtual communities and platforms which allow sex workers to screen clients and confirm references, many are forced to turn to pimps for vetting and protection. These pimps not only cut into the profits of sex workers and limit their autonomy but may also be abusive and controlling. Stories by Frank Miller and Missy Newel represent Stan, Selina's pimp/boyfriend, as physically abusive and emotionally manipulative and name his literal violence as the catalyst for Selina's initial decision to become Catwoman.

It is poignant that Catwoman's narrative history shifts from her 1940s unfettered independence to her subjugation as a reluctant sex worker in an abusive relationship with the pimp exploiting her labor. Though the content of these comics would no doubt horrify Wertham, the trajectory reflects his midcentury majoritarian conservative belief against sex work as a degrading and physically abusive power imbalance that cannot be consensual, recalled in his story of the young sex worker robbed by her clients (Wertham 1954, 185). In assigning Selina a "tragic" past which she must overcome by becoming Catwoman, Miller's and Newell's stories disrupt the initial representation of Selina Kyle as an unapologetically independent and successful woman: they blame and credit the patriarchy for her development, equating sex work with abuse and her pimp/boyfriend Stan (he who must be escaped) and liberation achieved through the examples set by the hyper-masculine examples of Batman and Ted, her gruff martial arts and self-defense trainer. But this narrative is challenged by the character's fashioning and how her bodily representation evolves in these comics narratives.

Catwoman finds power in fashioning herself as a monster/beauty—a strong femme who finds liberation in the exercise of her bodily strengths and the monstrosity of the gimp suit held against her, providing a compelling example of power and strength for femmes who similarly seek autonomy from oppressive power structures. Though these comics suggest she leaves sex work, the character is continually and unapologetically grounded in this past through her aesthetic representation. In Miller's *Batman: Year One,* Selina purchases a catsuit which recalls the dominatrix leathers she wears early in the book, and in Newel's "Catwoman: Metamorphosis," Selina's first catsuit is a gimp suit once forced upon her by Stan but later reclaimed as a signal of her agency: knowing her former pimp's hatred of cats, Selina proudly wears the costume as a mark of her independent identity (*Catwoman* 2014, 248–49).

Catwoman is not directly censored for being a sex worker, but scholarship is often critical of her sexualized costuming, denying the character's agency for her "awarish" sensuality. This extension of Wertham-reminiscent projections of respectability continues.[4] Like Catwoman censorship, the ramifications of faulty and fearful legislation show the law to be based on supposition rather than cultural understanding and a need to "rescue" femmes rather than protecting them in their work. As the ready acceptance of Wertham's challenges and the comics narratives of Miller and Newall demonstrate, the vilification of women has a long history, society's values reflected in their categorization of the monstrous and the immoral. "Respectability" and "decency" are cultural codes for the strict monitoring of dress, behavior, and speech that preserve a conservative status quo invested in the maintenance of patriarchal institutions. These terms communicate expectations of heteronormativity and adherence to a traditional gender binary, which largely romanticizes a nineteenth-century social order that has less to do with goodness and more to do with appearances, social hierarchies, and theocracies.

In "The Virtues of Unvirtuous Spaces," law professor A. F. Levy (2017) offers a careful analysis of SESTA-FOSTA and the case law that inspires the bill. Levy ultimately argues that the bill is one of visibility rather than active protection of sex trafficking victims, and that its enactment will do more to impede law enforcement in the recovery of trafficking victims. Levy recognizes that "The integration of sexual and nonsexual commerce brought sexual commerce onto the radar of people who were not looking for it. This sudden visibility may have been at the root of the myth that the US is experiencing an 'explosion in domestic sex trafficking'" (409) but argues that "[t]he war on Internet platforms is pageantry: a kind of theatre designed to satisfy people's need to identify and fight bad guys without regard to nuance or long-term outcome ... Censoring these platforms means forfeiting a resource that naturally facilitates the recovery of victims" (422). The action of the bill is to revoke protections for social media platforms, holding them responsible for the content posted by users, specifically in cases related to the selling of sex and adult entertainment. The concern is cultural rather than strictly criminal. It seeks to keep sexual industry out of sight—including images that help identify and locate actual victims. The expressed intention is to combat sex trafficking, but what's in a name? The writing of the bill itself communicates a desire to thwart the electronic practices established by consensual sex workers, shuttering their safe harbors and removing communications about sex work from public forums. The bill chastises providers for not doing enough to combat sex trafficking, placing on websites like *Craigslist* and *Backpage* the onus of jurisprudence. The bill itself offers no actual support for the identification and recovery of victims or punishment for traffickers; instead, it is focused on the punishment of advertisers, forcing media platforms to function as vice patrols in the censorship of user content with the threat of indicting the owners and managers of those platforms as conspirators in sex trafficking, pornography, and prostitution rings. Thus, it is not an anti-trafficking bill but a censorship bill. It is not stopping the coerced sexual labor of sex trafficking but making willing, professional, and autonomous sex workers more difficult to hire and forcing these workers to endure more dangerous conditions.

In "Speaking from silence: methods of silencing and of resistance" Marsha Houston and Cheris Kramarae (1991) write that "Adrienne Rich (1978: 18) has named some of the tragic and destructive forms of silencing that women experience: 'namelessness, denial, secrets, taboo subjects, erasure, false-naming, non-naming, encoding, omission, veiling, fragmentation and lying'. Silencing is used to isolate people disempowered by their gender, race, and class, even in the speaking contexts of their daily lives" (388). Rich's silencings are at the core of the CCA and SESTA-FOSTA efforts, as femme's narratives are omitted, veiled, and fragmented; their bodies become secret taboos, and they are named as deviant villains rather than autonomous figures profiting and empowered by their awareishness. In the days I first drafted this chapter, I watched such a silencing unfold, experienced by Los Angeles-based burlesque performer Vita Devoid. On 24 July 2019, Devoid (@vitadevoid) posted a video to her Instagram account and Facebook page in which she runs her left hand up her left leg, with the caption "This body earns a living on stage mostly nude. This body has stretch marks ... If you've got them, don't let em bother you. They don't bother anyone else." The clip features only a disembodied leg and arm, and Devoid shares it as a public affirmation, denying the public censure of "imperfect" bodies and celebrating her own, the display of which helps her earn a living. The next video posted on July 24, 2019 shows Vita's face as she addresses her 9,000 followers, saying "Within two seconds of uploading the video that's posted right before this one Facebook decided to BAN me for the next three days because of sexual activity. Because I posted legs... I guess legs are illegal on Facebook now." According to Devoid, the banning took mere moments from the time of her posting and allowed for no recourse for the performer who relies on social media for networking and marketing. When I reached out to Devoid through Instagram messenger, she replied that "it just keeps happening that anything posted by female-identifying members of facebook [*sic*] is immediately screened for any content showing skin (not even naughty bits)..." She remarks on the unevenness of Facebook content policies by stating that "Not ten seconds after that happened, a man sent me a friend request and his profile photo is his naked body wearing a sock on his dick."

Say Houston and Kramarae (1991), "In our personal lives also the power to silence another is not simply the power to *prevent* her talk; it is also the power to *shape and control* her talk, to restrict the things that she may talk about and the ways she is permitted to express them, to permit her to speak, but to suppress her authentic voice" (389). In this way, SESTA-FOSTA is silencing entertainers in the same ways in which Catwoman was silenced in the 1950s—by removing them from view, controlling what can be said, and punishing creators for the willful misreadings of others. Vita Devoid's experience is not unique among burlesque and variety performers, and the flippant suggestion that targeted performers simply leave social media platforms fails to recognize the professional necessity of maintaining a visible online presence to maintain a performance career that enables autonomy and self-expression.[5] Performers rely on social media to promote their brands, connect with audiences, advertise shows, and market content. Tickets to shows are sold online, and performers fly around the world in response to performer calls posted in private forums—forums made less private by SESTA-FOSTA's ownership provisions.

In response to the April 2018 passing of SESTA-FOSTA, social media platforms continue to enact policies that explicitly and directly challenge user-generated content, often without recourse. Says lingerie expert and historian Cora Harrington, "It might be easy to assume that a law that specifically targets sex work won't affect people who don't practice sex work. But when laws get passed restricting sexual expression, the outer edge of what's considered acceptable gets moved back" (Harrington 2018). Harrington goes on to quote lingerie designer Playful Promises, who "noted, 'The implication that sex workers are 'dirty' leads into the belief that a woman's body is 'dirty'—a slippery slope into the policing of our sexuality'" (Harrington 2018).[6] This is just what cultural censorship does and has done: the CCA retirement of Catwoman communicates to comics audiences that her power and agency—her awareishness—is deviant, dangerous, and inappropriate for public platforms and private readings. Similarly, SESTA-FOSTA deems femme awareishness as threatening, burlesque performers inappropriate, and sex-workers unworthy of protection.

Conclusion: living and working censored bodies

Though my subject is art and popular culture, I cannot lose sight of the violence and danger posed by SESTA-FOSTA. I am not attempting to minimize the lived experiences of sex workers—of all genders and sexualities—in my analysis. Rather, as a literary and cultural scholar, I seek to examine the creative space to better understand the lived and actual space. Outside of the sphere of art and entertainment is actual, real danger, as sex workers become the victims of misguided, judgmental, and poorly executed censorious legislation. Though there is no official consensus within the performance community, I argue that burlesque is not sex work.[7] This is not a statement of derision against sex workers but rather an acknowledgment of and respect for sex workers whose professions, lives, and well-being are far differently impacted by the cultural ethos of their work. While sex workers are derided and culturally outcast in contemporary cultural conservatism, burlesque performers, like Catwoman, remain marginally culturally acceptable. This may be in part for the style of performance, which is often categorized by performative glamour, continued ethos from vintage roots carried on from a romanticism of historic feminism, or performance venues, as burlesque shows are most often produced in theaters, bars, and restaurants, and not designated "clubs."

Wertham (1954) addresses the subject of prostitution in *Seduction*, arguing that "Childhood prostitution is always due to neglect by the family (which often cannot help itself) and by social agencies. It is on the increase at present. Comic books do their share in laying the psychological groundwork" (186). The claim is extraordinary and unfounded. But, he says further, the drive to engage the services of a sex worker—and further, to abuse them—is inspired by comics. Wertham relates an anecdote of four boys who borrow a family car, hire a prostitute, and take her back to the empty family home of one of their cohort (185). Like a guilty party offering an alibi, Wertham is highly specific in some details—"They paid her five dollars each"—while purposefully vague in others, spinning a narrative to draw readers in without crossing the line into pornography himself: "Two of them had intercourse with her and various sexual experiments were tried out, the girl being very co-operative." The climax of the morality tale, though, is what follows when the boys drive the young woman home.

> On the way they had a bright idea. They stopped the car, pounced upon the girl and while one held her forcibly around the neck the others beat her unmercifully about the face and body. They went through her handbag and took out all of her money. One boy, hitting her in the

> face, said to her, "You are too independent!" The girl did not fight back. She just sat and cried and said it was not fair after she had been so nice to them. Then they left her at a subway station, with just enough money to pay her faire. This is comic-book stuff. (Wertham 1954, 185)

"Comic-book stuff," Wertham says, but I counter that this is "political stuff," born of cultural lessons that women—and sex workers in particular—are inferior, available for patriarchal attention, and should be made subservient. These lessons do not *originate* in comics, as the abuse and murder of prostitutes far predates comic books. While Wertham sees the violence of the physical attack, I see the venom of "Well, what was she wearing?" What is happening in this moment of Wertham's anecdote is not a group of boys reenacting a scene from a violent comic, but members of a social majority exerting their influence over a person without social protection, whom the boys had been taught by society *at large* to disrespect and dehumanize. This is exactly the behavior from which sex workers seek protection, through client vetting and "bad date" lists, to appointment scheduling and reference letters, all made possible through online forums.

Just as the Comics Code isn't about protecting children, instead protecting an industry by upholding conservative social values, SESTA-FOSTA isn't about trafficking—the law does not target nor inhibit traffickers. It's about sex workers—full-service providers, cam girls, porn actors, call operators—and regulating femme bodies. It's about exposure. The primary purpose and function of SESTA-FOSTA censorship, forcing sex workers out of sight and out of public mind. While "Researchers at Baylor University recently found that Craigslist's personals section reduced the female homicide rate by 10% to 17% after studying its geographically-stratified rollout between 2002 and 2010" (Conlon 2019), SESTA-FOSTA offers no protections to at-risk populations or actual sex trafficking victims, instead punishing any involved in sex work for their violation of conservative respectability politics and enforcing a model of full-service sex work that pushes providers into the street and into dangerous situations with no legal or social protection or support. As a direct result of this legislation,

> In the last year, cities across the U.S. have seen an increase in street-based sex work. In September, law enforcement in San Antonio, Phoenix and Sacramento told the Associated Press that arrests for street prostitution had increased significantly since FOSTA-SESTA was passed. Police in Houston reported seeing more 14- to 17-year-olds working on the street. In October, San Francisco police said crimes related to pimping and sex trafficking had more than tripled in 2018 and called an increase in violence against sex workers a 'concerning trend.' In December, New York City arrest data showed a 180% increase in arrests for

> loitering for the purpose of prostitution, even though other prostitution-related crimes had been declining for years. (Conlon 2019)

It challenges the evolving model that allows workers a level of agency and professionalism endorsed in other industries. SESTA-FOSTA wants sex workers to carry a reputation for being seedy, dirty, and desperate.

It's working—and it's spreading. The actual impact has swept along other adjacent entertainment industries and is working to discriminatory censor all femme bodies for their display. Sex workers are domestic—they are neighbors and community members—but these laws are not isolated to their experiences. Regulating their virtual space is punching down and a way to ease society into further regulation of femme bodies and sexual expressions and work. Blaming popular media for undesirable social change is an easy scapegoat and means through which to romanticize a nostalgic status quo. Instead, these new media reflect changes that perhaps should be made. Catwoman eventually reappears in DC comics, thanks in no small part to the popular representation of the character as played by Eartha Kitt in the *Batman* television show that aired from 1966–1968. With an awareness of systems of power behind calls for censorship, agency may be returned to awarish femmes, too (Nashville Blue Law Coverage).

Notes

1 Here, I am analyzing the censorship of particular presentation and performativity that equally impacts people who identify as femme as an identification category facing targeted cultural restriction. My choice of the term "femme" throughout this chapter is a purposeful recognition of gender performativity and identity. While the reductive terms "male" and "female" are often used in an attempt to limit gender according to a culturally constructed binary (often as a means to dehumanize and trivialize the experiences and identities of trans and nonbinary people), the terms "man" and "woman" are similarly obtusely restrictive, failing to recognize a wide spectrum of gender performativity. Conversely, the terms "femme"(or fem, feminine) and "masc" (or masculine) refer directly to the purposeful performativity of an individual, as coded and signified within an active moment. "Femme" is an identification category that expresses an aesthetic or sartorial moment, enacted by people of all gender identifications (cis, trans, nonbinary, genderqueer, etc.). A person may be femme one day and masc the next or may identify as femme every day. A "high femme" is one who is further extraordinary in their gender presentation, adopting the aesthetics historically associated with traditional femininity in a highly performative manner, from the highest heels to the reddest lipsticks.

2 The regulation is so common, but so varied, that producers of burlesque shows will indicate acceptable levels of undress in their calls for performances; the standard final reveal may be that of a g-string and pasties, but some counties additionally require performers with breasts to cover the bottom third of their breast or the entirety of their butt-cheeks: Washington DC Blue Laws, for example, require that all genitals must remain covered, commonly achieved by wearing a g-string, and that humans with breasts must cover their nipples, which they accomplish with decorative pasties. At the Nashville Burlesque Festival

participants are warned that they must wear "an underbra covering from below the areola to the bottom of the breast" and that bottoms must cover the cleave of the buttocks from the top to where the buttocks meets the legs (the vortex)" ("Nashville Blue Law Coverage").

3 At the time of Wertham's direct attention, Catwoman's villainess costume consists of a calf-length, long-sleeved, purple dress, a purple cowl with rounded ears, and a green hip-length cape. She wears her whip as a fashionable belt, and though in motion the dress will often rise to show her knees and her cuffed purple ankle boots, her appearance lacks the salaciousness later associated with women's representation in comics. Mike Madrid says the same of the history of "supergirls":

> Although the prevalent image of the female comic book crime fighter is that of a sexy nymph in a revealing costume, this was not always the case. The Woman in Red, thought to be the first superheroine, wore a modest scarlet coat and matching mask and skullcap. Fantomah, described as "the most remarkable woman ever known," was a beautiful blonde protectress of the jungle. When evil struck, she transformed into a terrifying, skull-faced goddess who judged the guilty with lethal force ... Red Tornado is actually Ma Hunkel, a burly, working class mother who dresses in long johns and a cape, and disguises herself by wearing a cooking pot over her head. (4)

4 See Priscilla L. Walton and Michael Dorland's "A Slippage of Masks: Dis-Guising Catwoman in 'Batman Returns,'" *Canadian Journal of Film Studies*, Vol. 6, No. 1 (Spring 1997), 91–110.

5 The censorship is widely recognized and discussed within the burlesque community. Even after scrutinizing content restrictions, performers, sex workers, and models around the world are finding their content "flagged," and their accounts closed. Performers of color, such as Sydni Deveraux ("The Glorious Glamazon"), are particularly vulnerable; Deveraux had to build new social media accounts after being banned from old accounts with no recourse, losing followers, professional contacts, and opportunities as a result. In 2019 DC performer and producer Callie Pigeon had her illustrated (i.e., cartoon) show flyers rejected on Facebook for an "inappropriate" (but clad!) black femme heart-butt, while a similar flyer featuring the nude, white buttocks of a male revue were displayed on her timeline as a targeted advertisement. Both shows took place at the same venue.

6 Though not related directly to SESTA-FOSTA, the governmental punishment of consensual and legal sex workers is again illustrated in the COVID-19 pandemic relief efforts now being afforded by the Small Business Association. As a result of stay-at-home and shelter-in-place orders issued at the state level, "non-essential" businesses have been forced to close. To help small business owners and unpaid employees, Payment Protection Programs and forgivable loans are being offered—provided the workers and businesses are not related to sex. "SBA [Small Business Administration] has determined that financing lawful activities of a prurient sexual nature is not in the public interest ... The lender [of COVID-19 small business relief loans] must consider whether the nature and extent of the sexual component causes the business activity to be prurient," quotes *Penn Live* in "Strip club lawsuit claims coronavirus loans discriminate against businesses of a 'sexual nature.'"

7 The question of whether or not burlesque performers are sex workers is a frequent debate within the burlesque community itself. Some argue that burlesque is a form of sex work, akin to club stripping, for the sake of its definitive element of strip tease. Others argue that burlesque, privileged as a performance art, is not sex

work because it does not carry the same stigma as club stripping or full-service sex work. As a burlesque and variety performer since 2017, I believe the latter argument is most significant; though the line may be thin, burlesque is a performance art regulated differently than sex work and does not carry the same stigma. Some burlesque performers *are* sex workers, employed in parallel industries, but this does not mean all burlesque performers face the same social and legal hardships.

References

Allow States and Victims to Fight Online Sex Trafficking Act. 2018. Pub. L. No. 115–64, 132 STAT. 1253. *Congress.gov*, https://www.congress.gov/115/plaws/publ164/PLAW-115publ164.pdf.

Buszek, Maria Elena. 2006. *Pin-Up Grrrls: Feminism, Sexuality, Popular Culture*. Durham: Duke University Press. doi:10.1215/9780822387565.

Chute, Hillary. 2017. *Why Comics? From Underground to Everywhere*. New York: Harper Collins.

Conlon, Rose. "Sex workers say anti-trafficking law fuels inequality." *Marketplace.org*, April 30, 2019. https://www.marketplace.org/2019/04/30/sex-workers-fosta-sesta-trafficking-law-inequality/.

"The Comics Code of 1954." *Comic Book Legal Defense Fund*. http://cbldf.org/thecomics-code-of-1954/.

Frueh, Joanna. 2001. *Monster|Beauty: Building the Body of Love*. Berkley: University of California Press. doi:10.1525/9780520923904.

Halberstam, J. Jack. 2012. *Gaga Feminism: Sex, Gender, and the End of Normal*. Boston: Beacon Press.

Hajdu, David. 2008. *The Ten-Cent Plague: The Great Comic Book Scare and How it Changed America*. New York: Farrar, Straux and Giroux.

Hanley, Tim. 2017. *The Many Lives of Catwoman: The Felonious History of a Feline Fatale*. Chicago: Chicago Review Press.

Harrington, Cora. "Why Lingerie Addicts Should Care About SESTA/FOSTA." *The Lingerie Addict*, May 14, 2018. https://www.thelingerieaddict.com/2018/05/sesta-fosta-lingerie-addicts.html.

Houston, Marsha, and Cheris Kramarae. 1991. "Speaking from silence: methods of silencing and of resistance." *Discourse & Society* 2 (4): 387–99. https://doi.org/10.1177/0957926591002004001.

Jackman, Tom. 2018. "Trump signs 'FOSTA' bill targeting online sex trafficking, enables states and victims to pursue websites." *The Washington Post*, April 11, 2018. https://www.washingtonpost.com/news/true-crime/wp/2018/04/11/trump-signs-fosta-bill-targeting-online-sex-trafficking-enables-states-and-victims-to-pursue-websites/?u_term=.5534dcf36bbf.

Kane, Bob, and Finger, Bill. 2014. *Catwoman: A Celebration of 75 Years*. Burbank: DC Comics.

Levy, Alex F. 2017. "How Section 230 Helps Sex Trafficking Victims (and SESTA Would Hurt Them)." *Technology & Marketing Law Blog (*blog), August 15, 2017. https://blog.ericgoldman.org/archives/2017/08/how-section-230-helps-sex-trafficking-victims-and-sesta-would-hurt-them-guest-blog-post.htm.

Levy, Alex F. 2017. "The Virtues of Unvirtuous Spaces." *Wake Forest Law Review* 52: 403–34.

Madrid, Mike. 2009. *The Supergirls: Fashion, Feminism, Fantasy, and the History of Comic Book Heroines*. Minneapolis: Exterminating Angel Press.

Miller, Frank, David Mazzucchelli, and Richmond Lewis. 2005. *Batman: Year One*. Burbank: DC Comics.

"Nashville Blue Law Coverage." *Nashville Burlesque Festival*, n.d., https://www.nashvilleburlesquefestival.com/apply/nashville-blue-law-coverage/.

Nyberg, Amy. 1998. *Seal of Approval: The History of the Comics Code*. Jackson: University of Mississippi Press.

"Strip club lawsuit claims coronavirus loans discriminate against businesses of a 'sexual nature.'" *Penn Live Patriot News*, April 13, 2020. https://www.pennlive.com/coronavirus/2020/04/strip-club-lawsuit-claims-coronavirus-loans-discriminate-against-businesses-of-a-sexual-nature.html?fbclid=IwAR3Ns12iycEKiGWMS2L0BFG25Y9eMEe9LuajUQPzTLJE0rzeTB9VzjkB6sI.

Tilley, Carol L. 2012. "Seducing the Innocent: Fredric Wertham and the Falsifications That Helped Condemn Comics." *Information and Culture* 47(4): 383–413. https://doi.org/10.7560/ic47401

@vitadevoid. "Banned from Facebook for the next 3 days." *Instagram*, 24 July 2019.

@vitadevoid. "This body earns a living on stage…" *Instagram*, 24 July 2019.

Walton, Priscilla L., and Michael Dorland. 1997. "A Slippage of Masks: Dis-Guising Catwoman in 'Batman Returns,'" *Canadian Journal of Film Studies* 6 (1) (spring 1997): 91–110. https://doi.org/10.3138/cjfs.6.1.91.

Wertham, Fredric. 1954. *Seduction of the Innocent*. New York: Rinehart & Company.

3 Queer, Latina, and punching Nazis: a New America breaking borders[1]

Ande Davis

The image of Captain America punching Adolf Hitler that graced the cover of his first comic book in 1941 is a cultural touchstone that has resurfaced multiple times since its first printing (Simon and Kirby). Beginning in its initial comic printing as the wish fulfillment of two Jewish creators to take out the biggest threat to European Jewish citizens—at least on their pages—it found its most recent iteration in the 2011 movie *Captain America: The First Avenger*, where filmmakers recreated the moment from the comics by having Captain America, played by Chris Evans, repeatedly punch a Hitler stand-in for a traveling United Service Organizations Inc. (USO) show during World War II. The scene is integrated as an Easter egg for fans, a winking callback for those familiar with that first comic cover. While the initial comic's creation came out of a specific global and national politics around a US reluctant to enter the war in Europe to stop Hitler, *Captain America: The First Avenger* found itself born into a different political environment, shortly after the election of Barack Obama amid promises of change and a de-escalation in American military intervention that had enflamed political backlash around the world under his predecessor. While bringing back the iconic Nazi-punching image, its significance appeared to have waned, the "real" Hitler having been replaced by an actor and amounting to little more than a nod through the fourth wall.

By 2017, the political atmosphere in the US and the world had shifted dramatically. The inflammatory rhetoric of Donald Trump throughout the 2016 presidential campaign emboldened White supremacists, self-identifying Nazis, and KKK members to voice their views publicly at levels that hadn't been seen since the height of the Civil Rights Movement in the 1950s and '60s while incidents of hate speech and hate crimes saw a sharp increase to their highest levels in a decade. Meanwhile, immigrants from Latin America and the Middle East, both documented and undocumented, became a frequent target of Trump and his supporters, who argued for a closing of borders and a halt to immigration in order to "return" the US to a Eurocentric ethnostate that never really existed except in popular media depictions. Into this political atmosphere landed *America #1* in March of 2017—barely one month after Trump's inauguration and 76 years to the

DOI: 10.4324/9781003146520-3

day after Captain America's first appearance—the first standalone title for a newer Marvel superhero named America Chavez. The first issue's story finds Chavez traveling back in time and landing on a World War II battlefield, and at the book's climax, the queer Latina superhero pushes Captain America aside and punches Hitler in the jaw (Rivera and Quinones 2017a). In this act, and in the political moment where it emerges, it becomes much more than simply a nod to fans as in the *Captain America* movie, but instead comes much closer to embodying the spirit of the original image—the work's creators are presenting a mode of wish-fulfillment by having their hero take out a far-right demagogue that symbolizes the biggest risk to their status as citizens and people.

In the course of her one-year solo title run, however, this moment is a minor episode, but it foregrounds much of what and who America Chavez embodies as a superhero and what she contributes to readers' understanding of how superheroes both shape and are shaped by the surrounding political space. The Chavez who is fleshed out over the series becomes an embodiment of Gloria Anzaldúa's nepantla, navigating dimensions, time, and geopolitical space as both a source of her power and a means for reckoning with the slippage in issues of culture and identity that reevaluate both American and superhero ontologies. As a superhero figure, she must navigate the specific political and historical contexts she arrives in to negotiate these liminal, interstitial spaces and project a way of configuring issues of identity within both literal and figurative borderlands that are often occupied by those wishing to eradicate her.

Reading comics, reading bodies

America did not arrive into a blank space. In his book detailing the cultural history of comics, Jean-Paul Gabilliet (2010) describes comic books—particularly superhero comics—as a medium reflecting a transitional epoch of media consumption, from a period of popular consumption to our current mode of mass consumption (xviii). This transitional period, bridging a gap during the intra-war years and continuing into the middle of the twentieth century, coincides with the rise in popularity of comics, which as Gabilliet notes, were "deliberately and specifically designed to be purchased by youngsters, thereby becoming part of the long-term transformation of youths into active consumers as of the 1930s," (xviii)—in essence becoming a key component in the capitalist indoctrination of America's youth. This coincided with a period during which the economic and cultural conditions prolonged the average school experiences of teenagers, and with "more time in the company of their peers, they acquired new personal independence and a generational consciousness that struck some alarmed adults as evidence of diminishing respect for authority and declining traditional values" (Wright 2001, 27). These concerns were exacerbated by the comic producers' abilities to market directly to their adolescent consumers whose parents believed "young people deserved greater latitude to pursue their own happiness and means for self-expression" (Wright, 27) after the deprivation of their own childhoods in the Depression.

In their inception, these comic books "became objects of cultural consumption associated with an age class... rather than with a social class" (Gabilliet 2010, xviii). Because of both the stylistic and content similarities between comics and genres such as science fiction and fantasy, as well as a shared publication lineage—evolving from dime novels and pulps to be sold on store racks next to soda fountains and candy displays—the critical attitudes held toward all of these genres have tended toward the frivolous and inconsequential. Moreover, virulent opinions posited that "this cultural exchange was conducted in a language of violence, crudeness, and absurdity [that] understandably unsettled more than a few adult observers" (Wright 2001, 29). Popular opinions held forth that comics and superheroes were a trivial, disposable medium that was at best a waste of time but, at worst, had the potential to corrupt children.

Roland Barthes ([1957] 2012) points out, however, that such types of childhood fascinations are "essentially an adult microcosm; all are miniature reproductions of human objects" (59), highlighting the fact that pigeonholing comic books as youthful toys disregards the idea that comics often prefigure other, more broadly accepted literary pursuits. Critics who place comics as unliterary cultural detritus often frame the argument that engaging with literary texts "is seen as offering free play to the imagination, while comicbooks [sic] are overtly explicit and thus produce passivity" (Bongco 2000, 23), framing the medium as both ephemeral and inferior, with its wide appeal indicating its mediocrity. However, comic author and artist Scott McCloud (1993) points out that "the artform—the medium—known as comics is a vessel which can hold any number of ideas and images" (6). As comics moved drastically from caricatures and political cartoons toward superhero adventures featuring musclebound figures in brightly colored costumes, this criticism of comics as meaningless—yet somehow also simultaneously dangerous—only intensified.

The prospective result of corrupting youth readers, buoyed by Frederic Wertham's *Seduction of the Innocent*, resulted in the creation of the Comics Code Authority (CCA) in 1954. Its function, purpose, and language were similar to that of the Hays Code that governed the motion picture industry, in that the CCA was an attempt by the comics industry to self-regulate and cut down on depictions of violence, crime, horror, and sex. Even though "early research suggests that most of the critics exaggerated the effects of comics" (Nyberg 1998, 11), censorship and the CCA persisted in some form until it was finally fully abandoned by all publishers in 2011. Because of this outsized role in the comics industry, the CCA had a profound impact on how the superhero formed and stagnated during the latter half of the twentieth century. Within the scope of the CCA, "there was a unified view in the world of comic books, one in which social institutions and authority figures were always benign in their concern with upholding traditional values and in which rebellion against the 'establishment' was nearly impossible" (Nyberg, 159). These standards ensured the perpetuation of a model law-abiding, clean-cut, White, heteronormative masculinity, and "the code could be seen as an effort to feminize and domesticate the unruly world populated by comic book characters. In place of violence and rampant sexuality, there would be order and respect" (Nyberg, 115). Under these structures, the "Silver Age" of comics at Marvel debuted characters such as Spider-Man, the Fantastic Four, and the X-Men. While the Silver Age became known for its development of complex backstories and character arcs, particularly in Marvel Comics runs, the characteristics and actions of heroes at this time largely followed the structures of the CCA, with notably few female and minority characters acting outside of supporting and love interest roles. In the days of the CCA, it would have been impossible for a character like America Chavez to exist outside of underground comix.

Like any art form, the superhero matured and developed layers of character and complexity that "tackle complex moral dilemmas and diverse political shifts where changes and contradictions cannot so easily be labelled and appraised" (Bongco 2000, 94), even in the face of the CCA. Superheroes advanced from their early formations as simplistic upholders of law and order into complicated, nuanced characters that offer an opportunity for unpacking and analysis. By the last decades of the twentieth century and the beginning of the twenty-first, Marvel's heroes began to branch out to reflect the diverse readership that had always been there. Simultaneously, these heroes appeared to push back against the structures of authority—first against government and law enforcement with its antiheroes such as Wolverine, Ghost Rider, and the Punisher, and then against the scaffolding of White, cis-male, hetero supremacy itself with the growing prominence of minority, women, and queer characters in its titles. This is the environment that birthed America Chavez, whose appearance as Miss America contrasted with the original Golden Age version from the 1940s. The original Miss America fought alongside Captain America during appearances in Marvel's predecessor, Timely Comics, while also seeing her own title evolve into a magazine focusing on cooking, fashion, and makeup, before the heroine eventually died in childbirth. The new Miss America was destined to be something else entirely.

Working in the margins

Despite occasionally providing antiracist messages and eventually adding superheroes of color in small quantities, comic books were largely devoid of minority faces—whether as protagonists, villains, or faces in the crowd. These comics full of White heroes carry a debatable effect on the minority and marginalized children who were initially meant to consume these heroes. Some, such as Kenneth Ghee (2013), argue that "an out-group hero or mythos from an oppressive group (e.g., White culture[2]) can also have an intended or unintended *negative* effect on the Black psyche" (229). This formulation draws on ideas developed during Kenneth Clark's doll experiment in the 1950s that saw Black children overwhelmingly preferring White dolls when both White and Black dolls were offered, ostensibly demonstrating an internalized racism due to a lack of positive representation within mainstream culture (Nama 2011, 9–10). Within the superhero genre, this White predominance played out in the perceptions that, when a White hero engages in heroic acts to save the nation or the world, "it is an implicit assumption (in the mind's eye of those reading the story)[3] that he (and the story) is *culture bound* and he is (rightfully, intelligently and morally so) saving his own people and culture first" (Ghee, 230). In this reading, consumers of superheroes are taught to read the elided "White" before each item in Superman's call to protect "truth, justice, and the American way." Minority superheroes, when they exist, are rarely afforded this assumption of humanity according to Ghee, instead acting as a sidekick to White heroes or are, even if acting as the hero themselves, "not necessarily viewed in the [minority] culture bound context as necessarily helping, or serving, or even being relevant to the concerns of, or in the best interests of, [minority] America" (230). The historical dearth of representation, in this light, could be read as intensely damaging in its effects, especially due to the influential power of popular culture on the general population.

This idea is bolstered by the in-depth studies of Captain America by Jason Dittmer (2005). Upon his appearance in the movies from Marvel Cinematic Universe, Captain America has seen his status return as among Marvel's most popular heroes, though as an embodiment of the US itself, he has long been a mainstay of the comics, in which he entered as "a 1941 nativist fantasy of individualist patriotism, with Captain America's (and thus, America's) values contrasted against his un-American Others" (Dittmer, 631). Not only is the embodiment of the US captured within masculine, blond, blue-eyed Whiteness,[4] his essential nature as a hero—hard-working, selfless, and most importantly, patriotic—requires that "[s]upport for the geopolitical objectives of US exceptionalism becomes an understood, tacit extension of citizenship" (Dittmer, 630). This encapsulation of the American ideal signifies that "Captain America manifested the belief that science was a vehicle for political freedom and that scientific and technological enhancement of the human body could produce more capable citizens" (Fawaz 2016, 8). Such a fusion of American exceptionalism and scientific progress could not help but promote the idea that White Americanism is not only the historic root of goodness but also the best hope for a beneficent future. It would not be until the early mid-2000s that these aspects of Captain America's symbology are disrupted and figures such as America Chavez are primed to emerge, draped in the same metaphors as Steve Rogers.

Still, other critics such as Adilfu Nama (2011) argue that "even though superhero figures are predominantly white guys and gals clad in spandex and tights, a strict racial reading of the negative impact white superheroes may have on [minority readers] is too linear and reductive" (11). Likewise, Sheena Howard and Ronald Jackson (2013) posit that children from marginalized communities, finding themselves "seldom recognized for their historical contributions and achievements" outside of sports, entertainment, or manual labor found the spaces—despite being predominantly White spaces—provided by superhero comics to be sites with "the powerful potential to weave imaginary narratives that offer possibilities" (1) for their own futures. Such a cultural imperative emphasizes Frederick Aldama's (2017) insistence on co-creation in comics, particularly for readers from minority communities, wherein the act of reading and interpreting the multimodal text inherent in comics allows readers to "become chiasmic transformers, all while not changing the DNA of the story itself" (91). In doing so, readers of comics are able to subvert capitalist practices of mass consumption that Barthes details in which children conditioned as consumers by toys approximating the grown-up objects "cannot constitute himself as anything but an owner, a user, never as a creator" (Barthes [1957] 2012, 60). Comics, as productions of a transitional consumption space, as a medium between the visual and written modes of storytelling, create the conditions for readers to insert themselves into the creative process. The closure necessitated by these interstitial spaces between the panels, known as gutters, relies on the reader to be a participant in the process of story creation (McCloud 1993, 68). This active participation on behalf of the reader—the reliance on creating the "alchemy at work in the space between panels which can help us find meaning or resonance in even the most jarring of combinations" (McCloud, 73)—translates over for these critics into the ability of marginalized readers to transform their own experiences into the figures of White heroes on the comic pages. In being directed toward the medium of comic books, marginalized readers are prompted to participate and fill in the gaps, often with their own experiences, cultural markers, and ontological positions. The problem remains, one that each of the critics would agree upon—these comic spaces were founded and maintained for extended periods of time as White male spaces, despite the consistent and longstanding presence of readers in other demographics, and that positive representations of heroes of color would ultimately have a greater positive effect on minority readership than the practice of transcribing their own identities onto White bodies.

The enforcement and maintenance of comic book Whiteness has historically been abetted by the genre's young audience, as "the rise of comicbook [sic] production coincided with a time of extraordinary attention to juvenile delinquency" (Bongco 2000, 2). This focus, aimed at protecting children from errant behaviors and perceived deviancies, produced the infamous Comics Code that publications adopted to self-regulate and which limited the content and themes presented in comic books, ostensibly to protect innocent minds from damaging influences. These guidelines also coincided with such political and social touchstones as Reefer Madness, Yellow Peril, Operation Wetback, the Moynihan Report, and others designed to tie minorities and their associated communities to delinquency, crime, and moral shortcomings. This era of "self-censorship proved fatal to the medium's growth and development" (Bongco 2000, 4) and stymied any serious attempts at inclusivity in both the characters represented through comics and those hired to create them. A developmental stagnation, combined with the growing insistence upon US American patriotism as wholesome Whiteness, created the types of narratives within superhero comics "traditionally imbued with the cultural assimilation impulse advanced by the myths of the 'Melting Pot' and the 'American Dream'" (Espinoza 2016, 184). As Mila Bongco points out, "classic superhero narratives usually start with a disruption of the status quo and proceed to discovery and eradication of the perpetrator of this disruption" (92). The status quo, of course, is the White power structure that at the time of these classic narratives was being upset by minorities in various movements—namely, the Civil Rights, American Indian, Chicano, and Gay Liberation movements—as well as communist organizations advancing workers' and low-income citizens' rights and women demanding equal treatment in society and the workplace. Underneath the CCA, these movements were seen as the very authority-questioning, morally destabilizing elements that needed to be suppressed by heroes. However, Bongco notes further that the comic book genre "does not necessarily have conservative implications since only an extraordinarily fertile and productive genre could have spread and caught the attention of readers world-wide for so long" (92). Certainly, such an overtly supremacist project would not have garnered the non-White readership it maintained either, although this overlaying of comic books with the indoctrination of foundational US American myths and the upholding of a hierarchical status quo placed non-White, non-male, and queer heroes under a period of erasure while still managing to provide marginalized comic readers with a means of co-creating their own narratives of heroism in the spaces between panels. Even from within the strictures of the CCA, comics publishers such as Marvel found a means to encapsulate the spirits of these movements even while submitting to the letter of the CCA, where comics like *X-Men* served as proxies for confronting prejudice that provided a space for marginalized readers to engage in co-creation. As the CCA lost its influence, companies such as Marvel began to develop characters and storylines that reflected the non-White readership that existed from the beginning while also growing its representation of authors and artists from those groups to more authentically bring those elements to the page.[5]

Using the superhero figure becomes an especially liberatory moment for creators and readers from marginalized groups, particularly since, as Bongco (2000) notes,

> while the plots are naturally geared towards the restoration of the law, they are also about the breaking of the law, about the transgression of normal rules. Viewed from this perspective, the narratives become more interesting and take on more dimensions especially in relation to power and control. (93)

In the context provided by Aldama and McCloud, where the reading and consumption of comics takes place largely in the interstitial spaces between panels—particularly in regard to issues such as marginalized identities—creators are provided an interesting and useful mode of cutting against the grain and undermining the long-established White ubiquity within the mythos of superheroes. Within the narrative space that Bongco elucidates regarding power and control is a particularly useful area for non-White, non-male, and queer comic creators to navigate. This space provides a platform for the ability to speak back to power structures and interrogate the way in which superpowered bodies outside of White male heteronormativity are read, misread, and constructed in relation to those White dominant spaces. In this manner, the creation of space for marginalized voices—particularly represented as superpowered bodies—upsets racial paradigms that have plagued both comic books and society-at-large throughout their respective history.

Out of the margins, onto the panels

Given the history of marginalized comics readers to gain personal access to the heroic mythos in the gutters between panels, these interstices gain the ability to translate from the structures of the comics medium onto the heroes themselves as operating in these in-between spaces. One theory that gives additional motivation to those spaces is Gloria Anzaldúa's (2009b) idea of nepantla, "an unstable, unpredictable, precarious, always-in-transition space lacking clear boundaries" (243). For Anzaldúa, "living in this liminal zone means being in a constant state of displacement—an uncomfortable, even alarming feeling" (243). The way in which Anzaldúa presents her idea of liminality competes in a way with Victor Turner's (1967) concept rooted in anthropological study, in which he describes liminality in the context of rites of passage. For Turner, liminality is a transition that is "a process, a becoming, and in the case of *rites de passage* even a transformation" (94) that relies on movement between two states, which may be more or less defined by boundaries. As others have noted, though, Turner's ideas on liminality have come into contest with borderlands theories that recognize what "is missing in Turner is a conception and recognition of culture as *political* contestation: the battle over narrative power, the fight over who gets to (re)tell the story, and from which position" (Weber 1995, 532). For the purposes of analysis here, Turner's conceptions might prove to be too structural in comparison to Anzaldúa's borderland-centric view of the "betwixt-and-between" (to invoke Turner's key phrasing). This space is especially meaningful to Anzaldúa as it pertains to a *mestizaje* experience and the cultural imperative that results from living *en la frontera*, stuck between two lands without fully feeling a part of each.

Turner's formation of liminality can be seen in a number of superhero story arcs, particularly within origin stories where a hero such as Spider-Man is moving from his "before" life as teenager Peter Parker into a more self-assured superhero persona engaging with the numerous trials and rites of passage that bring him to this higher place while maintaining his previous connections. This encapsulation of liminality is embodied in Spider-Man's most frequently quoted maxim: "With great power comes great responsibility."[6]

With America Chavez, the story of her solo comic run does not fall so neatly within this framework. Turner (1974) situates the liminal population (who he refers to as "marginals") in a position in which "they often look to their group of origin, the so-called inferior group, for communitas, and to the more prestigious group in which they mainly live and in which they aspire to higher status as their structural reference group," and while they inhabit a space of in-betweenness, "unlike ritual liminars they have no cultural assurance of a final stable resolution of their ambiguity" (232–33). In formulating this position, Turner "is privileging his sense of social leveling and attendant cultural bonding over what we now recognize as an encounter with identity politics and the border" (Weber 1995, 530), misinterpreting the oppositional ontologies of those in border spaces as an incomplete and unstable position lacking societal structures. Nepantla, as Anzaldúa describes it, is indeed a stasis of discomfort and unease, similar to Turner's formulation of marginals, though through its distinct relationship to borderlands positionality,

> all people in it, whether natives or immigrants, colored or white, queers or heterosexuals, from this side of the border or del otro lado are personas del lugar, local people—all of whom relate to the border and to the nepantla states in different ways. (Anzaldúa 2009a, 180)

Despite the similarity in language to Turner—describing the spaces outside of nepantla as "states" and referring the process of transition that nepantla entails—Anzaldúa emphasizes the locality of all nepantleras and draws special attention to their political identities as opposed to the apolitical, ahistorical viewpoint Turner attempts to apply to liminality. In the always-already transitional medium of comics, nepantla may function as a space from which the superhero narrative might subvert and destabilize the foundational White supremacy and misogyny to which some within the industry still cling.

The interstitial space in which we contextualize these superheroes can additionally be aided through considering Homi Bhabha's (1994) ascribing of the Third Space, "based not on the exoticism of multiculturalism or the *diversity* of cultures, but on the inscription and articulation of culture's *hybridity*" (38). The space being offered up here allows for a move from the anthropological into the social-political framework dramatized in the common semiotic account of the disjuncture between the subject of a proposition (*énoncé*) and the subject of enunciation, which is not represented in the statement but which is the acknowledgement of its discursive embeddedness and address, its cultural positionality, its reference to a present time and a specific space, and through which these two positions must pass, "which represents both the general conditions of language and the specific implication of the utterance in a performative and institutional strategy of which it cannot 'in itself' be conscious" (Bhabha, 36). This reckoning does much to address the criticisms of Turner's liminality, in that the Third Space cannot be ahistorical or apolitical in its interrogations, but it also elucidates a space in which ambiguities and overdeterminations of identity can be more explicitly processed. By dislodging "our sense of the historical identity of culture as a homogenizing, unifying force, authenticated by an originary Past" (Bhabha, 37), considering the role of superheroes—particularly superpowered bodies coded to historically oppressed communities—within such a Third Space overcomes the *a priori* cultural determinations and static structures present for both Turner and Anzaldúa while allowing for the liminal/nepantla space to be one in which both the supernatural embodiment of superhero empowerment and the graphic medium of the comic text can help examine the hybridity of cultural and status positions being examined. The visual space of the comic allows for the unspoken aspects of White supremacist "othering" to be examined in full view, as it forces even the most subtle shifts in representation to encounter radical interpretations through the process of readership.

Rewriting America

Created by writer Joe Casey and artist Nick Dragotta in 2011, America Chavez made her debut in Marvel's *Vengeance* miniseries as part of a team known as the Teen Brigade. Strong and brash, Chavez quickly became a fan favorite and joined teams such as the Young Avengers, A-Force, and the Ultimates. As Aldama (2017) points out, she is portrayed during her run in *Young Avengers* "not as a hothead but as a Latina superhero driven to right wrongs and take supervillains—and without the usual spandex. And along the way she seeks to become her own person as a Latina and a lesbian" (86). Her relatively quick rise in popularity resulted in Marvel giving her a standalone series, titled simply *America*, handing the title off to artist Joe Quinones and writer Gabby Rivera, who self-identifies on her website as a "Bronx-born, queer Latinx writer." In putting Rivera in charge of Chavez's story, Marvel not only gave a queer Latinx character a stage crafted by a queer Latinx author, but they also appeared to be flaunting heteronormative editorial practices and creating space for transgression to happen. Anzaldúa (1987) adds that "for the lesbian of color, the ultimate rebellion she can make against her native culture is through her sexual behavior. [...] It is a way of balancing, of mitigating duality" (41). This sense of sexual identity directly reflects that of Chavez, who has been out as a lesbian since her stint in the *Young Avengers* series. Her new self-titled series did not shy away from incorporating America's sexuality and relationships in a way that encourages acceptance and inclusivity. Near the beginning of the first issue, we see her ending a relationship with her girlfriend and meeting up with a platonic female friend, illustrating a depth and breadth of female relationships often underrepresented in the hands of White male authorship. While Rivera did not create America Chavez as a character, the 12-issue run of *America* helped to define the character in new ways for readers. In much the same way that Bhabha (1994) discerns that "the narrative and psychological force that nationness brings to bear on cultural production and political projection is the effect of the ambivalence of the 'nation' as a narrative strategy" (140), Chavez, and her position as nepantlera, subverts the societal tropes that govern national and cultural identities, offering alternatives to those concepts throughout her solo comic title's run.

Chavez, of course, is not the first Latina hero from Marvel, nor is she the first to headline her own series, which debuted in March 2017. Over the past few decades, Marvel (and its main competitor DC) has made a more conscious effort to include non-White male heroes in its titles, to admittedly mixed success. As Isabel Millán (2016) points out, Marvel has a history of "contributing to the erasure of prior Latina superheroes, even within its own comic franchise" (204), as they did when they claimed Araña as their first Latina hero, despite the existence of others in their catalogue. Millán argues that, in marketing for Araña's first title, the character "is meant to target a Latina/o niche market," with an accompanying blurb that is "purely a marketing ploy" (204). This is compounded by the fact that "superheroes such as Araña remain confined within popular discourses of normativity or what constitutes acceptable deviance," and "where queerness is suggested for Araña, it borders on the side of insult" (Millán, 218), as evidenced when Araña is derided by a villain for coming to her friend's rescue, as he refers mockingly to the two as "girlfriends." By first not even doing its homework as to what representation even existed in its own catalog, Marvel signaled that its attention to Latinx audiences was rote and cursory, and by further sidelining any other aspects of Araña's identity as trivial or as punchlines, they missed an opportunity to develop actual representation in favor of race-blind and heteronormative tokenism. These observations by critics echo the constraints that still remain from the days of the CCA, as well as the conditions Anzaldúa (1987) observes when she states, "We're afraid of being abandoned by the mother, the culture, *la Raza*, for being unacceptable, faulty, damaged. [...] To avoid rejection, some of us conform to the values of the culture, push the unacceptable parts to the shadows" (42). While there is no canonical evidence of Araña's homosexuality within the books themselves, Millán points out that the slippages present in her identity and inability to be pinned down to a single identification leave open possibilities for her sexuality to be renegotiated, whether in the comics or in the hands of fandom (Millán, 205, 219).

America Chavez is, whether by design or happenstance, a considerably Anzaldúan character, navigating multiple identities, borders, and *(des) conocimientos* in her role as a superhero and as a fully fleshed-out character that embodies Anzaldúa's (2015) imperative that "Nepantleras function disruptively" (84). She possesses as superpowers, after all, the ubiquitous super strength, flight, and invulnerability found in so many other characters. What makes her unique, however, is her additional power—to kick open portals in space and between dimensions, literally traversing boundaries between realities and engaging in the very act Anzaldúa describes when she urges others to challenge "the basic premises on which our concepts are built" as well as to "overcome the limits of perception, extend perception beyond bodily confines, transform our consciousness and our perception from ordinary reality to a spiritual/magical/other reality, and enter states of nonordinary reality" (44–45). America is given the power to embody nepantlera in her very existence, moving inside, outside, and between boundaries at will. She is what Anzaldúa calls for when she demands

> nepantleras whose strength lies in [their] ability to mediate and move between identities and positions [... who] *choose* to occupy intermediary spaces between worlds, *choose* to move between worlds like the ancient chamanas who *choose* to build bridges between the worlds, *choose* to speak from the cracks between the worlds, from las rendijas. (93)

Moreover, her space- and dimension-hopping powers allow her to transcend ideas of nationness, which, by becoming "an apparatus of symbolic power, ... produces a continual slippage of categories, like sexuality, class affiliation, territorial paranoia, or 'cultural difference' in the act of writing the nation" (Bhabha 1994, 140). She personifies both Latinidad through her language, affinities, and body, while also embodying US Americanness through her dress, her name, and the actions she takes to supplant Captain America. Chavez embodies these slippages, and Rivera takes the opportunity throughout the series to illustrate the potentials that Chavez represents.

This is not to suggest that America Chavez is without her problems. Her position within the Marvel Universe shares much in common with the hero Black Panther, her teammate on the Ultimates group. In his own story, Black Panther is king of the fictional African country of Wakanda, depriving any single nation the opportunity to claim him as their own while still tapping into an idea of "Africanness" for readers of the comic. Likewise, Chavez is not from a particular country but rather an interdimensional space known as the Utopian Parallel. Though her origins allow her to figure more literally as in-between, as nepantlera, her lack of national origin while still being identified as Latinx manages to play into notions of Hispanic homogeneity, signaling Latinidad without indicating a distinct national identity, a tactic that can often seem to prioritize racial markers over actual social/political/cultural history. While at once a surface erasure of nationality in favor of racial presence, it is also a broader call toward a transcultural feminism that emphasizes "what we have in common is experiences of disempowerment and being under dominant patriarchal ideology" (Anzaldúa 1995). Even though America's identity as Latina is embodied in vagaries that universality is itself a call toward Anzaldúan solidarity.

This attribute is admittedly potentially problematic, although—as is often the case with America Chavez—there's a unique duality at play. After all, the Utopian Parallel she comes from is populated only by women, which means both of America's parents are female, and mainstream comics are presented with a family that breaks heteronormative boundaries. *America* issue seven (Rivera and Quinones 2017e), in fact, flashes back to America's birth, unabashedly providing alternatives to societal norms about family, sexuality, and gender, flaunting conventions of appropriateness held in the past. This construct—shared by both Black Panther and America Chavez—runs into Bhabha's (1994) reckoning with the notion of "the people" in relation to the borders of the nation-state as a double narrative movement:

> We then have a contested conceptual territory where the nation's people must be thought in double-time; the people are the historical "objects" of a nationalist pedagogy, giving the discourse an authority that is based on the pre-given or constituted historical origin *in the past*; the people are also the "subjects" of a process of signification that must erase any prior or originary presence of the nation-people to demonstrate the prodigious, living principles of the people as contemporaneity: as that sign of the *present* through which national life is redeemed and iterated as a reproductive process. (145)

This is the issue being challenged by both these heroes, and Chavez in particular: their national boundaries as a real-world referent have been erased—contrast their lack of identity to others in the Marvel universe (Captain America, Iron Man, the X-Men, Spider-Man) who receive real world birthplaces—and along with it any sort of specific historicity in favor of a general "otherness" meant to draw on general cultural overtones. As such, readers are not provided an opportunity at true cultural affiliation, but at the same time, nationalist tendencies are stripped away in favor of a broader effort toward futurity. National borders, after all, are a shifting historical project, always in progress and therefore temporally locked in their specificity. This erasure of borders produces an elasticity in the present for these characters who are not confined to a specific mode of identification but are instead able to serve as a much more readily available avatar for readers who might see some resemblance to their own lived and cultural experiences, developing a greater scope in accounting for issues such as race, ethnicity, nationality, and potentiality.

In addition, like Black Panther, Chavez's status as hero is elevated—their exploits are frequently of global concerns, the save-the-world variety of heroics that place them on par with other heavyweights in the Marvel universe such as the Avengers and the Fantastic Four. Unlike heroes such as Luke Cage, or even Spider-Man, whose exploits are often confined to threats within their communities and neighborhoods, Chavez is not constrained by such limitations. This status as hero once again presents itself as a duality—on the one hand, by not directly impacting and serving the Latinx community, America seems to distance herself from that identification. On the other hand, she is able to transcend racial or ethnic labels that might try to box her in, allowing her to traverse boundaries and take on the kind of heroic roles that White male characters often approach without being challenged. Her heroic tasks aren't focused solely on problems within Latinx communities or nations but often take on global implications, such as her role on the Ultimates squad that battles enemies both on and outside of Earth. By breaking these boundaries, her disruptive capabilities are opened up in a way that Anzaldúa (2015) describes as her identity narrative of *nos/otras*. In this theory, she places a slash to bisect the word *nosotras* into *nos* and *otras* to signal the ways in which "we cross into each other's worlds all the time" and become "mutually complicitous" (Anzaldúa, 79) in the formation of each other's identities, both as outsider and as insider.

In a number of ways, this type of identification of self in others is notable throughout the *America* series. To start, she enrolls in the fictional Sotomayor University—a college for superpowered individuals located between dimensions—to continue her studies. Not only does this University have as its namesake the highest-ranking Latina official in US history, but her first class encourages her not to use her powers but to instead "rely on ancestral knowledge and not just brute force" (Rivera and Quinones 2017a). Her professor is urging her to find a link to a pre-nationalist past from before the concept of borders became, as Anzaldúa (1987) frames it, "*una herida abierta* where the Third World grates against the first and bleeds" (25). From there, America starts to better understand the potentials and the limits of her powers. Later in the first issue, she uses her portal in tandem with an invention by her friend and teammate Prodigy to go back in time—an expansion of her power she was unaware she had. In doing so, she finds herself in the middle of World War II alongside Captain America. In this issue, Quinones and Rivera make use of the iconic image of Captain America punching Hitler that graced the cover of his comic during the war (Simon and Kirby 1941)—only in their interpretation, Chavez pushes Cap aside and does the punching herself (Rivera and Quinones 2017a). In this one act, she manages not only to insert herself in the place of one of Marvel's most famous White men but also to position herself as the defender of US American ideals in the face of iconic evil. Ms. America supplants Captain America; Latinidad supplants Whiteness; queerness supplants overt masculinity; nepantla supplants nationalism. The timing of the issue is no coincidence either, as portraying a Latina figure punching a symbol of far-right authoritarianism comes shortly after the ascendance of Donald Trump to the presidency, who as a candidate played to a far-right base using racial animus against Latinx people and often targeted women in particular for harassment. This could be read as a reactionary response to that particular political rhetoric,[7] but in these transgressions, America Chavez creates a paradigm shift away from traditional comic book power dynamics; no longer are marginalized readers forced to imagine themselves in the role of the White hero. Instead, the hero is one of them, and they are able to co-create a future for themselves in the spaces between panels more easily through the explicit representation of Latinx identity within the comic page.

Chavez's newfound power to traverse time in the early issues of the series is uncontrollable; she points out that she has no way of knowing where she will end up. She discovers this is due to her not fully understanding herself and those that proceeded her. The reader learns that her jumps in time are guided not by her, but rather by a shamanic old woman who is sending her to meet with women from different points in the Marvel Universe timeline who can help her to reach this better understanding. In World War II, she meets with Peggy Carter (Rivera and Quinones 2017b), an early compatriot of Captain America; later, she is sent to meet the mutant X-Man Storm (Rivera and Quinones 2017c). In these journeys, Chavez is forced to go through a series of trials that leads to "the demotion of the ego as the self's only authority" (Anzaldúa 2015, 29). She is fractured and reassembled, both psychically and physically with the result that "healing is a deep change of attitude that involves an adjustment and abandonment of 'ego-heroics.'" (Rivera and Quinones 2017d). By meeting with and learning from her spiritual ancestors and comadres—a group not tied to a racial or ethnic lineage, but rather a sense of female solidarity that emanates from the Utopian Parallel—America is able to gain control of her existence transgressing borders between worlds. In later issues, the shamanic woman who navigated Chavez through her time travels is revealed as her own grandmother (Rivera and Villalobos 2017), giving her the chance to reconnect with her literal ancestry after her parents were killed defending the Utopian Parallel when Chavez was young. These links to the past are crucial to Anzaldúa's concept of nepantla, and Chavez's ability to transgress from within this liminal space is tied to how well she can link to the past. Her crossing of dimensions and time during this process serves as an instrument to allow "an accounting with all three cultures—white, Mexican, Indian" (Anzaldúa 1987, 44). Anzaldua discusses how she is unable to go home, so "I will have to stand and claim my space, making a new culture—*una cultura mestiza*—with my own lumber, my own bricks and mortar and my own feminist architecture" (Anzaldúa 1987, 44). America here faces the same challenge, unable to return to the Utopian parallel, and thereby creating her own space with her own feminist architecture, borrowed from the bricks and mortar that are her heroic women predecessors.

America relies on its placement both within history as much as its sociopolitical space. As Aldama (2009) asserts, comics "don't float free in some ethereal platonic space. Like all cultural phenomena, they are produced and circulate within specific social and historical material conditions" (4). The *America* series is no different; it lives very much in the political and pop cultural moment. The cover of the second issue pays homage to the visuals of Beyonce's "Formation," as well as some humorous references to the lyrics from another song off the same album (Rivera and Quinones 2017b).[8] There is a moment when the characters debate the political expediency of punching Nazis (Rivera and Quinones 2017b), calling upon popular discussions about public civility and nonviolence circling in liberal and progressive media around the time of publication and in the aftermath of hard-right White supremacists emboldened by the campaign and election of Donald Trump. But as Aldama points out, these comics don't have any agency to transform on their own. They can instead "be manipulated in ways that restrict or unleash the imagination" (Aldama, 4).

Perhaps nowhere in *America* does this idea combine with the current political moment than in the image of a queer Latina draped in the American flag produced during a time of increased nationalism tied ever closely to straight male Whiteness. As Anzaldúa (2015) explains, "this country does not want to acknowledge its walls—its limits, the places some people are stopped or stop themselves, the lines they're not allowed to cross" (81). During a time when talk of literal walls to create lines that *las otras* can't cross, a nepantlera hero who can punch through and cross boundaries, who lives in between borders in a transitional medium, becomes a useful tool for negotiating a new understanding for what these borders truly mean.

Notes

1 The author would like to thank the Center for Mexican American Studies and the Benson Latin American Collection at the University of Texas for providing a research fellowship and access to Gloria Anzaldúa's personal papers, as well as the University of Missouri-Kansas City School of graduate studies for awarding a research grant, both of which helped make this work possible.
2 The situating here as "White culture" is an overdetermined view of culture with rigid boundaries that ignores both the process of borrowing and appropriation that has happened in the history of the culture Ghee is identifying, and the degree to which minority groups have read themselves into the cultural artifacts (as Nama, Howard and Jackson, and Aldama will discuss later) despite a lack of representation in them.
3 This reading isn't even necessarily implicit, as a viewing of classic comic books shows that victims, hostages, and other faces in the crowd are almost ubiquitously white, while Black and brown faces are quite explicitly erased almost entirely from representation even in the backgrounds of panels.
4 For a detailed discussion of Captain America and his relationship to a masculine nationalism, see the chapter in this volume by Michael Rinehard and Monica Sandler.
5 As with all of publishing, the face of comics editorship lags behind in terms of representation, and as this level is where most storytelling decisions get made across the multiple interwoven books produced each year, that disparity is typically far more predictive of representation within comics than is the number of authors and writers (and often can be pointed to as the reason for a lack of diverse creators). This topic, however, is the subject for other research devoted to that phenomenon.
6 See, e.g., Lee and Ditko 1962.
7 This cannot be entirely ruled out, though it is unlikely to be the sole purpose for existence given the long writing and publication timeline for comic books, leaving little room for insertion in the three-month time period between Trump's election and the appearance of the book. In all likelihood, the plot point was related to the rhetoric, but other motivations were obviously at play in including it in the book.
8 In a panel, a blonde female agent asks Peggy Carter if Chavez needs to be detained for questioning, to which Chavez responds, "Try me, Becky." Carter subsequently refers to the agent as "Agent Goodhair;" this is a reference to lyrics from Beyoncé's song "Sorry" off the *Lemonade* album: "He only want me when I'm not there/He better call Becky with the good hair."

References

Aldama, Frederick Luis. 2009. *Your Brain on Latino Comics*. Austin: University of Texas Press.

Aldama, Frederick Luis. 2017. *Latinx Superheroes in Mainstream Comics*. Tucson: University of Arizona Press.

Anzaldúa, Gloria E. 1987. *Borderlands/La Frontera: The New Mestiza*. San Francisco: Aunt Lute Books.

Anzaldúa, Gloria E. 1995. "Aliens: The Dynamic Construction of U.S. Chicana/Latina Experience." Talk presented at University of Wisconsin-Milwaukee, October 6, 1995, Box 112, Folder 1, Gloria Evangelina Anzaldúa Papers, Benson Latin American Collection, The University of Texas at Austin.

Anzaldúa, Gloria E. 2009a. "Border Arte: Nepantla, El Lugar de La Frontera." In *The Gloria Anzaldúa Reader*, edited by AnaLouise Keating, 176–186. Durham: Duke University Press. doi:10.1215/9780822391272.

Anzaldúa, Gloria E. 2009b. "(Un)Natural Bridges, (Un)Safe Spaces." In *The Gloria Anzaldúa Reader*, edited by Ana Louise Keating, 243–248. Durham: Duke University Press. doi:10.1215/9780822391272.

Anzaldúa, Gloria E. 2015. *Light in the Dark/Luz En Lo Oscuro: Rewriting Identity, Spirituality, Reality*, edited by Ana Louise Keating, 44–45. Durham: Duke University Press. doi:10.1215/9780822375036.

Barthes, Roland. (1957) 2012. *Mythologies*. Translated by Richard Howard. New York: Hill and Wang.

Bhabha, Homi K. 1994. *The Location of Culture*. London: Routledge. doi:10.4324/9780203820551.

Bongco, Mila. 2000. *Reading Comics: Language, Culture, and the Concept of the Superhero in Comic Books*. New York and London: American Popular History and Culture. doi: 10.4324/9781315805030.

Dittmer, Jason. 2005. "Captain America's Empire: Reflections on Identity, Popular Culture, and Post-9/11 Geopolitics." *Annals of the Association of American Geographers* 95 (3): 626–43. doi:10.1111/j.1467-8306.2005.00478.x.

Espinoza, Mauricio. 2016. "The Alien Is Here to Stay: Otherness, Anti-Assimilation, and Empowerment in Latino/a Superhero Comics." In *Graphic Borders: Latino Comic Books Past, Present, and Future*, edited by Frederick Luis Aldama and Christopher González, 181–202. Austin: University of Texas Press.

Fawaz, Ramzi. 2016. *The New Mutants: Superheroes and the Radical Imagination of American Comics*. New York: New York University Press. doi:10.18574/nyu/9781479814336.001.0001.

Gabilliet, Jean-Paul. 2010. *Of Comics and Men: A Cultural History of American Comic Books*. Translated by Bart Beaty and Nick Nguyen. Jackson: University Press of Mississippi. doi:10.14325/mississippi/9781604732672.001.0001.

Ghee, Kenneth. 2013. "'Will the "Real" Black Superheroes Please Stand Up?!': A Critical Analysis of the Mythological and Cultural Significance of Black Superheroes." In *Black Comics: Politics of Race and Representation*, edited by Sheena C. Howard and Ronald L. Jackson II, 223–37. London: Bloomsbury. doi:10.5040/9781472543424.ch-013.

Howard, Sheena C., and Ronald L. Jackson II, eds. 2013. *Black Comics: Politics of Race and Representation*. London: Bloomsbury. doi:10.5040/9781472543424.

Johnston, Joe. 2011. *Captain America: The First Avenger*. Paramount Pictures.

Lee, Stan, and Steve Ditko. 1962. *Amazing Fantasy #15*. New York: Marvel.

McCloud, Scott. 1993. *Understanding Comics: The Invisible Art*. New York: William Morrow.

Millán, Isabel. 2016. "Anya Sofía (Araña) Corazón: The Inner-Webbings and Mexi-Ricanization of Spider-Girl." In *Graphic Borders: Latino Comic Books Past, Present, and Future*. Austin: University of Texas Press.

Nama, Adilifu. 2011. *Super Black: American Pop Culture and Black Superheroes*. Austin: University of Texas Press.

Nyberg, Amy Kiste. 1998. *Seal of Approval: The History of the Comics Code*. Jackson: University Press of Mississippi.

Rivera, Gabby, and Joe Quinones. 2017a. *America #1*. New York: Marvel.

Rivera, Gabby, and Joe Quinones. 2017b. *America #2*. New York: Marvel.

Rivera, Gabby, and Joe Quinones. 2017c. *America #3*. New York: Marvel.

Rivera, Gabby, and Joe Quinones. 2017d. *America #4*. New York: Marvel.

Rivera, Gabby, and Joe Quinones. 2017e. *America #7*. New York: Marvel.

Rivera, Gabby, and Ramon Villalobos. 2017. *America #6*. New York: Marvel.

Simon, Joe, and Jack Kirby. 1941. *Captain America #1*. New York: Timely Comics.

Turner, Victor. 1967. *The Forest of Symbols: Aspects of Ndembu Ritual*. Ithaca: Cornell University Press.

Turner, Victor. 1974. *Dramas, Fields, and Metaphors: Symbolic Action in Human Society*. Ithaca: Cornell University Press. doi:10.7591/9781501732843.

Weber, Donald. 1995. "From Limen to Border: A Meditation on the Legacy of Victor Turner for American Cultural Studies." *American Quarterly* 47 (3): 525–36. doi:10.2307/2713299.

Wright, Bradford W. 2001. *Comic Book Nation: The Transformation of Youth Culture in America*. Baltimore: The Johns Hopkins University Press.

4 Unweaving the world: militant ecofeminism in the anti-fairy tale *Beautiful Darkness*

Shane Gomes

As a narrative medium, graphic literature is unique in the demands it places on a reader. Most narrative unfolds word by word or frame by frame, with little work necessary on the part of the consumer to fill in the blank spaces between. As a contrast, graphic literature unfolds across disjointed, deliberately separated moments of time in a narrative, leaving the reader to infer what happens between those moments and to fill in the spaces with their own imagination. Barbara Postema (2013) argues that "In their fragmented nature, comics ... create an implied reader more explicitly than many other forms" (107) by which means comics are "...inviting readers to reconstruct the text" (2013) and thereby making each reader the cocreator of the narrative. The medium is "based on 'the insistence on the active cooperation provided by the reader,'" (Groensteen 2007, 10) without which the narratives recounted therein are instead just series of illustrated panels, sometimes with words included. As Scott McCloud posits, a reader forces a relationship between representations when they are seen in sequence, but without that active participation relationships between the narrative fragments that make up a graphic novel's sequential layout breaks down and renders the medium unintelligible. Graphic literature requires a reader's attention, investment, and identification to function at all.

The reader engagement required by the comics medium stands in contrast to the narrative genre of fairy tales. Fairy tales, by design, are didactic, and blatant in their ethical ideals. As a genre they primarily serve the purpose of providing a method for inculcating young children into the ideologies from which the stories arise. They often provide this indoctrination by presenting short, accessible stories with easily understood morals to their audience, in the simple formulations of action followed by consequence, good deed followed by reward, and bad deed followed by punishment. The genre's simplicity makes it a powerful and effective tool of enculturation. Intrinsic to its effectiveness is the genre's formulaic, predictable structure, which implicitly proposes that the ethics of these stories are the product of natural, immutable laws.

Graphic literature has great narrative impact as well, albeit for different reasons. They exist as "the union of story and structure" (Kannenberg

DOI: 10.4324/9781003146520-4

2001, 175) and dramatically emphasize the participation that all narrative mediums require of their consumers. Therefore, utilizing the structure of the fairy tale genre in the comics medium provides an especially potent storytelling opportunity. *Beautiful Darkness*, by the team of Fabien Vehlman and Kerascoët, takes this opportunity and instead rebels directly against the culture into which both its genre and medium are usually used to indoctrinate children and young readers, subverting not only explicit cultural values but the method and narrative structures often used to convey those myths and ideals. It "deliberately invokes binary opposition in order to dismantle it" (Warhol 1996, 859), by portraying the ongoing conflict inherent in the dyad of western culture and nature as the foundation of hierarchical societies and systemic oppression and seeking to violently dismantle those systems that thrive on the exploitation of the natural world.

The novel concerns a tiny race of people that have been forced to flee their homes and find subsistence in an unsettled forest. The text has many of the traits of a fairy tale: a princess in distress, helpful animals, a wild forest, and in many ways, it resembles many of the revisionary versions that are currently popular, such as *Into the Woods* (2014). But despite initial appearances, the novel attempts to completely unmake not just the fairy tale genre but also the ideology which the genre directly supports. Fairy tales present social guidelines and expectations to children from a young age, and the novel strives to illustrate many of the cultural norms and expectations that are present in their ideological make-up. From a cultural standpoint, fairy tales have usurped much of the former import of myths, which "communicate not only what a culture believes but also what it wants to believe, what it *needs* to be true" (Murray 2000, 154). Therefore, the fairy tale plays a foundational role in formalizing the expectations and values of western culture. As Chris Murray elaborates, comics have often been, and usually are, tools of that same culture, explicating and expounding on the cultural givens to which fairy tales first expose many children. Hence the tremendous dissonance of this novel, which uses a genre and medium both generally aimed at children and used to actively reinforce myths of western culture, and dismantles those myths entirely. The primary cultural norm that *Beautiful Darkness* aims to subvert is the purported resilience of western patriarchal system based on the violent exploitation of nature and instead examines how that social structure should be dismantled.

In *Culture of Violence*, Francis Barker (1994) details the systemic usage of violence by political states in order to protect themselves and the ideologies that support them. This system creates expectations regarding how and when violence can be used, by whom, against whom, and to what ends. Notably, the primary way into which people are inculcated into this system is through texts and other cultural artifacts (Barker focuses on works by Shakespeare, especially *King Lear*, but the system is omnipresent). Texts that do this ideological work generally begin by creating a functioning social context, portray some sort of threat to the social status quo, and then violently depict the destruction of the threat, thereby restoring the supposedly "natural" equilibrium that was present at the beginning of the text. As Wolfgang Mieder (1987) points out, this restoration of a status quo is especially required by the generic fairy tale ending. His "Grim Variations: From Fairy Tales to Modern Anti-Fairy Tales" reveals this trope within most western fairy tales, particularly in *Kinder und Hausemarchen*, the foundational anthology first published by the Grimm Brothers in 1812 (Grimm 2014). The violent means portrayed in order to restore equilibrium in these children's tales is portrayed in order to exemplify what happens to those that threaten foundational social systems, in and out of the texts.

But in addition to the restoration structure, other foundational cultural norms are questioned in *Beautiful Darkness*, specifically the opposition between culture and nature, whose terms are often arbitrarily conflated with male and female, respectively. The novel directly dramatizes how these norms are enacted socially, as well as their failure to productively maintain a society of any kind. In its negative portrayal of these cultural expectations, *Beautiful Darkness* works to undo these binaries, and it does so by posing as a fairy tale while radically subverting generic assumptions. By using the common plot structures to undermine the ideological basis of these children's stories, the novel uncovers how fairy tales consistently protect the status quo, which is built on a foundation of structural binaries and the exploitation of the less empowered, in this case women and the natural world.

Fairy tales are tools used to indoctrinate children into specific social values. But as an anti-fairy tale, *Beautiful Darkness* rejects the social values present in western ones which in the text become clearly based on violent modes of exploitation. Instead, nature refuses to be exploited, violating the expectations of the genre. This is demonstrated by both the violent natural world of the forest setting, and the brutal nature of the characters Aurora and her subjects (whom I'll refer to as Tinies) that is revealed throughout. "Comics and graphic novels foreground... retellings and revisionings," (Taylor 2009, 172) and as a fairy tale graphic novel, *Beautiful Darkness* takes full advantage of both modes of storytelling. A dramatic revamping of the stock fairy tale may have been less palatable in a more staid medium, but graphic novels, especially those working in the Franco-Belgian *Bande Dessinée* tradition as this does, are much more open to experimentation, revision, and change in general. This medium then provides the space in which to perform this radical revamping. The novel ultimately proposes, as a counter to genre expectations, an anti-societal, anti-economic-progress equilibrium by which Aurora can exist alongside of nature, even if she can't use it as she wishes.

The novel works diligently to situate itself in the both the culture and genre it works to undermine. It begins with Aurora waiting on her intended,

Prince Hector, as the latter visits her for an afternoon. Immediately the reader can see exemplified the "patterns of male dominance and female subservience" (Kykendal and Sturm 2007, 39) that fairy tales are so adept at perpetuating. But nearly as quickly, the genre framework begins to fracture. During this initial scene, the Tinies' world dissolve around them, literally. The walls begin to collapse into red muck and Aurora's subjects are forced to flee from their homes into the woods. But it is shown, through Kerascoët's deceptively delicate artwork, that what they had made their homes in was in fact the decaying corpse of a young girl.

The novel here employs the characteristics of its medium to great effect and sets up a tension that runs throughout the text. Often as the narration or diegetic dialogue directly supports the fairy tale ideology, the artwork presents an ironic counterpoint, or foregrounds the ways in which the medium subverts cultural norms. In this case, Aurora and Hector's date is interrupted as the walls around them begin to collapse, represented vividly as more of each successive panel is filled with red muck, looming over the Tinies and demonstrating the claustrophobic nature of their predicament. The redness swallows the panels, leaving only a small gap in the center for Aurora, but she eventually emerges from the collapsing sequence of panels into a storm, seeking shelter in a dark forest. Finally, readers are shown the nature of that decaying shelter, in a full-page depiction of the body. The startling image, along with implication that these Tinies may have killed Sleeping Beauty, begin to quickly attack the basic ideas that structure and support these traditional stories. Though fairy tales often include horrific imagery (the list there is long), they do still have a "formative civilizing character," and Zipes (1997) also argues that "literary fairy tales...were complex symbolic social acts intended to reflect upon mores, norms, and habits organized for the purpose of reinforcing a hierarchically arranged civilizing process in a particular society" (3). Therefore, they were meant to provide behavioral and ideological blueprints for children. Do this and you will be safe and happy; don't do this or you will die. With the casual, unexplained death of a young girl presented so vividly, though, this text immediately begins to work against the genre's frames.

Graphic novels especially present opportunities to visually emphasize specific narrative instances through their reliance on sequential panels, and in the case of the girl's corpse, the comic takes advantage of several opportunities afforded specifically to storytelling in this medium. In regard to the layout of panels, this comic is fairly regular. Panels may change from oval to rectangle, and there may be two or four per row, but for the most part the panels progress naturally in rows from the top left of the page. When first the comic portrays the young Sleeping Beauty, however, her corpse is presented on a page comprised of one panel. This presents what David Kunzle (2001) calls "a crystalline isolation of climactic physical moments" (5). In this case, that strategy works to show that the Tinies, simply by emerging into their new reality, make several pivotal points for the reader. First, the events of the first few pages are put in a new, unpleasant light as the reader now understands what exactly was happening (that being the natural course of decomposition of a body). Second, the single-panel page both informs the reader of the scale of the main characters and presages the importance of their tiny size to the upcoming conflicts in the plot. Most importantly, it inextricably ties the novel into the fairy tale genre via the consistent trope of a young girl being lost in the woods, while simultaneously undermining the expectations thereof. The form, the full-page depiction of the corpse, not only underscores the horror of a dead, decomposing girl but also emphasizes both the connection to and subversion of the fairy tale convention. Sleeping Beauty is dead, and the text wants to make sure the reader understands the implications of that.

The use of the fairy tale tropes, even if they are often employed just to be immediately deconstructed, is especially useful as a genre approach strengthens an ecofeminist reading of the narrative. Robyn Warhol (1996) states that "feminist theory seeks to undermine Western culture's penchant for binary opposition (and the inevitably resulting hierarchies)" (858) which ecofeminism expands by examining the relationship between nature and culture, as "men are, ex officio, on the side of culture whereas women ... are cast on the side of nature" (Bourdieu 1984, 40). As such, a large part of the project of western civilization has been to subjugate nature to human whims and to frame it simply in regard to its use value to us. Similarly, women have been conflated with nature and therefore as a group that is to be subject to male/cultural domination via violent means. While the logic of domination may hold, it is based on the entirely faulty supposition that nature exists only in its relation to humans and their cultures and that women are defined solely in regard to their relationships with men. Instead, ecofeminist perspectives work to reframe cultural understandings of nature as that of a partner, something humanity can work with without exploitation. That becomes crucial when considering the linkage of oppressions as a single system, as exploitation of nature becomes exploitation of other under-privileged groups. As such, the fairy tale characteristics of *Beautiful Darkness* alert us to the ideology that is being discussed. Then, by reimagining and rejecting the generic tropes, it actively works to unmake them in a more radical way.

The reimaginings often do this by demonstrating much of the unspoken submission of nature that society, as western culture imagines it, demands. After their exodus from the corpse, the Tinies try to survive in the surrounding forest. Aurora does her best to organize her people into some sort of stable society, as it is implied the community was quite structured before with a social, economic, and gender hierarchy in place. As the princess, this would be her responsibility and privilege, and as such she is performing her fairy tale role. The issue, though, comes from her subjects, who do not conform, nor do they follow her leadership, nor do they act in the interest of the others around them. Instead, they solely pursue their own self-interests, which fails to benefit them in a natural setting that is openly hostile to them.

From a needs-based perspective, the fundamental role of a social group is to provide protection and resources for each other, and even at this most basic level, the Tinies fail. In order to survive, the Tinies attempt to actively exploit and essentially pillage the forest around them, to an extent that the resources gathered exceed what is needed for their survival. One of the Tinies, Zelie, sets herself as the leader of a small splinter group, ostensibly obeying Aurora, but instead exploiting the others to enrich herself at their detriment. Zelie demands small tokens from her followers that put them in dangerous situations, including asking Prince Hector to retrieve her scarf from predator infested waters, which leads to his death. As Zelie demonstrates, another key reason for social constructs is to keep members within a group safe from one another. In this sense, Aurora and her people fail.

Zelie's depiction throughout the text is especially telling, both of her purported and actual character, a dichotomy that would be especially difficult to convey outside this medium. Aurora is portrayed as a fairy tale trope visually, but one that would fit more comfortably in newer revisions. Though decidedly delicate-looking, she time and again proves her agency and resilience in taking care of herself. In contrast, Zelie is introduced as she cries in terror when confronted with a harmless insect, and her visual representation is akin to that of a porcelain doll. The contrast in the physicality of the two Tinies is marked. While Aurora looks competent, Zelie appears to be an over-grown child, one that is entirely helpless, which furthers her goal of enriching herself while not engaging with her new surroundings. But her depiction renders her anger more telling of both her true intent and the extent to which she has knowingly manipulated Aurora and the others, such as when she sends Prince Hector to die (Vehlman and Kerascoët 2014, 70). Her duplicitousness is visually realized dramatically. Her representation varies subtly, but said variation reveals her to be an entirely untrustworthy character. Scott McCloud (1993) argues that comics function in large part through a "form of amplification through simplification" (30) in which representations are made as simplistic as possible to, in part, amplify any variations in depiction. When Zelie narratively reveals the extent to which she is willing to exploit those around her, the subtle change in her simplistic depiction is interpreted as a dramatic shift in her character

Also, it is necessary to note the extent to which Zelie's evolving visual representation further emphasizes her commitment to a social structure based on exploitation. While initially dressed simply, as the novel continues, she acquires decorative and otherwise unnecessary accoutrements and begins usurping the labor of an increasingly large portion of her people to benefit her alone, until in her final appearance she is shown to have a train of sycophants, portrayed with vacant expressions, prepared to perform any and all necessary tasks for her. She becomes a stand-in for those that are enriched by systemic oppression, and the visual representation of her extravagance, such as a luxurious fur coat and tame bird, underscores her connection to the systems of exploitation.

It soon becomes clear that Aurora must act violently and destroy Zelie for the good of the group. "The fairy tale's magic act requires not only social violence and appropriation but a careful balance of threats and rewards" (Bacchilega 1997, 6), and as Zelie has become a social threat, generic and ideological expectations should lead to Zelie's violent destruction. Furthermore, such an act should lead to a restoration of the society which Aurora had been struggling to revive. However, by this time, much of the group has rejected Aurora and her attempts not only to sustain her people but also not damage much of the world around them. For the most part, her subjects do this due to her continued insistence on holding onto authority despite no longer having any practical claim to it. Although Aurora's idea of ruling was less openly exploitive than Zelie's, it was still baseless and ultimately ineffectual. A large number of the Tinies are claimed by the forest at every opportunity, evincing Aurora's failure, because they cannot work cohesively.

The reason for Aurora's failure is layered, but primarily she failed to grasp the qualitative differences between her lifestyle and that of her subjects after they left the protection of the corpse. The extent to which the Tinies' means of survival is impacted is emphasized by the depiction in the artwork of the contrast between the Tinies and their surroundings in terms of scale. Generally, fairy tales make some sort of narrative compensation when depicting characters of a non-standard size. Something about the world around them will help them to function, usually magically. But there is no such concession here. Aurora and her people are thrown into a wild forest, and its exactly as unforgiving and brutal as one would expect a wild space to be to three-inch-tall creatures. Vehlman and Kerascoët (2014) underscore this with repeated imagery of the Tinies struggling tremendously with everyday objects such as twigs or of them being preyed upon by everything from birds to frogs to flies. A forest can be a dangerous place in general, but the scaling of the comic, or just how big the characters are compared to the backgrounds in panels, demonstrates the mortal peril they are all in from the moment they leave the corpse. Exposed to the elements, the Tinies' feeble attempts to mimic their previous station simply recreated and exacerbated inequalities between them, as Zelie slowly accumulated more and more of the increasingly scarce resources, including the authority of a state; she could command violence against others and often exercised this power. Aurora was then marginalized within a version of the system she hoped to reinstate and was left without means of redress as her few remaining followers either joined Zelie or were taken by the forest's violence.

Aurora, though, does more than "claim justice from a social... system that has systematically failed to meet (her) needs" (D'Amore 2017, 391).

While her culture collapsed around her, Aurora had slowly been building a relationship with nature and more quickly than most grasped that their life in the forest was not going to mirror that inside the corpse. She managed to build a trading relationship with a kind mouse and learned what resources around her could be safely used or not. At one point, it did seem as if Aurora was going to be able to restore her subjects to a state of safety and comfort, with the help of the Cinderella-esque forest animals at her behest. Even if it was in a different context, the fundamentals of her society looked as though they may not have needed to change. Aurora believed, at her new society's zenith, that she and her people had been restored to their place of dominance over nature and that they were now protected and had reliable access to forest resources.

In order to mark their new status as cultured rulers of the forest, Aurora invited the animals which had been instrumental in helping them to a tea party. The symbol is not a subtle one, with its relation not only to so many fairy tales specifically but as representative of an elitist and cultured society that has divorced itself from many natural concerns. But, as one might expect if various forest creatures were brought to a tea party, pandemonium ensues, and the party is destroyed, which destroys Aurora's illusory hope in regaining what she had lost.

While the scene has great weight thematically, it also demonstrates vividly the impact of the intersection of fairy tales and the graphic literature medium. Throughout the novel to this point, animals had been either predators or helpers, two categories that the genre makes space for. Often animals in fairy tales are evil villains, and even more often they are magically helpful. Almost never do they act simply as animals, and especially not wild ones. But here, the tea party guests act as small rodents and birds would act in such a situation. The artwork takes special pains to underscore just how uncontrolled and chaotic this party becomes, as the animals overwhelm the panel space, encroaching on the boundaries thereof, seeming to flee the page while simultaneously dwarfing and crowding out Aurora and the other Tinies that are present. While a description of the events could be likewise impactful, the usage of panel framing enhances the impact significantly, emphasizing Aurora's inability to tame their nature despite her best efforts. The animals force their way into the panels, looming over Aurora and her party with only parts of their bodies visible, making them seem larger and more foreboding. Immediately thereafter, they scatter to the forest, taking much of the party food with them, and the destructive nature of their departure is vividly depicted as they quickly flee the page, only legs, tails, and wings being represented as the animals flee, leaving the princess behind.

Yet Aurora had more to lose besides her party and trust in wild animals, namely her self-image as a person who acted in accordance with social rules. When it's discovered that one of the animals that destroyed her party is the mouse Aurora considered her friend, she gouges out its eyes and leaves it to be eaten alive by her followers. This act finally divorces her from her own social consciousness, and she begins to mimic the creatures that she had been relying on, living stealthily off the land and taking the pelt of her former friend as a cloak. As a ruler attempting to restore her fallen society, Aurora fails completely, and afterwards her only real goal is survival.

In Balinisteanu's (2012) terms, Aurora's failure was caused by her not "reimagin[ing] women's relation with nature as one engendering agency instead of subjection" (6). The conflation of women with nature is oppressive for various reasons, but of most concern here is that it is othering from the point of view of those with real political and economic power. Nature is a semantically blank space from which culture and society draw necessary resources, but the belief is that it is something fundamentally at odds with society's desired "progressive" (in the sense of economic expansion) ends. The Other, Women or Nature, is posed as a construct to be conquered, not something to be understood and accepted, and certainly not something to partner with or to respect. Culturally, the conflation poses women as resources to be exploited. Separating the two though is counterproductive if that is done within the current ideology which thrives off of the exploitation of both. Without addressing larger systemic causes, a separation of women and nature culturally would regardless leave the binary of oppressor/oppressed in place. This is the source of Aurora's failure, in that she tried to create an egalitarian society (albeit with her as a ruler) but failed to address the structure of the society which made its survival contingent on the exploitation, not just the use, of nature and the residents of the forest.

Eventually, Aurora does learn to integrate her needs with what is available in the forest. Narratively, the novel reaches its climax when Aurora discovers the cabin of a woodsman and hides there for shelter, but when Zelie and her coterie discover the cabin as well, Aurora's comfort and safety are threatened. While the cabin may seem a civilized place, the distinction that is made between nature and civilization in the novel strongly conflates the woodsman with nature, despite his living with some comforts. Throughout the text, despite that the Tinies met several creatures that exhibited intelligence, the fact that they could not directly communicate with the Tinies meant that they were then considered a part of the forest, not a part of a society. The same is true of the woodsman; because of his inability to communicate with Tinies, he is portrayed as simply another part of the woods, a natural being, while the Tinies are the exploitive invaders. In response to the ongoing violence Zelie commits against the other Tinies, Aurora contrives to have her and her followers be eaten by this representative of the forest, leaving herself alone, but no longer fearing or wishing to exploit what's around her, and achieving finally an equilibrium between her and the natural world. This is in direct conflict with the genre in which the comic is functioning.

The fairy tale structure "perpetuate(s) the patriarchal status quo" (Rowe 1979, 237), and as the novel begins in that traditional mode, the latent expectation of the reader then would be that, in some way, *Beautiful Darkness* will do the same; from the start, many of the characteristics are emphasized. Contemporary fairy tales and adaptations are in many ways far removed from D'Aulnoy, Perrault, and the Grimms. "Postmodern revisions 'unmake' some of what fairy tales have traditionally held dear" (D'Amore 2017, 386) and a common descriptor of the genre now is "disobedient." The most famous example of these types of reimaginings, which often do a great deal of work to address the most egregious implications of the classical version, often invert many of the tropes to underscore their ideological underpinnings and trouble our acceptance of these stories as ethical guidebooks. However, they still do little to address some of the structural binaries inherent in the genre, which, returning to the ideas of linked exploitation, means that little social progress is still being made as other methods of entrenched oppression are not being challenged. The woodsman, however, is a trope which the text uses to both further enmesh itself in the fairy tale genre and to exploit the affordances of the comics medium to redeploy this trope as a tool for dismantling Zelie's resurgent oppressive society.

The woodsman functions in multiple ways, especially when taken as a bridging character between graphic literature and the usually oral or written genre of fairy tales. His first introduction is as just another part of the forest, a natural force with which the Tinies must contend. He seems to have no interest in them, or even any knowledge thereof, acting as a synecdoche for the forest and its indifference to the concerns of Aurora and her people. His home, however, is the final setting of the novel, and he acts as the natural force to which Zelie and her followers fall prey. In the course of simply doing what he needs to, in this case eating, he undoes the last ties Aurora had to her previous existence, ending that society and perhaps giving her a chance to exist in a new one productively. It narratively comes as no surprise, then, when Aurora begins to refer to him as her "prince," a title she previously applied to Hector. Thematically, and generically, this reapplication of the term furthers the disruption of social structures, which the novel consistently pursues.

Hector, before his death, was a consummate fairy tale prince, clearly based on a number of familiar characters. The woodsman, however, while reminiscent of the woodsmen in Little Red Riding Hood, is completely divorced from the society of the Tinies. Using the same moniker then underscores several important aspects of the text. A common technique in graphic literature is that braiding, in which there is a determined repetition of certain symbols, situations, or contexts, in order to emphasize the thematic linkage between two separate parts of a novel. "Braiding thus manifests into consciousness the notion that the panels of a comic constitute a network" (Groensteen 2007, 148) feeding off of the connotations, themes, and events of the other panels with which they are braided. The usage of "prince" to refer exclusively to Hector and the woodsmen then ties together their positioning relative to Aurora in two wildly different contexts.

Hector was a prime example of social norms against which the novel is working. While not in and of himself a very problematic character, he was representative of systems that function through hierarchies which conflate women with nature and relegate both to positions in which they are exploited systemically. Aurora's relationship to Hector was subservient. But by referring to the Woodsman with the same honorific in her new context, Aurora is tying the woodsman into how she relates to a new power structure with which she must exist. The woodsman is a part of the forest, and across the fairy tale genre characters such as he may protect others from the worst of the woods but are inextricably a part of it. But using the conventions of graphic literature, he has usurped Hector's role and by extension represents the woods' conquest of the Tinies and their hierarchical society.

The conquest, in the end, was largely of the Tinies' own making. They had been used to lives which relied on structures that thrived due to the exploitation of the natural world around them, as much of the world does. When their most basic social need, shelter, decomposed, they were forced to reckon with that which they had been exploiting, which now had the opportunity to fight back. Unused to having violence turned against them, the Tinies at Zelie's urging began to consolidate resources and were prepared to use violence against one another, until all but Aurora are gone. The woods merely existed as they do, the generic symbol of the untamed.

Yet the woods are also anything but passive. While they may not be a character *per se*, they certainly directly impact the Tinies. Haraway (1991) suggests that one way to break down the dualisms employed to "naturalize" exploitation, which fairy tales work so hard to do, is to acknowledge nature and women as active subjects rather than passive objects (199), and *Beautiful Darkness* strives to do this in two primary ways. The dualisms, or binaries, that are primarily addressed in the novel are those of culture: nature and exploitation: cooperation. A major goal is to expose just how deeply these binaries are rooted in our culture, to the extent that they seem to be cultural givens or have become what Roland Barthes referred to as "myths." They are ideas that have lost their history in order to become unquestionable and natural, seemingly part of the basic workings of the world: "Myth… gives … a natural and eternal justification" to social norms (Barthes 1972, 143). The first step to undoing these "myths" is to make them visible, to defamiliarize them, and to make readers recognize what they have been taking for granted in their culture.

Beautiful Darkness works in two ways to expose these two binaries, both thematically and formally. First, it calls into question the genre in which it works. Despite the frequent modern reworkings of fairy tales, the genre remains primarily aimed at children and young adults, people whose relationship to the ideology and culture they live within is still being formed, hence the basic "civilizing character" (Zipes 1997, 3) referred to before. *Beautiful Darkness* blatantly markets itself as such, as well. The artwork especially is reminiscent of Margaret Keane or other whimsical art, and it strongly conveys the novel's presumed adherence to the generic expectations someone familiar with fairy tales would hold. The novel, however, relies heavily on shocking acts of violence. Granted, those are a fairy tale staples, but they usually are sanitized and are rarely presented visually. In this novel, they are gruesomely rendered, such as a Tiny being gutted via the mouth by a bird that had mistaken him for a hatchling or another Tiny seemingly without reason eating several of her compatriots. *Beautiful Darkness* stakes its claim convincingly as a member of the fairy tale genre, but then by its own violence calls into question the genre itself. With the entire corpus being directed at children, this graphic novel posits by its own horror that fairy tales as a whole either contain or endorse similar acts.

What allows *Beautiful Darkness* to so directly question the ideology endorsed by most fairy tales is its cultural positioning as a graphic novel. Comics and graphic novels are substantially less critiqued compared to more the mainstream art forms of film, literature, or drama, in which most revisionary fairy tales are produced. But returning to Taylor, graphic novels, and the entire medium of comics, rely on and excel at revisionary storytelling to an extent beyond most mediums. An effect of the long history of superhero comics, and of the same characters being written by numerous writers and artists, the medium expertly demonstrates various methods for revising a well-known story or character to the extent that this tendency has become part and parcel with the entire medium. This characteristic is vital to stress as "[r]epeated revisioning allows [stories] to be reimbued with subversive potential" (Taylor 2009, 173) as is occurring here. In its original form, Sleeping Beauty is anything but subversive, but after multiple retellings it becomes this text, which is working to undermine the very ideology that produced and was perpetuated by the fairy tale genre. As a graphic novel, *Beautiful Darkness* is using its positioning as a text which is "flying 'below the critical radar'" (Taylor 2009, 177) to propose an ideology in dramatic opposition to the dominant one of its time. As a medium, comics in general are especially powerful for telling revisionist narratives in that they are often "using the original ... as mirrors for counter- and contradistinction-and ... the comparison to teach larger concerns like... suppressed histories, dominant versus oppressed viewpoints, and myth in relation to cultural concerns" (Taylor 175). The novel exploits its position as a part of a medium which is often critically underanalyzed to undermine and undue dominant cultural assumptions about western culture's relation to nature. It accomplishes this successfully and using a method that readers will accept due to the historical tendency of the medium in which it is published.

After undermining its own genre through the opportunities afforded to its medium, the novel goes further to address the ideology into which the form innocuously inculcates its consumers. Classic fairy tales, such as those published by the Brothers Grimm and Charles Perrault, often evince a radically conservative ideology, which even modern fairy tales often actively renounce. *Beautiful Darkness* works against the fairy tale genre as it stands now, as an indoctrinator into a relatively progressive society, intimating that current ideology still is based on fundamental structures of exploitation and domination even if it is less exploitive than before. Textually, Zelie's actions and views are clearly based in the ideology presented by older tales: one in which oppression is the status quo and where she has set herself atop an unquestionable hierarchy. The hierarchy Aurora tries to institute, though, is meant to provide for the common good of her people and is a hierarchy only in that it has been set up with her as the leader. But even in that role she acts as the person that makes sure resource distribution is as fair as possible as opposed to acting as another autocrat. The fact that this structure fails as well, however, is meant to directly trouble the culture by which current fairy tales are used as indoctrinating tools. Aurora's failure is that, while she tries not to exploit nature, she still expects it to relate to her in terms she understands. She makes little effort to understand nature and stays firmly on the cultural side of that binary until she's lost almost all of her subjects.

Exploitation of nature is posed by extension as intrinsic to western culture, and our right to nature becomes mythic in Barthes' sense of the term. Since the novel is using this genre to perform its ideological critique, it further underscores that fairy tales are thematically and semantically rich form of storytelling, deeply embedded with cultural prescriptions. However, they are not always presented as such, and "[t]he ostensibly innocuous fantasies symbolically portray basic human problems and appropriate social prescriptions" (Rowe 1979, 237) and that supposed innocence is the source of their power. By being seemingly wholesome and shallow, fairy tales inculcate young people into social and ideological standards regarding gender roles and similar oppositions regarding the role of culture versus nature.

Beautiful Darkness's impact then is twofold. The text is presented in such a fashion that the reader is clearly meant to recognize its connection with European fairy tales, but it quickly evolves into abject horror and disgust. It therefore undermines the key assumption of innocence that fairy tales use for indoctrination. The horror is such that the text makes certain that the reader is aware of what they are seeing and reading, and therefore that they are a knowing, willing participant. With its vivid visual depictions of gratuitous violence, presented in ironically delicate brush strokes, the novel shows that there is no veneer of innocence at play here. It acknowledges the horrific nature of its visual palate and forces the reader to do the same. Secondly, by making its own ideology evident, it begs the question of what ideologies other narratives in its genre have been covertly exporting to their readers.

One of the most widely criticized ethics supported by the fairy tale genre is its inherent "patterns of male dominance and female subservience" (Kuykendal and Sturm 2007, 39). These are perhaps the most easily recognizable, and certainly most widely criticized, aspects of fairy tales, which are deeply rooted to the extent that they are present even in modern retellings and are ostensibly revisions designed to do away with just that patterning. In other words, as a whole, the genre is markedly misogynistic. A common rebuttal to the idea that revisionary fairy tales are not particularly feminist is that they do often underscore the issues of feminine subservience taken for granted in older versions of these tales, such as those made into most animated Disney films. However, while that is the case, allowing female characters agency in these stories is not nearly enough when the social structures (everything from market forces controlling where books are published, who gets to read them, to how gender roles are further crystallized through everything from naming conventions, to toys, to our education systems) which support these stories are not engendering actual change. Representation matters; it is the first step to crucial revolutionary alteration of the ways our society functions. But representation in and of itself provides little progress. It is an impetus for some further action, certainly, but that further action is not necessarily anticipated by representation alone.

Largely, the issue of representation has been addressed by placing female characters in leading or more powerful roles. But as Kuykendal and Sturm (2007) note, "The simple reversal of gender roles does not result in a feminist fairy tale" (40). In fact, this sort of genre play may in fact strengthen the ideology that underpins these stories. There has been a growing number of dark, adult, or simply more complex fairy tales in the contemporary cultural marketplace. For example, *Wicked: The Life and Times of the Wicked Witch of the West* (1995) and *Into the Woods*, two of the best known, engage in extensive play with the structures and constraints of their source materials, in large part to underscore aspects of the original texts that may have been lost, to underscore ideologies that have always lain dormant, or (*Wicked* being the most famous case here) to reclaim a character whose current evaluation may have been unfairly rooted in their initial evaluation performed through a very different ideology. Many of these texts examine how many seemingly villainous female characters are far more understandable through a lens that reads them as being subjected to patriarchal power structures. But the core issue at play remains, that of the oppressor/oppressed binary. These tales, which do have as one of their major functions the inculcation of children into traditional gender roles, nevertheless do far more ideological work than that. The 2007 Disney film *Enchanted* works as an especially useful example.

Enchanted is notable as it does present, at first glance, a stereotypical fairy tale princess: Giselle. The stereotype is fulfilled, however, to the point that it is clearly meant as satire. While towards the climax of the film she does need to be rescued, it is instead her love interest, not Giselle herself, that plays the traditional damsel in distress. Giselle instead acts as the hero, slaying a dragon/sorceress who also happens to be a wicked stepmother. This film portrays a much more positive message for its audience than, say, *Snow White* or *Sleeping Beauty*, each of which valued most of all women that were dead or un-wakeable: Giselle is a character with substantial agency. But a problematic ideology is still at work. By simply reversing the gender of the hero, the narrative does little to nothing to undo notions of oppression. This of course would be perhaps too much to ask of a mainstream children's film, especially one produced by the company whose stock-in-trade has been these very tales. There is little oppression portrayed directly in the film that isn't defeated by Giselle's sword. But what, in truth, changed besides swapping a prince for a princess as the hero?

A simple gender reversal would not be problematic if that was the only issue in the genre which the film is using as a springboard for its (admittedly powerful) message of feminine empowerment. But by using a majority of the tropes uncritically, the film, and others like it, are instead expanding the boundaries of this genre, empowering it further, without addressing other binaries that also further modes of exploitation, such as consistency of restorations (which *Enchanted* also portrays). By making space for more women in the genre, the genre itself, and the oppressive ideology it supports, becomes more resistant to criticism and therefore less likely to change. The swapping of the genders of primary characters may not only *not* make for more feminist fairy tales but may in the long run make that goal harder to achieve at all. Even more troubling, they may make the binary oppositions that support the genre of fairy tales even more resistant and more reified.

Beautiful Darkness takes a different approach, instead choosing to address systemic issues that a character like Giselle doesn't have a chance to narratively. Aurora is, by the standards of her genre, a positive character. While initially somewhat lacking in resolve, she quickly takes control of not only her own situation but also that of those around her who need her help. She takes and tries to earn authority, exercising power where no one else will, within her rights as the ruler of her people. Yet, she is an abject failure despite acting as such a positive representation. The critical tea party underscores the limits of this type of power when confronting not just an immediate situation but deeper structures as well. Those deeper structures that the Tinies clung to granted them what they believed was the right to hold power over others: in this case, the forest creatures and by extension nature itself. Positive representation is only so positive when it is still a representation endorsed, or at least allowed, by the status quo. That representation may then infiltrate the status quo, that is true, but instead of undoing any binary it instead changes who is being oppressed rather than addressing oppression directly. The dissolution of their homes didn't allow any Tinies to really free themselves from the system of exploitation that had already been at work (as evinced by Aurora's indentured servant). It just brought them face to face with what they had been taking advantage of and allowed Zelie a chance to set up her own dictatorship.

Texts such as *Wicked: The Life and Times of the Wicked Witch of the West* and *Into the Woods* attempt to call into question our acceptance of fairy tales in general. However, a fundamental fairy tale attribute remains in most of these that *Beautiful Darkness* rejects. While much of the genre does feature horrific events (large scale destruction, mass murders, cannibalism, etc.), the foundational trope is that of restoration. In the end of almost all fairy tales, whatever threat that had been conjured against the status quo, be it a wolf, a witch, a giant, or any other, is destroyed, usually violently. Prince Charming slays the dragon, and despite the destruction that had already been wrought, it is somehow all set right. While many of these disobedient narratives may well reckon with the destruction wrought, the restoration is still vital and ever-present. This is the key exemplification of the ideological underpinnings of the genre: violence against the status quo may be tragic and horrific, but is never successful, while violence used by those defending it is just and to be celebrated. The immutability of the status quo is the primary ideology that fairy tales are working to subsume people within, but *Beautiful Darkness* rejects the restoration.

The text details how the Tinies' attempts at restoration are themselves destructive and further confronts the impulses that drove the creation of societies in the first place. Furthermore, it reckons with the inherent violence of culture and civilization against nature. The novel is an explication and critique of the cruelty of humanity (ostensibly aimed at the young readers that tend to read in this genre) and the extent to which human expectations and forms of interaction cause violence against people and the surrounding world. The depiction of violence against nature especially gains importance in light of "Kristeva's concept of intertextuality," which "explains how the transformed characters and tales still rely on and continue to inform other-original and revised-texts that have those characters and tales" (Taylor 2009, 173) and supports why it's so important ideologically that *Beautiful Darkness* is part of the fairy tale genre. With its anti-progress, anarchic stance, it is still something that has to be reckoned with as a fairy tale, especially with the dead girl's strong ties to Sleeping Beauty and the overall setting so strongly evoking Snow White and Little Red Riding Hood. It becomes something that has inserted itself into the web of texts, and while it may be a fringe one, it still troubles the genre and the genre's overall ideological project. These anti-fairy tale ethics are now some of the values that this genre is espousing, as opposed to the simple patriarchal status quo inherent in the genre as it is usually understood. Framing the text within an ecofeminist lens reveals a further social critique. Only by destroying the systems that had allowed their civilized previous life and those that sought to re-instate them is Aurora finally able to reach a state of balance with the world around her, and the novel implies that only by actively destroying patriarchal, economically progressive institutions and ideals, not simply altering them, can actual change be sustained.

The artists arrange the text in the mode of the fairy tale genre to imply that this is inculcating readers into a new ideology—a complete break from patriarchal systems. By conveying it within the medium of the graphic novel, with its powerful usage of identification and participation, the impact of this anti-fairy tale is enhanced, creating a partnership in this destruction of the patriarchal status between reader and text. The combination is especially powerful as graphic literature is so engaging to readers due to the need to participate in order to activate these texts, which cooperates with the familiar fairy tale genre and tropes. In this novel, the opportunities afforded by the graphic medium are integrated into an already familiar narrative arc, which makes the reader especially unsettled when the genre conventions are disrupted. Marion Perret (2001) argues that "when the comics artist manipulates our imaginative involvement effectively, we do more than fill in gaps between pictured actions: we become co-creators of the story's meaning, which we therefore find relevant to us" (136). In this case it means readers are the coconspirators in the subversion of their own western ideology, which was originally deployed through this same genre.

Catherine Diamond (2017) argues that the ideology of western culture is embedded with "[t]he hierarchy of dualisms that divide the world and valorize the male side, such as nature/female and culture/male," which "has to be dissolved to allow more nuanced interconnections" (136). But the rhetoric employed here is altogether too passive. Hierarchies as Diamond poses them are not inherent in the natural world; they are created by people and founded in methods which are used to enrich and preserve social structures that operate through exploitation and oppression of nature. In that regard, that hierarchy dissolved (literally, as shelter is one of the foundations of social hierarchies) when the corpse the Tinies lived in decomposed beyond use. But the ideology lives on, even in the face of certain death in the forest, as the Tinies don't know another way to exist, and these hierarchies do not reward considering alternatives. Instead of just *dissolved*, as Aurora discovers, these hierarchies must be actively fought, actively destroyed. What follows must not be just an inversion or reorganization, but a "possible something else" (Diamond 2017, 72) that may allow for work to begin on a system that functions without perpetuating oppression.

References

Bacchilega, Christina. 1997. *Postmodern Fairy Tales: Gender and Narrative Strategies*. Philadelphia: University of Pennsylvania Press.

Balinisteanu, Tudor. 2012. "Goddess Cults in Techno-Worlds: Tank Girl and the Borg Queen." *Journal of Feminist Studies in Religion* 28 (1): 5–24. doi:10.2979/jfemistudreli.28.1.5.

Barker, Francis. 1994. *Culture of Violence: Shakespeare, Tragedy, History*. Manchester: Manchester University Press.

Barthes, Roland. 1972. *Mythologies*. Translated by Annette Lavers. New York: Noonday Press.

Bourdieu, Pierre. 1984. *Distinction: A Social Critique of the Judgement of Taste*. Cambridge: Harvard University Press.

D'Amore, Laura Mattoon. 2017. "Vigilante Feminism: Revising Trauma, Abduction, and Assault in American Fairy-Tale Revisions." *Marvels & Tales: Journal of Fairy-Tale Studies* 31 (2): 386–405. doi:10.13110/marvelstales.31.2.0386.

Diamond, Catherine. 2017. "Four Women in the Woods: An Ecofeminist Look at the Forest as Home." *Comparative Drama* 51 (1): 71–100. doi:10.1353/cdr.2017.0003.

Gaard, Greta. 2015. "Ecofeminism and Climate Change." *Women's Studies International Forum* 49: 20–33. doi:10.1016/j.wsif.2015.02.004.

Grimm, Jacob, and Wilhelm Grimm. 2014. *The Original Folk and Fairy Tales of the Brothers Grimm: The Complete* 1st Edition. Translated by Jack Zipes. Princeton: Princeton University Press.

Groensteen, Thierry. 2000. "Why are Comics Still in Search of Cultural Legitimization?" In *Comics and Culture: Analytical and Theoretical Approaches to Comics*, edited by Anne Magnussen and Hans-Christian Christiansen, 29–42. Copenhagen: Museum Tusculanum Press.

Groensteen, Thierry. 2007. *The System of Comics*. Translated by Nick Nguyen and Bart Beaty. Jackson: University Press of Mississippi.

Haraway, Donna. 1991. *Simians, Cyborgs, and Women: The Reinvention of Nature*. New York: Routledge.

Kaijser, Anna, and Annica Kronsell. 2014. "Climate Change Through the Lens of Intersectionality." *Environmental Politics* 23 (3): 417–33. doi:10.1080/09644016.2013.835203.

Kannenberg, Jr., Gene. 2001. "The Comics of Chris Ware." In *The Language of Comics: Word and Image*, edited by Robin Varnum and Christina T. Gibbons, 174–98. Jackson: University Press of Mississippi.

Kunzle, David. 2001. "The Voices of Silence." In *The Language of Comics: Word and Image*, edited by Robin Varnum and Christina T. Gibbons, 3–18. Jackson: University Press of Mississippi.

Kuykendal, Leslee Farish, and Brian W. Sturm. 2007. "We Said Feminist Fairy Tales, Not Fractured Fairy Tales!" *Children & Libraries: The Journal of the Association for Library Service to Children* 5 (3): 38–41.

Lima, Kevin dir. 2007. *Enchanted*. Burbank: Walt Disney Pictures. DVD.

Maguire, Gregory. 1995. *Wicked: The Life and Times of the Wicked Witch of the West*. New York: HarperCollins.

Marshall, Rob dir. 2014. *Into the Woods*. Burbank: Walt Disney Pictures. DVD.

McCloud, Scott. 1993. *Understanding Comics: The Invisible Art*. New York: William Morrow Publishing.

Mieder, Wolfgang. 1987. "Grim Variations From Fairy Tales to Modern Anti-Fairy Tales." *The Germanic Review: Literature, Culture, Theory* 62 (2): 90–102. doi:10.1080/00168890.1987.9934196.

Murray, Chris. 2000. "*Popaganda*: Superhero Comics and Propaganda." In *Comics and Culture: Analytical and Theoretical Approaches to Comics*, edited by Anne

Magnussen and Hans-Christian Christiansen, 141–56. Copenhagen: Museum Tusculanum Press.

Postema, Barbara. 2013. *Narrative Structure in Comics: Making Sense of Fragments*. Rochester: RIT Press.

Perret, Marion. 2001. "'And Suit the Action to the Word.'" In *The Language of Comics: Word and Image*, edited by Robin Varnum and Christina T. Gibbons, 123–44. Jackson: University Press of Mississippi.

Rowe, Karen. 1979. "Feminism and Fairy Tales." *Women's Studies* 6 (3): 237–57. doi:10.1080/00497878.1979.9978487.

Taylor, Laurie N. 2009. "Snow White in the City: Teaching Fables, Nursery Rhymes, and Revisions in Graphic Novels." In *Teaching the Graphic Novel*, edited by Stephen E. Tabachnik, 172–78. New York: Modern Language Association of America.

Vehlman, Fabien and Kerascoët. 2014. *Beautiful Darkness*. Translated byHelge Dascher. Montreal: Drawn and Quarterly.

Warhol, Robyn R. 1996. "Double Gender, Double Genre in *Jane Eyre* and *Villette*." *Studies in English Literature, 1500-1900* 34 (4): 857–75. doi:10.2307/450979.

Zipes, Jack. 1997. *Happily Ever After: Fairy Tales, Children, and the Culture Industry*. New York and London: Routledge.

Part II

National histories and personal autographies

5 Drawn into being: the transformative voices of Native American and First Nations women in comics and visual narratives

Nicole Dib

In part through their merging of the written and drawn word, the fictional worlds that Indigenous comics creators imagine contribute to decolonization, a process that works against coloniality by centering the power of storytelling. Mishuana Goeman (2013) of the Tonawanda Band of Seneca explains how "The narrations of national myths normalize colonial closures, but the many creation and migration stories of Native people attest to their presence" (33). In the face of normalized accounts of history that erase Indigenous voices and that contribute to the closure to which Goeman refers, fiction in the form of comics is a way to witness the continued presence of Native stories. Native American and First Nations comics creators actively resist discourses of domination and disappearance by imbuing their contemporary comics with narratives of Native "survivance," the term that Chippewa theorist Gerald Vizenor (2010) employs to understand how Indigenous communities simultaneously survive and resist settler-colonialism. This continued presence is also legible in a surge in Indigenous comics anthologies in the present moment, a format of publishing short comics in anthologized collections that are often collaborations between writers and illustrators. These collections are distinguishable by, among other features, a traceable presence of a Native American feminism that emerges in plot-based and formal transformations. I consider the impact of this transformational aesthetics in the comics anthologies entitled *Moonshot: The Indigenous Comics Collection Volume 1* (2015) and *Volume 2* (2017); *Deer Woman: An Anthology* (2017); and *Sovereign Traces, Volume 1: Not (Just) (An)Other* (2018) together with *Volume 2: Relational Constellation* (2019). By following character transformations in comics from these anthologies, one can see how the visual narrative is a medium through which Native writers and illustrators illuminate the issues faced by women members of their Indigenous nations. The comics medium becomes a ground on which artists and authors detail the threats of domestic and sexual violence faced by Native and Indigenous women; they simultaneously advance a message of resistance toward these threats in part through the aesthetics of transformation that run through their comics.

DOI: 10.4324/9781003146520-5

Indigenous comics creators including Weshoyot Alvitre (Tongva/Scots-Gaelic), Elizabeth LaPensée (Anishinaabe, Métis, Irish), and Arigon Starr (Kickapoo Tribe of Oklahoma) combat narratives of Native disappearance that persist in the US and Canadian cultural imaginary. They combine creation stories in their comics with transformation narratives, speculative fiction cues, and feminist messages of resistance in the face of domination; the latter is particularly important when considering how fiction approaches issues relevant to Indigenous women. Native American and First Nations women writers and artists have always played a necessary role in the work of combatting violence and sexual assault, which disproportionately affects Native women, both in their fiction and outside of it. Shortly after the publication of her National Book Award winning novel *The Round House* (2012), Louise Erdrich (Turtle Mountain Band of Chippewa Indians) wrote an opinion piece for the New York Times called "Rape on the Reservation" (2013), in which her scathing survey of the ways that legal gaps have "attracted non-Indian habitual sexual predators to tribal areas" supports her plea for stronger jurisdiction for tribal authorities. After listing statistics about sexual violence against Native women, including the Justice Department's report that "one in three Native women is raped over her lifetime," Erdrich (2013) closes with a striking image: "If our hearts are on the ground, our country has failed us all. If we are safe, our country is safer." Placing Native women at the center of the fight and at the center of her fiction, Erdrich's call for action has an ethical imperative thanks to the imagery her words invoke.

While Native American fiction in the form of novels, poetry, and plays has been a well-studied space where women create stories that resist domination, the medium of comics and graphic narratives has seen less scholarly attention. The three anthology collections that this chapter discusses house short comics pieces from Native American and First Nations women writers and artists. The comic anthology functions quite differently from the graphic novel, the latter defined by the *Oxford English Dictionary* (2019) as "a full-length ... story published as a book in comic-strip format."[1] The anthologies I discuss in this chapter have some features in common, though the three sets I look at have different formats and listed aims. They each include works by different authors and artists, each have an editor (or multiple editors), and for the purpose of my argument, I chose anthologies that feature comics about and by Native American and First Nations women writers and illustrators.[2] Each anthology represents the realized potential for collaboration between and among Native and non-Native writers and artists; indeed, Patty Stonefish's (2017) (Lakota, Russian, and Polish) introduction to *Deer Woman: An Anthology* insists that "This is a group of powerful Indigenous women sharing their power with others" (3). These anthologies, then, signify collaboration in form (as they are pieces often created by the collaboration of writers and illustrators, which are then joined in a collection) as well as creation. Contemporary

Native comics have found tremendous support on social media, with Kickstarter campaigns and Twitter publicity lending a helping hand in the publication efforts of both lesser-known and famous artists. Weshoyot Alvitre, for example—at the time that this chapter was written—has completed funding for a graphic novel about Toypurina, the Tongva medicine woman who led a revolt in 1785 against the San Gabriel Mission, and has also published a historical graphic novel entitled *Ghost River: The Fall and Rise of the Conestoga* (Pratt and Weshoyot 2018).

The ample participation of Native American and First Nations women comics creators and the collaborative possibilities of these comics anthologies have led to a recurring appearance of an Indigenous feminist transformational aesthetics, which emerges thanks to the medium's unique blend of written word and drawn art. Transformation can equal social change, as Louise Erdrich (2013) called for it; it can also be an illustrated approach that counters the way in which "Elements of indigeneity become props in colonial discourse," as C. Richard King (2009) explains in "Alter/native Heroes: Native Americans, Comic Books, and the Struggle for Self-Definition" (218). The resistance-based transformations in the pages and panels of these comics come about in part due to their specificity. A particular benefit of the anthology format is that it makes room for multiple varied voices and styles, which for Native American and First Nations writers and illustrators, means there is space to create visual stories unique to their Indigenous nations' histories and stories. In what follows, I consider the intersection of race and gender as it emerges in anthologized works by Native women comics writers, who work in a historically white and male-centered field; their growing presence combats what Neal Curtis and Valentina Cardo (2017), in their intersectional analysis of women-centered superhero comics, call the "social and institutional hurdles that still exist within the [superhero comics] industry" (382). Native and Indigenous creators challenge the formal conventions of different comics genres as well as the popular image of the industry as a "boys' club." I then work through the feminist messages and visual forms in selected comics from *Deer Woman*, *Moonshot*, and *Sovereign Traces*, to demonstrate the richly beautiful resistance enacted by these comics creators.

Native American feminisms and the drawn word

Thanks to their interplay between image and text, comics are a space of collaboration between the "real" and the "fantastical" in a way that has endeared the medium to genres such as the superhero story, fantasy, science fiction, and speculative fiction as well as realism. In his introduction to *Multicultural Comics*, Frederick Luis Aldama (2010) asserts that comics artists of color "take from the real world *and* fictional worlds: author-artists of color talk about real, biographical experiences living at the margins of a xenophobic society informing their comics as much as they talk of the influence of fiction, film, and art" (2). For comics creators who are members of marginalized communities, the "real" that inspires their graphic narratives is necessarily influenced by the lived realities of precarity. Furthermore, an intersectional understanding of the perspective that comics creators of color bring to their works is necessary for an analysis of the concerns that emerge in comics by women of color.

Recent studies of multiethnic and multicultural comics have theorized Native American, First Nations, and Indigenous comics, generally in the scope of US or North American comics studies. Graphic novels such as David Alexander Robertson's (2012) *7 Generations: A Plains Cree Saga* have been acclaimed, as Dedra Dudek (2016) explains, for "subvert[ing] a linear and singular notion of history/ies and identity/ies by inviting a close-reading practice that also refuses linearity and singularity" (40). Analyses of Native American comics such as Dudek's often find that the double marginalization at work (that is, the marginalization Indigenous communities experience coupled with the often disregarded comics form) fosters this medium as a space within which precarious writers and illustrators feel at home. In tandem with growing interest in comics by and about Native American and First Nations peoples, there has been keen scholarly work on representations of Indigenous communities in works of popular culture. Aldama (2010) points out in *Multicultural Comics,* "There has been a tradition of Native Americans appearing as sidekicks, the easily disposable, and the preternaturally ecological in comics" (8). Michael Sheyahshe's (2013) (Caddo Nation) *Native Americans in Comic Books: A Critical Study* further surveys representations of Native Americans as they appear in the roles of villains, sidekicks without agency, and (more rarely) protagonists in comic books, while a critical take such as Brady DeSanti's (2015) (Lac Courte Oreilles Ojibwe) zooms in on recurring depictions of the windigo "as just another stock monster comparable to many other notable fiendish creatures," despite the windigo's importance in the religious beliefs of Native American nations (186).[3] These approaches to Native representation in comics and other popular culture artifacts by Native American and First Nation critics establish a framework for my analysis of Indigenous comics that will focus on women-created and women-centered Native comics stories.

Critical analyses which focus on Indigenous women comics creators have been somewhat sparse, though Margaret Noori's (2010) "Native American Narratives from Early Art to Graphic Novels" and Susan Bernardin's (2015) "Future Pasts: Comics, Graphic Novels, and Digital Media" lay some necessary groundwork for a feminist reading of Native American comics. Noori (2010) offers a link between the oral tradition and comics studies, explaining that "the layered construction of the sound and meaning is perfectly suited to the comic format, where text, line and color combine to communicate action and relationships" (58). The attention she pays to oral forms of storytelling and the connection she finds between these forms and illustrated narratives emerges in various comics featured in the anthologies this chapter surveys. In particular, there is a recurring use of a somewhat framed narrative (where one character narrates a story to another character), which in the comic form is represented through multiple layers of images and stories in panels and on the page. In Bernardin's (2015) indispensable survey of Native American graphic narratives, she identifies an "indigenous comic aesthetic" which emerges in the meeting between the contemporary challenges Native people face and the way they become "super people" as they fight evils in the realm of the "environmental, legal, political, or social" (484). Genre comics meet realism in many of the anthologized comics of these collections, and the attributes associated with genres such as the superhero story, science fiction, and fantasy do not preclude Indigenous writers from discussing political issues.

Furthermore, the intersectional approach that this essay takes toward understanding the entwined roles of gender and race in the following comics is influenced by form as well. Studies on formally intriguing graphic narratives such as Michael Nicoll Yahgulanaas' *Red: A Haida Manga* (2009) often take into account the contentious relationship between Indigenous and non-Indigenous perspectives or layouts. Richard Harrison (2016), for example, calls attention to Yahgulanaas' "tension between the Indigenous and European concepts of space and time—both of which are represented in comic art, not by drawings within the panels, but in the structure of comics itself" (53); much like my own attention to the generative possibility of the anthologized comic, Harrison's study reminds us of the unique comic form that is as worthy of attention as the content. Together, the form and content of Indigenous comics create political as well as aesthetic statements.

Indeed, we will see how comics—for Native American women creators in particular—lend themselves well to addressing the violence that Indigenous women are susceptible to as a result of systemic injustices perpetrated toward Native American and First Nations communities. Examining cultural productions such as comics by and about Native American communities requires an understanding of differential racialization or the ways that ethnic groups are racialized and the way this racialization leads to different treatment and different forms of representation. In the foreword to *Moonshot: Volume 1*, Hope Nicholson (2016) writes that "There is no single, homogenous native identity," a statement that addresses the specter of homogenization that has been an issue for Indigenous representation in media (7). The varied art styles, narrative techniques, and genre choices for each comic across these anthologies reflect the diverse Native voices that each strive toward a visual sovereignty. Furthermore, the comics take up issues such as domestic abuse, sexual assault, and the National Inquiry into Missing and Murdered Indigenous Women and Girls, whose final report—released in 2019—"reveals that persistent and deliberate human and Indigenous rights violations and abuses are the root cause behind

Canada's staggering rates of violence against Indigenous women, girls and 2SLGBTQQIA people." There is a growing representation of these issues in popular media, such as the films *Wind River* (2017) and the *On the Farm* (2016), which unveil the crucial task of seeking justice for Indigenous women and which add to an archive of fictional works that deal with this very real cataclysm that the comics in this chapter address as well.

Comics by Native American and First Nations women writers thus play a role in a literary landscape that Laguna Pueblo literary theorist Paula Gunn Allen claimed was in dire need of transformation. In her book *The Sacred Hoop: Recovering the Feminine in American Indian Traditions*, Allen (1986) writes that "Media images, literary images, and artistic images, particularly those embedded in popular culture, must be changed before Indian women will see much relief from the violence that destroys so many lives" (193). Her call for a change in images is taken up by the writers and illustrators surveyed here, whose comics address the challenge that Allen elaborates: "To survive culturally, American Indian women must often fight ... the colonizer's revisions of our lives, values, and histories have devastated us at the most critical level of all—that of our own minds, our own sense of who we are" (193). The fight against these revisions plays out in the graphic tales anthologized across these three comics collections, and it is further legible in their different transformative strategies.

In addition to combatting settler-colonialism's revisions and narratives of disappearance, the comics in these anthologies are also particularly well-suited to countering the flattening homogenization that contributes to these same damaging narratives. In Jace Weaver's (1997) analysis of Native American "communitism"—his portmanteau of "community" and "activism"—entitled *That the People Might Live: Native American Literatures and Native American Community*, he affirms how storytelling counters hegemony:

> The telling of stories is both spiritual and essential: spiritual because of their ability to form identity and community, and essential as a means of claiming representational sovereignty against the forces in the dominant culture that suppress them and collapse the diversity and richness of Native lives into homogenized banality. (140)

Sovereignty, here linked to the issue of representation, which is so important for Native artists, writers, and theorists, has long been a legal contestation that mirrors the violent homogenization Weaver refers to, and that has contributed to a "flattening" of Native American sovereign nations into "a" Native American identity over which the US nation-state has dominance. Indeed, the legal sovereignty "granted" to Native nations can seem to function more as a dependence on, than an independence from, the US government. If, as Nick Estes (2019) (Lower Brule Sioux Tribe) argues, in response to changing manifestations of colonialism "each generation continues to build dynamic and vital traditions of resistance" in part by "drawing upon earlier struggles and incorporating elements of them into their own experience," then the contemporary comics narratives created by Indigenous artists and writers today continue a long tradition of claiming sovereignty through representation (21). The transformation of resistance movements that Estes traces—one that begins before and continues toward contemporary movements like #NoDAPL and Protect Mauna Kea—happens when there is a merging of old stories with new strategies, a transformation that is well-represented in these comics anthologies.

Beginning with *Deer Woman*, moving on to the *Moonshot* collections, and ending with the *Sovereign Traces* anthologies, we will see how women comics creators imbue their graphic narratives with the stories, oral narratives, and visual transformations that create much-needed representation in the world of comics. The different, often revisionary, takes on the *Deer Woman* oral story across the short comics collected in the *Deer Woman* anthology opens this chapter, while the second section will examine the intersection between science-fiction genre cues and women's stories. Finally, the chapter will close with a section that analyzes the power of adaption in comics anthologized in the *Sovereign Traces* collections.

A unified collection: *Deer Woman*

Elizabeth LaPensée published *Deer Woman: A Vignette* in 2015, a digital comic written by LaPensée, illustrated by Jonathan R. Thunder (Ojibwe), and edited by Allie Vasquez. The anthology that grew from this vignette compiles the original comic with other pieces centered on Native women's issues, as well as two introductions (one by Patty Stonefish, which was referenced earlier in this chapter) and a closing reflection. The first introduction to the anthology by Lee Francis IV (Pueblo of Laguna) provides the same statistic quoted by Louise Erdrich, that "1 in 3 Native women are sexually assaulted in their lifetimes," and goes on to say, "When we first published *Deer Woman: A Vignette*, I knew we had something powerful that could work toward disrupting the hegemonic narrative and give Native women hope" (1). The hegemonic narrative to which he refers opens up the 18-page comic, which begins with a scene of sexual assault: a man drives a woman to an empty park under the guise of taking her to a party, rapes her, and leaves. In the vignette's first two pages, there is a meeting of the three themes that this chapter will focus on as they emerge in comics by Native American and First Nations comics creators. These are the real and present-day threats of violence disproportionately affecting Native women, the message of survival, and the aesthetic of transformation that addresses—and fights back against—this violence.

In the vein of the resistant strategies outlined by Nick Estes, where contemporary movements build from—and adapt, when necessary—past coalitions and movements, the comics in the *Deer Woman* anthology take inspiration from an oral story whose narrative was rather different from the stories that these contemporary comics creators tell. The Lakota story of the *Deer Woman*, an oral story transcribed by Ella Cara Deloria (Sioux) in 1932, functions as a cautionary tale for men; in this story from the oral tradition, a man is ensnared by a beautiful woman who is revealed to be a deer and who curses the man with sickness until he is healed by his community. Deloria (2006) provides a footnote that explains how "the deer-spirit represents the enticing woman" and that "A man who allowed himself to be ensnared too deeply died; but those who did not go so far, came through" (163). This story is further situated by Carolyn Dunn (Creek/Seminole/Cherokee/Choctaw) and Carol Comfort (1999) (Cherokee/Choctaw) in their introductory chapter to *Through the Eye of the Deer: An Anthology of Native American Women Writers*, in which they explain that Deer Woman is "the spirit we are warned about as children, the spirit that bewitches those who are susceptible to her sexual favors and who can be enticed away from family and clan into misuse of sexual energy" (xi). It is interesting, then, that Alvitre's vignettes and the other comics collected in this anthology invoke the Deer Woman figure—along with other feminine figures and characters who signify change and transformation—for the entirely different message of promoting women's agency in the face of violence, particularly violence by men. The comics creators in this collection borrow Deer Woman's strength, subversion, and trickery while updating the perimeters of her story to account for contemporary struggles faced by Native women.

This modern update is evident in *Deer Woman: A Vignette*, which has the beats of an origin story in the framing of its first few pages. On the page where the sexual assault takes place, the woman at first sits fully shaded in the car, her face revealed in the next two panels as the man's violent intentions become clear. LaPensée and Vasquez (2017) begin layering transformations on the first page, drawing the woman as a human with cloven deer legs during the rape. After this scene, the woman walks home as the following text lays over drawn panels of her human body giving off a Deer Woman shadow, her gaze in the mirror, and her stance among boxing gear and weights: "In that moment, when it's already too late, what could I do? Survive. Transform. So that it never happens again. To anyone" (10). The words teach us that there is no separation between the one and the community and that an assault on one woman is an assault on one's community. Deer Woman's immediate reaction is to extend her self-defense to everyone else, transforming the meaning of *self*-defense, which is especially important for the vignette and its reprinting in this anthology. When the comic was originally published online, it included an additional page illustrating self-defense moves such as groin strikes, eye gouges, and ear slaps. This didactic page is followed by a message of empowerment from Patty Stonefish, a martial artist and self-defense instructor whose nonprofit organization Arming Sisters teaches women's self-defense.[4] LaPensée's vignette thus introduces the spirit of collaboration beyond writers and artists that is also important to these Indigenous comics anthologies, which teach and take lessons from women even outside of the comics community.

The two-page origin ends with a close-up of a deer's eye, and from there, Deer Woman goes to work. The vignette follows her avenging actions against figures of institutional violence that affects Native women and their communities. In a wordless sequence, Deer Woman lures a fraternity member away from another woman, leads him to a bathroom, and leaves him in a puddle of blood from which deer footsteps walk away. She enacts similarly violent justice against a police officer who is tasing a helpless victim and a man wearing a biker vest sexually assaulting a woman. Before and during each intervention, the panel work juxtaposes the human and animal to present a seamless transformation that makes us reconsider the way that transformation itself functions. In Figure 5.1, we can see how Deer Woman's right human ear and left deer ear parallel each other, demonstrating her heightened ability to sense violence against women; on the following page, the human who goes to strike the rapist finishes her attack standing on deer hindlegs. Rather than presenting an isolated scene of transformation, LaPensée and Thunder create a figure who is always in the process of transformation, and who uses both sides implied by the act of transforming (the pre- and the post-) to defend women who are vulnerable to the same violence that she faced.

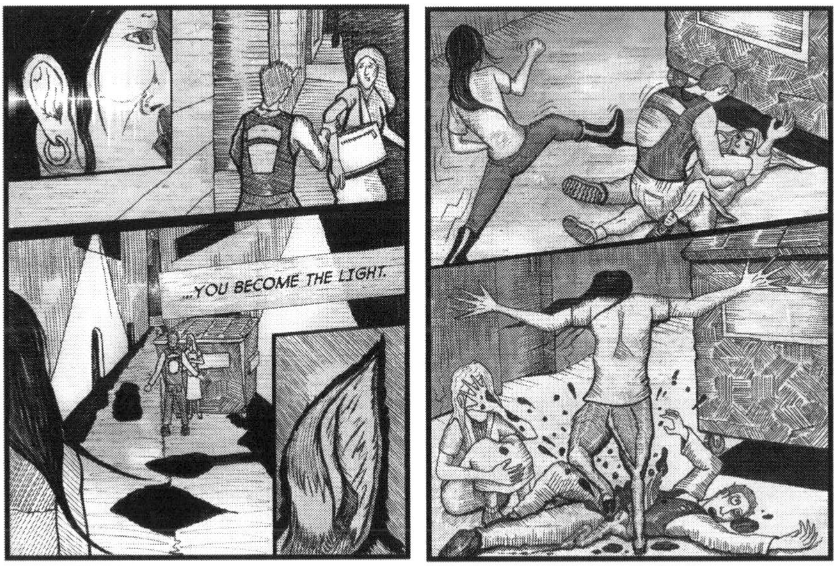

Figure 5.1 "Deer Woman" By Elizabeth LaPensée and Jonathan R. Thunder, 2017.

Deer Woman: An Anthology thus has a very identifiable theme taken up in a number of its short comics that are quite different in style and form. Some have a linear narrative, while others are more abstract; but they all touch on the transformative potential of marginalized women in a racist patriarchal society. Certain comics in *Deer Woman* appear as text overlaying images, such as Maria Wolf Lopez's version of the Deer Woman story midway through the anthology. Like LaPensée, Lopez articulates transformation as an ongoing state of being rather than an outcome. Her comic mixes full-page drawings that are more symbolic than narrative with panels that tell the story of a woman who is abused, who then meets with other women (who appear as wolves and as humans), and who then becomes *Deer Woman* herself. Reading the nameless—and by this point, familiar—figure of the woman fighting back against normalized violence corresponds to a feminist decolonial perspective, one which, according to Katherine Kelp-Stebbins (2018), "insists on the foregrounding of the specific types of subjects that are inscribed and described by reading comics" (211). Drawing strong women fighting back counters the hegemonic violence of toxic masculinity, and the subject in Lopez's comic, who is woman, wolf, and *Deer Woman* simultaneously, presents readers with a subject that positions Native women as powerfully transformative.

Tatum Bowie (Navajo Nation) contributes a piece to the anthology called "Changing Woman," which features a linear style of storytelling that is more akin to a traditional comic book. Her visual narrative demonstrates an appreciation for oral storytelling as a necessary element of her address of Native women-centered issues. Bowie (2017) opens her piece with a woman who hides the evidence of partner-inflicted abuse on her wrists from her grandmother and who then asks her to tell her about Changing Woman "again" (86). Bowie conveys the worrisome sense of repetition that is part of the cycle of abuse, both in the way she draws the young Navajo woman's practiced pulling up of her sleeve and in the use of the word "again." The grandmother explains that although there are different versions of Changing Woman (which acknowledges the varied roles that change and transformation play in Indigenous world-building), she is a deity who is part of the cycle of life and death: notably, the grandmother states that "though there aren't many depictions of her, she is said to have very long hair and is very beautiful and strong" (87). This part of the comic is accompanied by an image of Changing Woman holding figures of a baby, a girl, a young woman, and an old woman to represent the life cycle that she watches over. Bowie's depiction, then, is an example of a transformative story given a new edge in the way it mixes oral storytelling, written narration, and drawn images. The young woman who comes to her grandmother for a story in a time of duress hears about the importance of Changing Woman to the Navajo Nation's way of viewing the world, and the text that overlays an image of the young woman with tears in her eyes is her grandmother's message that "Changing Woman didn't get her name by staying the same ... And you can't change by letting things stay as they are!" (89).

Rather than following up this call for transformation with a reference to the present struggle her granddaughter endures, the grandmother continues her explanation of Changing Woman by connecting it to important milestones in her granddaughter's life. In Figure 5.2, a mirrored image depicts Changing Woman watching over the protagonist's Kinaalda and Blessingway Ceremonies, which amplifies the final part of the grandmother's story: that her granddaughter already has the strength of Changing Woman thanks to her presence at important coming of age ceremonies. Change and transformation, here, are framed as a discovery of what is already there, rather than a physical manifestation of an entirely new form. And when the young woman ultimately goes to confront her abusive boyfriend, as seen in Figure 5.3, her language and Bowie's art enhance the transformation via "finding" that emerges both from the woman's question ("you're not going to change, are you?") and by the manner in which her hair now matches Changing Woman's as seen in Figure 5.2: a gradient of a starry sky that is shown off as she walks away from the dangerous situation she had been in.

Speculative fiction and Sci-Fi cues in *Moonshot*

Like *Deer Woman: An Anthology*, the *Moonshot* collections are remarkably collaborative, both in the way that most of the short comics are written by pairs of artists and writers and in the very manner of their creation thanks to the participation of readers. *Moonshot: Volume 1* was published in 2015 after a crowdfunding effort through Kickstarter, with *Volume 2* published in 2017 (and *Volume 3* similarly crowdfunded and forthcoming at the time this chapter was written). *Moonshot* has received scholarly attention, evidenced, for example, by Kyle Bladow's reading of the collection's "future-oriented tone" (2019, 45). Bladow and others such as Judith Leggatt (2016), in "Suicide Prevention in Nêhiyawi (Cree) Comic Books," cite the significance of *Moonshot* to the contemporary surge in interest in Indigenous comics, with Leggatt considering how important it is for young-adult readers to be "seeing their people and traditions positively represented in a popular genre," a representation which "strengthens young Indigenous peoples' ties to their culture and heritage" (32). The women-centered comics in *Moonshot: The Indigenous Comics Collection Volume 1* and *Volume 2* are especially committed to recuperating genre through the graphic narrative, taking elements from science fiction, speculative fiction, and fantasy in tandem with a range of art styles.

The science-fiction comics in *Moonshot* are relevant for a feminist reading of Indigenous comics in part because they recuperate a genre that has had a hold in the North American popular imaginary as a space of white, masculine fantasies and futures.[5] The comics creators who

Figure 5.2 "Changing Woman" by Tatum Bowie, with additional credit to Elizabeth LaPensée and Native Realities, 2017.

Figure 5.3 "Changing Woman" by Tatum Bowie, with additional credit to Elizabeth LaPensée and Native Realities, 2017.

contribute to *Moonshot* respond to Danika Medak-Saltzman's (Turtle Mountain Chippewa) concern about Indigenous representation in genres like science fiction and speculative fiction. Medak-Saltzman (2017) explains that "the variety of our [Native] narrative traditions have always incorporated elements of futurity, prophecy, and responsibility-rooted strategies for bringing forth better futures," yet she points out that "mainstream narratives represent a profound and pervasive inability to portray Native peoples and our continued existence in the present, let alone to project us forward into any potential futures" (140–41). We find multiple examples of resistance to this lack of representation, such as Steve Keewatin Sanderson (Plains Cree) and Peter Dawes' (2017) contribution to *Moonshot: Volume 2* titled "Where We Left Off" which dramatizes a post-apocalyptic future in the US. Their comic follows the generations of a Cree family that survives, thrives, and creates a new future by passing on the practical lessons of trapping and hunting and by embracing a communal mode of living in a post-apocalyptic world. The Cree family's adaptation and survival in this brief science-fiction comic exemplify Joni Adamson's (2017) encapsulation of a key difference between Native and non-Native approaches to this genre, as she posits that "Native speculative fictions embrace the 'science' in 'science fiction' as 'indigenous scientific literacies' rather than the modern or futuristic technologies that are typically the focus of science fiction or speculative fiction" (217). The post-apocalyptic narrative and the Indigenous story merge, for example, in the futuristic armor that the family wears as they hunt bison in a former wasteland, armor which is adorned with images of embroidered flowers, a visual representation of the Native survivance that takes place within the comic and that is enacted by its publication.

Indigenous feminism plays a role in the sci-fi comics and stories of reclamation that compose *Moonshot*'s powerful projections. Even in comics that do not directly invoke women's issues, Native women are represented, such as in *Volume I*'s "Ue-Pucase: Water Master" (2016). Arigon Starr (Kickapoo Tribe of Oklahoma) and David Cutler (Qalipu Mi'kmaq First Nation) create a comic that intervenes in the absence that Saltzman points out, not just by projecting Native American people into the future but by sending women-centered Native stories and lessons there as well. "Ue-Pucase: Water Master" depicts two forms of presence for Indigenous peoples: the first is their continued presence in an unspecified future, where Earth has become a planet that humans visit via spaceship, in the case of our protagonists, to go junking. The second is the role that stories relayed by women play in such sci-fi staples as "off-worlding" and planetary exploration, a realm of storytelling that often excludes them.

"Ue-Pucase: Water Master" follows two Native American space junkers who are visiting Earth to collect cargo. The naïve junker of the pair is introduced in direct relation to his grandmother, as his more experienced partner sourly listens to him exclaiming, "Gaw-lee, Buck! Grandma Ida **said** that planet would look like a tiny blue bead" (67). Though it is two men who are taking part in the adventure at hand, they are both connected with the grandmother: the more experienced junker warns his partner not to eat a can of Spam in part thanks to his grandmother's warning: "Junkin' 101: No off-world food. Didn't Ida ever tell you that story about the Honvnwv who didn't listen?" (68). The characters in this comic mix Creek with English, just as the comic mixes a Muscogee Creek story and the trappings of science fiction stories to tell a familiar story of transformation. The comic's introduction explains the original story about a man who eats unusual eggs and is transformed into a snake. Starr and Cutler reimagine the eggs as a can of Spam, a long-lasting staple which—while it invokes the hardships of food scarcity some Indigenous communities experience—is a contemporary reimagining that sees the past meeting the future.

The transformation in this comic is linked to the power of women's knowledge and stories, reminiscent of the "transformational entities" that Joni Adamson (2017) finds—in indigenous art and stories—"an imaginative force for thinking about how the Earth was formed through a series of relations" (218). When the junker eats the Spam, he dreams of sharing it with his grandmother and partially transforms in his dream. His partner is able to bring Grandma Ida to Earth, where she reunites with her fully transformed grandson and disappears into a lake together with him, while the experienced junker closes the comic with the statement, "I'm telling you now—those old stories are true" (72). As we can see in Figure 5.4, Starr and Cutler's sci-fi comic, despite centering two male characters, shows the imperative behind heeding women's advice while simultaneously transporting Native stories about transformations into a future fiction. The transformation that the naïve junker undergoes is nightmarish but also, in this comic, part of a true story that the Creek junker who survives passes on to his listeners (Figure 5.4).

Several of the comics in *Moonshot* adopt a humorous tone even as they address current issues faced by Native communities, such as Darcie Little Badger (Lipan Apache) and Rossi Gifford's "Worst Bargain in Town" (2017) from *Volume 2*. Like many of the comics in the *Moonshot* anthologies, the background statement at the beginning of "Worst Bargain in Town" explains the metaphor of the comic. In this case, the spiritual significance of hair to the Lipan people opens the door for the transformative conflict between two Lipan women, Kat and Laura, and a white barber who steals the health of the townspeople by cutting their hair. In the foreword to this comic, the writers bring up a 2009 case where a Lipan Apache boy and his family resisted his school's claim that his long hair was in violation of a dress code, defending his rights and resisting a horrific history of Indigenous persecution via methods such as cutting hair, preventing Indigenous children from speaking their own language in school, and forcing them to attend boarding schools.[6]

Figure 5.4 "Water Master" by Arigon Starr and David Cutler, 2016

This history is countered in Little Badger and Gifford's comic, in which the Lipan duo take down the thieving hairdresser by accepting the challenge she proposes: cut off her braid, and she will cease to steal the spirits of the townspeople. In a scene that reenacts and addresses a flashback to the Lipan characters getting bullied and having their hair cut against their wishes, Kat braids a small piece of her own hair into Laura's hair, who then successfully cuts the hairdresser's braid and robs her of her power. The hairdresser, visibly sapped of energy, transforms into a weakened version of her malicious self. As in the "Changing Woman" comic, interweaved throughout the action is a woman family member's message that serves as a lesson. After Kat was bullied, the comic recaps how her mother taught her that "Hair is a source of strength. It's a uniquely spiritual part of our bodies. Cut it to mourn or celebrate change" (36). This lesson about the importance of hair to the Lipan way of approaching the world helped the women recognize the monstrous transformation that the hairdresser was enacting and was forcing upon the townspeople and helped them find the collaborative solution to ending her reign, one that metaphorically represents white colonialism at work in Indigenous communities (Figure 5.5).

Adaptation and form in *Sovereign Traces*

The continued presence of Native stories takes on a new form in the visual narrative retellings in *Sovereign Traces, Volume 1* and *Volume 2*, which merge written works by contemporary Native American and First Nations writers, including novelists and poets, with art. Like the other Indigenous comics collections, these anthologies are collaborative, while they also incorporate the added dimension of adaptation. *Volume 1: Not (Just) (An) other* is edited by Gordon Henry Jr. and Elizabeth LaPensée and is composed of graphic adaptations of a variety of written stories, poems, and prose pieces by authors such as Louise Erdrich, Gerald Vizenor, and Joy Harjo. LaPensée edited *Volume 2: Relational Constellation*, which features stories that focus on Indigenous love. While these two anthologies differ slightly in the comics they collect, they too feature a traceable interest in transformation as a way to explore Indigenous feminisms through graphic narratives.

Across the two volumes, Indigenous writers and artists center the role that Native women play in stories which speak to the past and the future, such as Stephen Graham Jones' (Blackfeet Native American) and illustrator Delicia Williams' "Werewolves on the Moon" in *Volume 1: Not (Just) (An) other*, a comic based on an excerpt from Jones' 2017 novel *Mongrels (Jones and Williams 2018)*. A werewolf in hiding and her son have a parent-teacher meeting during which the teacher calls the boy's drawing of a werewolf on the moon a "joke." Leaving the meeting, the mother and son witness the school janitor, with whom they had spoken earlier, bounding away by the highway as a transformed werewolf, suggesting the presence of

Figure 5.5 "Worst Bargain in Town" by Darcie Little Badger (Lipan Apache) and Rossi Gifford, 2017.

Native kinship even in spaces of conflict and misunderstanding. In *Volume 2: Relational Constellation*'s "Changing Woman," Shaun Beyale (2019) (Navajo Nation) takes a science-fiction approach to a Navajo woman character, drawing her as a warrior who travels across time and space. Her partner, describing her to his grandchildren, is reunited with her at the end of the comic, as she returns from the future to Dinétah, the ancestral home of the Navajo Nation. In conversation with comics in the *Moonshot* collection, Beyale's "Changing Woman" is drawn in an action-comic style and features a Navajo woman protagonist fighting against what she identifies as "the past wrongs that mankind brought upon themselves in their search for greatness" (20). Their comics invoke themes of Indigenous feminism and foreground the roles of fighters, protectors, and negotiators that Native women play.

Volume 1: Not (Just) (An) Other features a visual adaptation of the poem "Deer Dancer" by Joy Harjo (Mvskoke Nation), who in 2019 became the first Native American US poet laureate. Illustrated by Weshoyot Alvitre, "Deer Dancer" (2018) is unique in its combination of poetry—a written form already well suited to imagery—and visuals. Alvitre's comic works as a visual poem which, rather than moving from scene to scene, gives us bursts of images. These range from hyper-realistic scenes (as on page 76 of the anthology, which scans over the faces of different people sitting at a bar), to less narrative portraits such as the full-page portrayal of Joy Harjo on page 77. Figure 5.6 shows the role that transformation plays in Alvitre's visual interpretation of Harjo's poem: a small panel of a woman meekly entering a bar leads way to a half-page panel that evokes a sacred figure, with *Deer Woman* surrounded by profane artifacts such as dollar bills, horseshoes, and cigarettes (trappings of the bar that underlays much of the poem), while she is backlit with a glowing light and antlers hovering above her head. In a similar manner to other illustrated imaginings of *Deer Woman*, Alvitre's depiction sometimes suggests, rather than outright portrays, the transformative play between woman and deer. The woman in her comic transforms the space by entering it, represented by the way men's faces turn toward her (a visual reference to the dangers that can await women in male-dominated places). Transformation is also cued by the various vignettes that Alvitre visualizes from Harjo's poem, such as the one in Figure 5.6, in which a man who saw *Deer Woman* dance was moved and thus convinced to pay back a loan: Deer Woman's transformative qualities would seem to be transferable.

The visual autonomy that emerges from such a collaboration, which involves adapting, refiguring, and illustrating poems and prose—which were already acts of female sovereignty—recurs in other comics in the *Sovereign Traces* anthologies. *Volume 2: Relational Constellation* collects comics about Indigenous love, and self-love meeting transformations embodied by earthly and organic connections emerge in two of this volume's comics. Darcie Little Badger contributes to this anthology as well, and her

Figure 5.6 "Deer Dancer" by Joy Harjo and Weshoyot Alvitre, 2018.

comic "Oceanographer" (2019) merges the personal and the political through a visual exploration of the way knowledge and education play a role in Native women's lives. An illustration of the story of badger teaching humans about the "wonders she witnessed"—a personal connection to a Lipan story—transitions into a full-page spread of a hand within which are drawn multiple ecosystems (45). Without stating it as such, the comic suggests the connection between the badger that shared information with our human ancestors and Darcie Little Badger, who, as an oceanographer and earth scientist, does the same. In the full-page spread, she writes that "Unlike collectible coins, knowledge is less valuable when it's rare" (46). This democratizing message that Little Badger implements in her role as a teacher and a comics creator is also one of representation on multiple levels: sharing Lipan stories with more people, teaching earth science as a Lipan woman scientist, and drawing the connection between fine arts and the sciences in the very form of a short comics work.

The comics by Indigenous women collected across these anthologies write the different stories of different Native Nations into the archive of North American popular culture, and they are each a space for these comics creators to address issues of women's rights, sovereignty, and safety in a world that is historically and presently hostile to women of color. The aesthetics of transformation that emerge from the visual narratives across the different comics styles is one that enables representation, both of the women who have been telling stories and teaching lessons over the years and of the new generation of storytellers who understand the importance of representation both in media and in media creation. In a 2018 interview, Weshoyot Alvitre stated,

> I didn't have any Native artists, writers or examples to look up to growing up. Most books about Natives, were not written or illustrated by Native people. So I am doing my small part to try to change that so my children have a different experience with representation when they grow.

Her experience and her future dreams emerge in her comics, and the range of Native American and First Nations voices in *Deer Woman*, *Moonshot*, and *Sovereign Traces*—with future volumes on the way—are transforming the world of comics and visual narratives into one that speaks to Native women.

Notes

1 See "Teaching the Comics Anthology: The Readers, Authors, and Media of *McSweeney's* 13" by Alexander Starre in *Teaching Comics and Graphic Narratives: Essays on Theory, Strategy and Practice* (2012) for a brief theorization of comics anthologies from a pedagogical perspective.

2 There are several other comics collections by Native American and First Nations writers and illustrators, including *Trickster: Native American Tales, A Graphic Collection* (2010) edited by Matt Dembicki and *Graphic Classics, Volume 24: Native American Classics* (2013) edited by Tom Pomplun. See also the Annotated Bibliography of Indigenous Comics and Graphic Novels created by Taylor Daigneault (Métis), Amy Mazowita, Candida Rifkind and Camille Callison (Tahltan), which is updated twice a year.

3 Sheyahshe includes a chapter on representations of Indigenous women in comics, noting that "Indigenous female characters face far more adversity than just serving as eye-candy for male readers. The representation of the Native female gender has long been far baser in nature than just one founded in physical perfection. It has reached further into overt sexual icons" (2016, 168). For more critical work on representations of Native Americans in comic books and other media, see Chad A. Barbour's *From Daniel Boone to Captain America: Playing Indian in American Popular Culture* (2016) and Cornel Pewewardy's "From Subhuman to Superhuman: Images of First Nations Peoples in Comic Books" (2002).

4 Patty Stonefish's organization has more information at her website: https://armingsisters.org/

5 In the introduction to the *So Long Been Dreaming: Postcolonial Science Fiction & Fantasy* anthology, Nalo Hopkinson summarizes the tensions of science fiction and fantasy tenets with the realities of Indigenous peoples' histories: "Arguably one of the most familiar memes of science fiction is that of going to foreign countries and colonizing the natives, and as I've said elsewhere, for many of us, that's not a thrilling adventure story: it's non-fiction, and we are on the wrong side of the strange-looking ship that appears out of nowhere" (2004, ii).

6 For more on the 2009 case see "Public schools in Texas adjust policies after Apache boy's case" (https://www.indianz.com/News/2015/04/10/public-schools-in-texas-adjust.asp). To read more about Indian Boarding Schools and other modes of persecution against Indigenous communities, see Roxanne Dunbar Ortiz's *An Indigenous History of the United States* (2015).

References

Adamson, Joni. 2017. "Collected Things with Names Like Mother Corn: Native North American Speculative Fiction and Film." In *The Routledge Companion to the Environmental Humanities*, edited by Ursula K. Heise, Jon Christensen, and Michelle Niemann, 216–26. Abingdon: Routledge.

Aldama, Luis Frederick. 2010. "Multicultural Comics Today: A Brief Introduction." In *Multicultural Comics: From Zap to Blue Beetle*, edited by Frederick Luis Aldama, 1–25. Austin: University of Texas Press.

Allen, Paula Gunn. 1986. *The Sacred Hoop: Recovering the Feminine in American Indian Tradition*. Boston: Beacon Press.

Alvitre, Weshoyot, and Joy Harjo. 2018. "Deer Dancer." In *Sovereign Traces Volume 1: Not (Just) (An)Other*, edited by Gordon Henry Jr. and Elizabeth LaPensée, 73–82. Lansing: Michigan State University Press.

Alvitre, Weshoyot, interview by Alex Dueben. "Smash Pages Q&A: Weshoyot Alvitre on 'Sixkiller' and more." Smash Pages, August 9, 2018. http://smashpages.net/2018/08/09/smash-pages-qa-weshoyot-alvitre-on-sixkiller-and-more/.

Bernardin, Susan. 2015. "Future Pasts: Comics, Graphic Novels, and Digital Media." In *The Routledge Companion to Native American Literature*, edited by Deborah L. Madsen, 480–93. Abingdon: Routledge.

Beyale, Shaun. 2019. "Changing Woman." In *Sovereign Traces Volume 2: Relational Constellation*, edited by Elizabeth LaPensée. 16–24. Lansing: Michigan State University Press.

Bladow, Kyle. 2019. "Framing Storytelling: Indigenous Graphic Narratives." *The Journal of Popular Culture* 52 (1): 35–52.

Bowie, Tatum. 2017. "Changing Woman." In *Deer Woman: An Anthology*, edited by Elizabeth LaPensée and Weshoyot Alvitre, 82–90. Albuquerque: Native Realities Publishing.

Curtis, Neal, and Valentina Cardo. 2017. "Superheroes and Third-Wave Feminism." *Feminist Media Studies* 18 (3): 381–96.

Daigneault (Métis), Taylor, Amy Mazowita, Candida Rifkind, and Camille Callison (Tahltan). 2019. "Indigenous Comics and Graphic Novels: An Annotated Bibliography". *Jeunesse: Young People, Texts, Cultures* 11 (1): i–xxxvi. http://jeunessejournal.ca/index.php/yptc/article/view/504.

Deloria, Ella Cara. 2006. *Dakota Texts*. Lincoln: University of Nebraska Press.

DeSanti, Brady. 2015. "The Cannibal Talking Head: The Portrayal of the Windigo 'Monster' in Popular Culture and Ojibwe Traditions." *Journal of Religion and Popular Culture* 27 (3): 186–201.

Dudek, Debra. 2016. "'Good Relationships Mean Good Lives': Warrior-Survivor Identity/ies in David Alexander Robertson's *7 Generations*." *Canada Review of Comparative Literature/ Revue Canadienne de Littérature Comparée* 43 (1): 39–50.

Dunn, Carolyn, and Carol Comfort.1999. "Introduction." In *Through the Eye of the Deer: An Anthology of Native American Women Writers*, edited by Carol Comfort and Carolyn Dunn, ix–xviii. Iowa City: Aunt Lute Books.

Erdrich, Louise. 2013. "Rape on the Reservation." *The New York Times*, February 26 www.nytimes.com/2013/02/27/opinion/native-americans-and-the-violence-against-women-act.html.

Estes, Nick. 2019. *Our History Is the Future: Standing Rock Versus the Dakota Access Pipeline, and the Long Tradition of Indigenous Resistance*. Brooklyn: Verso.

"Final Report of the National Inquiry." 2019. *National Inquiry into Missing and Murdered Indigenous Women and Girls*, May. www.mmiwg-ffada.ca/final-report/.

Goeman, Mishuana. 2013. *Mark My Words: Native Women Mapping Our Nations*. Minneapolis: University of Minnesota Press.

Harrison, Richard. 2016. "Seeing and Nothingness: Michael Nicoll Yahgulanaas, Haida Manga, and a Critique of the Gutter." *Canadian Review of Comparative Literature / Revue Canadienne de Littérature Comparée* 43 (1): 51–74.

Hopkinson, Nalo. 2004. "Introduction." In *So Long Been Dreaming: Postcolonial Science Fiction & Fantasy*, edited by Nalo Hopkinson. i–vii. Vancouver: Arsenal Pulp Press.

Jones, Stephen Graham, and Williams, Delicia. 2018. "Werewolves on the Moon." In *Sovereign Traces Volume 1: Not (Just) (An)Other*, edited by Gordon Henry Jr. and Elizabeth LaPensée, 3–14. Lansing: Michigan State University Press.

Kelp-Stebbins, Katherine. 2018. "Comics as Orientation Devices." In *Comics Studies Here and Now*, edited by Frederick Luis Aldama. 206–25. Abingdon: Routledge.

King, C. Richard. 2009. "Alter/Native Heroes: Native Americans, Comic Books, and the Struggle for Self-Definition." *Cultural Studies ↔ Critical Methodologies* 9 (2): 214–23. doi:10.1177/1532708608330259

Leggatt, Judith. 2016. "Suicide Prevention in Nêhiyawi (Cree) Comic Books." *Bookbird: A Journal of International Children's Literature* 54 (1): 31–41.

LaPensée, Elizabeth, and Jonathan R. Thunder. 2017. "Deer Woman: A Vignette." In *Deer Woman: An Anthology*, edited by Elizabeth LaPensée and Weshoyot Alvitre. 5–22. Albuquerque: Native Realities Publishing.

Little Badger, Darcie and Rossi Gifford. 2017. "Worst Bargain in Town." In *Moonshot: The Indigenous Comics Collection: Volume 2*, edited by Hope Nicholson. 33–43. Toronto: Alternate History Comics Inc.

Little Badger, Darcie and Rossi Gifford. 2019. "Oceanographer." In *Sovereign Traces Volume 2: Relational Constellation*, edited by Elizabeth LaPensée. 44–49. Lansing: Michigan State University Press.

Medak-Saltzman, Danika. 2017. "Coming to You from the Indigenous Future: Native Women, Speculative Film Shorts, and the Art of the Possible." *Studies in American Indian Literature* 29 (1): 139–71.

Nicholson, Hope. 2016. "Foreword." In *Moonshot: The Indigenous Comics Collection Volume 1*, edited by Hope Nicholson, 7. Toronto: Alternate History Comics Inc.

Noori, Margaret. 2010. "Native American Narratives from Early Art To Graphic Novels: How We See Stories / Ezhi-g'Waabamaanaanig Aadizookaanag." In *Multicultural Comics: From Zap to Blue Beetle*, edited by Frederick Luis Aldama, 55–72. Austin: University of Texas Press.

OED Online, *s.v.* "Graphic, adj. and n." Accessed June 2019. www.oed.com/view/Entry/80829.

Pratt, Stacy, and Weshoyot Alvitre. 2018. "Weshoyot Alvitre, Illustrator of 'Sixkiller' Comic." *First American Art Magazine*, July 24. firstamericanartmagazine.com/weshoyot-alvitre-sixkiller/.

Sanderson, Steve Keewatin and Dawes, Peter. 2017. "Where We Left Off." In *Moonshot: The Indigenous Comics Collection: Volume 2*, edited by Hope Nicholson. 115–23. Toronto: Alternate History Comics Inc.

Sheyashe, Michael A. 2016. *Native Americans in Comic Books: A Critical Study*. Jefferson: McFarland & Company.

Starr, Arigon and David Cutler. 2016. "Ue-Pucase: Water Master." In *Moonshot: The Indigenous Comics Collection: Volume 1*, edited by Hope Nicholson. 66–72. Toronto: Alternate History Comics Inc.

Stonefish, Patty. 2017. "Introduction." In *Deer Woman: An Anthology*, edited by Elizabeth LaPensée and Weshoyot Alvitre. 3–4. Albuquerque: Native Realities Publishing.

Vizenor, Gerald Robert. 2010. *Manifest Manners: Narratives on Postindian Survivance*. Lincoln: University of Nebraska Press, 2010.

Weaver, Jace. 1997. *That the People Might Live: Native American Literatures and Native American Community*. Oxford: Oxford University Press.

6 Comics and gendered subjectivity: the multifaceted truth of Alison Bechdel's graphic memoirs

Cody Shrum

An inherent characteristic of memoir is the creative liberty taken by the author when presenting facts and the truth to the audience. Given the subjective nature of memory and experience, objective truth is abstract and difficult to achieve, even with a vast archive of evidence to draw from. But even the guesswork filter through which the memoirist depicts their experiences constitutes a subjective truth which may or may not sync with "facts" but is nevertheless *a truth*. With graphic memoir, the stakes are even higher because the author not only presents their past but does so using pictorials and therefore commits to a set of images to solidify the narrative visually on the page. As Ian Horsman (2018) puts it, memoir "possesses a veneer of truth." In her graphic memoirs, *Fun Home* (2006) *and Are You My Mother?* (2012), Alison Bechdel experiments with this veneer of truth to meticulously interrogate a past haunted by uncertainty.

Much of the exhaustive scholarship on *Fun Home* pertains to Bechdel's extensive inclusion of references to literature and the intertextual conversations therein, queer studies, autography as an emerging genre, and Bechdel's rendering of archived materials, to name a few. David Ball (2013), Julia Watson (2008), Robyn Warhol (2011), Hélène Tison (2015), and others have said much about the inclusion of artifacts in the graphic memoir, specifically rendered photographs, and especially the "centerfold" of Roy, Bruce Bechdel's teenage lover. In comparison, very little has been said about Bechdel's follow-up graphic memoir, *Are You My Mother?*, which relies on many of the same graphic, archival, and intertextual techniques and styles as *Fun Home*. After first analyzing Bechdel's graphic archival techniques in *Fun Home*, I will turn to *Are You My Mother?* to show the ways in which Bechdel uses archival evidence—and her reactions to it—to establish, complicate, and question her past. I argue that Bechdel's purpose in meticulously rendering archived evidence, despite the books' differences, is to engage in forensic inquiry regarding her father's death, her own sexuality, psychological issues associated with her relationship with her mother, and the question: what constitutes truth? This forensic inquiry and tendency toward openness, revealing the truth at all costs, is closely tied to Bechdel's parents (a closeted father and a mother who staunchly denied

DOI: 10.4324/9781003146520-6

that) and is also performative and gendered in many ways. Ian Horsman states that

> reading memoirs can serve as windows into the varied ways in which people perceive their world and choose to narrate their lives. In that way, a memoir would not claim sole authority over its historical subject and instead would allow for a range of perspectives to emerge. (2018)

An important component of this question regarding truth is the reader's role in deciding and deciphering what the truth is and how Bechdel's experiences fit into the larger picture. The reader's role in actively unraveling the tensions that arise between the pictorials, artifacts, and the text Bechdel juxtaposes with them becomes essential. Because Bechdel composed her memoirs with such an emphasis on rendered archival evidence to present the past, the form actually *becomes* the content. Additionally, examining Bechdel's memoirs through the feminist lenses provided by Marianne Hirsch and Valerie Smith (2002), who are concerned with cultural memory, and Lisa M. Diamond (2006), who writes about autobiographical narratives and memory, reveals that Bechdel's reasons for using overt techniques of authenticity are multifaceted and push back against the fallibility of memory.

This idea of the reader playing a role in the memoir, a participation of sorts, essentially equates to Scott McCloud's (1994) definition of "closure" in comics: the "phenomenon of observing the parts but perceiving the whole... mentally completing that which is incomplete" (63). McCloud argues that not only are works of graphic literature composed with closure in mind—actively deciding how to tell a story and what to leave out—but also that the reader is a key participant in producing the work's meaning. Between pages, chapters, and panels on the page, Bechdel purposely leaves gaps that represent segues of time and space that also serve as invisible ellipses, indicating gaps in the story the reader must fill in. Often this closure in which the reader participates is simple, what McCloud would call moment-to-moment, action-to-action, or subject-to-subject transitions in which the reader can easily jump from one point to the next, cognitively. Others are more difficult, scene-to-scene or aspect-to-aspect transitions, for example (McCloud 1994, 70–72). No matter the difficulty of closure transitions, the most important aspect of closure is the meaning-making process the reader undergoes, deciding what the author is communicating through these gaps and transitions. Bechdel relies heavily on closure in *Fun Home*. In her investigation of her father's death and sexuality, Bechdel provides all the evidence that forms and shapes her dilemma for the reader: all of the photographs, journal entries, letters, maps, along with her telling alongside those things of her version of the story and what growing up with her father was like. But she never comes out and gives any answers or conclusions to the reader; it's the reader's job to deal with all of the information and interpret it themselves. This process mirrors Bechdel's own task of making sense of the variety of evidence from her past. Perhaps the most important example of closure in *Fun Home* comes on the final page. Consisting of two panels, the final page shows a close up of the front of a truck—presumably the truck that ran over Bechdel's father—and a pictorial of young Alison jumping into a pool to be caught by her father with outstretched hands. Because of this specific, purposeful, subject-to-subject transition between panels, Bechdel makes it clear that the top panel is from Bruce Bechdel's perspective, facing the truck before he died. With the bottom panel the way it's presented, Bruce facing Alison and about to catch her, the reader participates in closure and understands that Alison has become the truck. As McCloud says, in such a moment, the reader is "an equal partner in crime [to the author]," and it isn't Bechdel who tells us that she killed her father (1994, 68). The reader participates in that moment, and because of the deliberate construction of those final panels, the powerful realization arrives that yes, Alison believes she played a role in killing her father. She *is* the truck.

Fun Home is a technical, meticulous graphic text. The memoir is composed of regular panels, nearly no bleeds, and is full of reproduced artifacts that provide the reader with information and a look into actual sources from Bechdel's past. This interplay between objective artifacts and subjective memory or interpretation is the means by which Bechdel explores her past, and the audience goes on this journey with her, mirroring her experience as they read, trying to "solve" the same puzzles. In regard to this process of memoir in *Fun Home*, David Ball (2013) asserts that "Bechdel is keen to make her readers understand the longheld positions of memoir scholarship: the unreliability of memory, the gulf that invariably separates the speaker of the text from its author, and the multiple ways in which memoirs are ordered and construct narratives that complicate uncritical notions of facticity and testimony" (5). Even as readers enter into the text with the understanding of Horsman's "veneer of truth," Bechdel makes it clear throughout that her exploration intersects both truth and uncertainty. An extended example of this is Bechdel's exploration of her adolescent journal. At a young age, Alison begins writing in a journal her father gives her, which is the beginning of what Bechdel (2006) calls "[her] own compulsive propensity to autobiography" (140). On page 141, Bechdel draws five panels that show uncertainty begin to rise up and take over her journaling. Rather than straight narration, she begins talking about her day with "I think" phrases cropping up between. Bechdel says, "It was a sort of epistemological crisis. How did I know that the things I was writing were absolutely, objectively true?" (141). Later on she develops a circumflex symbol to replace the "I think" phrases, as shorthand for signifying the lack of faith in her perceived truth, eventually drawing it over entire journal entries, as if to say, "I think these things happened this way, but I'm not sure." In the lower-left panel on page 141, Bechdel narrates, "All I could speak for was my own perceptions, and perhaps not even those." Even in her childhood, Alison experiences this epistemological dilemma of subjective truth, and Bechdel looking back uses these moments to illustrate the problem with truth and reality: people only have their own perceptions to go on. Yet, her commentary on this in the text as part of her exploration serves as metacommentary on memoir: memory and human perception are unreliable sources of objective truth. In all this, Bechdel presents her perceptions, which are undeniably part of the truth of her reality.

Though mostly devoid of bleeds, *Fun Home* does have one notable bleed, which comes at the center of the memoir and is central to Bechdel's inquiry into the truth of her past. On pages 100–101, Bechdel depicts herself holding a photograph her father had taken of Alison's babysitter, Roy, lying half-naked on a bed, often referred to as the "centerfold" of *Fun Home*. The photograph is detailed and realistically rendered, suggesting that, like the depiction of her journal pages, this is recreated from an actual document. But the rendered photograph is perhaps more real than the photograph itself because the illustration contains Bechdel's emotional projection—the viewer sees not only the photograph but also Alison's experience of seeing it. Hélène Tison (2015) shows that this move on Bechdel's part cleverly takes an artifact of objectivity and presents it to the audience in such a way that it falls beneath a subjective filter:

> She appropriates the image, inscribing herself upon and within it, saturating it with her presence: she draws her hand holding the photo, whose surface is also eaten up by her comments, so that, in fact, it reaches the reader/viewer through a triple filter.
>
> The photograph is filtered through her hand that penned the reproduction—there is no technical reason why the actual photo couldn't have been reproduced in the book—and which appears in the image, holding the photo. This drawn hand, immense and white … directs our gaze into the image and thus functions as a sort of framing device, putting the photograph and its subject into relief. (349)

Part of the crisis in *Fun Home* is Bechdel's coming to terms with her father's death and sexuality, as well as her relationship to both. By looking at this photograph, Alison reaches an understanding of the homosexuality he was hiding, and because of Bechdel's bleed technique, which shows Alison's hands holding the reproduced photograph, the reader effectively experiences the moment *as* Alison does. This moment, with the detail of Alison's hands, is real to Alison and real for the viewer. This bleed panel isn't just a tool for conveying this moment; it actually *is* the moment. Alison's hands, holding the photograph, wrists and arms disappearing off the page like the reader's hands holding the book, *are* part of the story.

However, Bechdel's use of realistically rendered photographs isn't used explicitly to achieve an objective sense of reality. As Julia Watson (2008) discusses in her essay, "Autographic Disclosures and Genealogies of Desire in *Fun Home*," Bechdel's inclusion of photographs rendered realistically isn't necessarily to posit evidence for what really happened but instead does so to challenge the photographs:

> Bechdel, in the many drawn photos that punctuate *Fun Home*, probes the interplay between personal memory, a kind of subjectivity imaged in cartoons, and photography, an indexical form of documentary evidence .... And in her readings of photos—through both words and drawings—she undermines the claim of photographs to one kind of tacit authority, and opens them to interpretation that grants them a different kind of encoded subjectivity, a legacy of family history. (52)

At the same time that Bechdel gives factual evidence of her past, evidenced by archived photography, she challenges their authority by opening them up for examination. The photographs show what literally happened—a snapshot of reality that can't be altered. But Bechdel includes them as a contrast with her own subjectivity: what she believes or remembers to have happened. This juxtaposition of artifact and text boxes written by the adult author looking back are epistemological, creating knowledge and meaning that would be absent without it. The centerfold photograph of Roy reveals that, although she was there on that trip with her father and brothers, she doesn't recall any homosexual behavior or any intimate moments between her father and Roy. A textbox explains that Alison found the photograph "in an envelope labeled 'Family' in Dad's handwriting," so it's all the more intimate that a photograph of her father's teenage lover was in that specific envelope (Bechdel 2006, 101). Watson (2008) also comments on Bechdel's technique of disclosing and challenging the specific photograph of Roy in the novel:

> ...by contrasting Bechdel's drawings of photographs... as archival documents with the cartooned story of a remembered—and fantasized—past, we can observe how Bechdel reinterprets the authority that photos as "official histories" seem to hold, and opens them to subjective reinterpretation. In her focus on varying visual versions of her father and her wildly changing impressions of him (recorded in her diary) at different moments, Bechdel composes a textured autobiographical reflection that moves by an ongoing process of her own recursive reading. (37)

In other words, Bechdel's inclusion of the photographs and other drawn artifacts both gives literal truth—"this is how it really happened"—an epistemological certainty, and challenges that truth—"this isn't how I remember experiencing it."

As another example of Bechdel's questioning the accuracy of the photographic record, on page 64 Watson (2006) depicts Bruce's annual school portrait and comments, "But he was more attractive than the photographic record reveals." This, too, shows that photography as a means of "truth" isn't always accurate. Or more precisely, it doesn't seem accurate to Bechdel, so her perceptions challenge the objective truth presented by the photograph. Of this moment in the memoir, Hélène Tison (2015) states,

> Despite its connection with reality, with what is or has been, photography can prove inadequate; it can be artful and deceitful; it can also fail to bring to light the deception it is made to record. Alison Bechdel's cartooning is also an attempt at revising such flaws and inadequacies in the "photographic record" of her father's life, despite the fragmentation constantly at play in this elliptical and repetitive medium and in defiance of photography's inability to reveal "the truth of the individual." (360)

Bechdel includes the reproduced photograph, along with her commentary on its inaccuracy, because both are equally important, thereby purposefully encoding her revision on the artifact. However, all of this constitute Bechdel's "truth" as a whole. Truth is presented in both the inclusion and challenging of her archived reality—both subjective and objective truth comingle together on the page.

Specifically with the Roy centerfold, it's important to note that while rendered realistically, the photograph, and likely others, was altered in its rendering. David Ball (2013) astutely points out this seemingly obvious fact, which is hardly, if ever, mentioned in other scholarship. Ball states that

> Given… the affective and confessional authority of the photograph, the representational power of Bechdel's art, as well as the central role of these pages in the text… it is easy to forget that images such as this one do not mimetically represent lived experience. For legal reasons such as the protection of the identities of many of the memoir's subjects, as well as a host of other considerations, "Roy" and his likeness are a pseudonym and an avatar respectively. "Roy" is not Roy, and the bodily representation of him reproduced in the text is not as he appears in Bechdel's private archive. (7)

So even this artifact of objectively lived experience has technically been given to the reader as altered artifice on the page. Given the transparent, subjective nature of memoir in general, reading *Fun Home* means following Bechdel down the rabbit hole of her life as she explores the truth, both as her subjective experience and the objective reality through archived artifacts. However, even some of these mimetically rendered artifacts have been altered—for good reason, but the fact remains. These alterations seemingly serve to acknowledge and highlight Bechdel's editorial role in crafting this story and deciding what information to impart to the reader, and how to do so. These revised documents, then, contain with them Bechdel's subjectivity, a slight alteration from epistemological fact through her point of view, which interestingly contains her truth encoded within the pictorial.

There are moments in *Fun Home* where Bechdel, by necessity, relies fully on artistic license in order to depict scenes. Either Bechdel didn't personally experience these moments, or else she must imagine them or reconstruct the moments from minute details. One such moment, a panel on page 116, depicts Bruce Bechdel moments before his death. Bechdel herself wasn't there, nor were her mother or brothers, and the only witness was the truck driver who hit him. Nonetheless, Bechdel (2006) depicts the moment to the best of her ability, and the moment is crucial to her forensic study in the book because her theory of her father's suicide teeters on this moment. Bechdel depicts the same moment—Bruce, shirtless, holding a clump of tree branches over his shoulder, walking across the highway moments before being hit by a Sunbeam truck—three other times in the book (28, 59, and 89). In depicting these moments, Bechdel must imagine what the scene had been like. Based on her studious methods of staging scenes and posing to get angles, shapes, and shadows right, she likely took photographs of the scene and posed to make her rendering as accurate as possible. Still, she wasn't there, and because of her lack of evidence, this moment eludes her, and she can't say for certain whether Bruce's death was a suicide. Perhaps this fleeting scene and her inability to capture and own it is why she returns to it so many times. Despite evidence, though, her interpretation of the event and others like it where she couldn't have been present are not inaccurate or false. Bechdel's subjectivity, her truth, shrouds the book, and this moment especially can be said to feel absolutely true to Bechdel's lived experience. In examining these aspects and examples from the book, it's clear that Bechdel has gone to great lengths to achieve multiple layers of truth. The use of archival documents, even when edited, communicate a sense of objective truth, which she challenges in a number of ways to complicate that truth and establish a new sort of epistemology within her past and lived experience. However, this technique and epistemological conversation between herself, her past, and the archive plays an even more substantial role in her follow-up graphic memoir, *Are You My Mother?*

Bechdel's *Are You My Mother?* (*AYMM?*) has received far less critical attention than *Fun Home*, yet Bechdel's forensic exploration of the past and use of graphic and storytelling techniques to do so are no less important in her sequel. With *AYMM?*, Bechdel takes even greater pains to document the truth for the reader than in *Fun Home*, with even greater emphasis on archival evidence as central to her past inquiry. *AYMM?* features the same focus on recreated artifacts from Bechdel's archive, such as photographs, journals, maps, newspaper clippings, diagrams, covers and excerpts of books, and others. Much like the Roy Centerfold in *Fun Home* that shows

Alison's hands bleeding off the page, thereby placing the reader there with her to witness this image for the first time, *AYMM?* also incorporates moments like this but to a higher level. Throughout the book, Bechdel depicts at least 27 moments like this, which accomplishes a similar effect as the Roy centerfold, though one could say less impact is achieved because of the frequency. However, Bechdel's impulse here is to document even further what it was like for her as an artist looking back at these photographs and puts the reader in an unusual position of looking over Alison Bechdel's shoulder while creating this book.

This impulse to accurately document her life plays into *AYMM?* in a way that is absent from *Fun Home*: Bechdel depicting the act of her transcribing her phone conversations with her mother. Bechdel could have simply written that, over the phone, her mother had commented on her friend's granddaughter getting her period at age 12, which she finds too early, and the reader would believe her—why would someone lie about that? But instead, Bechdel chooses to depict this process in action, thereby committing it to the page, showing herself transcribing the words to enter them into the record that is *AYMM?* (Figure 6.1). In these panels, she depicts herself typing at her computer while listening to her mother talk and also depicts the word processor's typeface on the screen as she's typing it. This act of providing meticulous evidence not only shows her commitment to the objective truth but also serves as a moment of record-keeping for herself. On page 11, Bechdel (2012) also shows this transcription process in action and, in a textbox at the top of the page, says, "... my mother considers memoir a suspect genre" (11). This is followed by another textbox, which indicates her mother is talking on the other end of the line, answering Alison's question regarding someone else's memoir, asking what it's about, which reads, "Oh, you know. Inaccuracy, exhibitionism, narcissism, those fake memoirs" (11). This is a metacommentary on memoir and specifically her own memoir: inaccuracy and being "fake" are chief concerns for the memoirist, and her own mother is skeptical of memoir for this reason. Bechdel likely uses her mother's voice and views to represent her imagined readers. The act of actually showing this on the page sidesteps this issue in a way that indicates Bechdel is aiming to avoid this. On page 12, Bechdel justifies her act of transcribing the conversations: "But I want to capture her voice, her precise wording, her deadpan humor. I don't think I could possibly recreate it on my own" (12). This moment, used to accurately "capture her voice," is in keeping with the other archival evidence she uses to craft both memoirs, aimed at accurately capturing the past and avoiding the "inaccuracy, exhibitionism, narcissism ... fake memoir" that memory alone might have produced.

With both books, Bechdel famously posed for most of the panels in order to have a photograph to draw from, thereby leaving less guesswork in the equation and having the perfect angle, motion, and pose to recreate on the page. According to Ruggemeier (2016), "...Bechdel describes her work

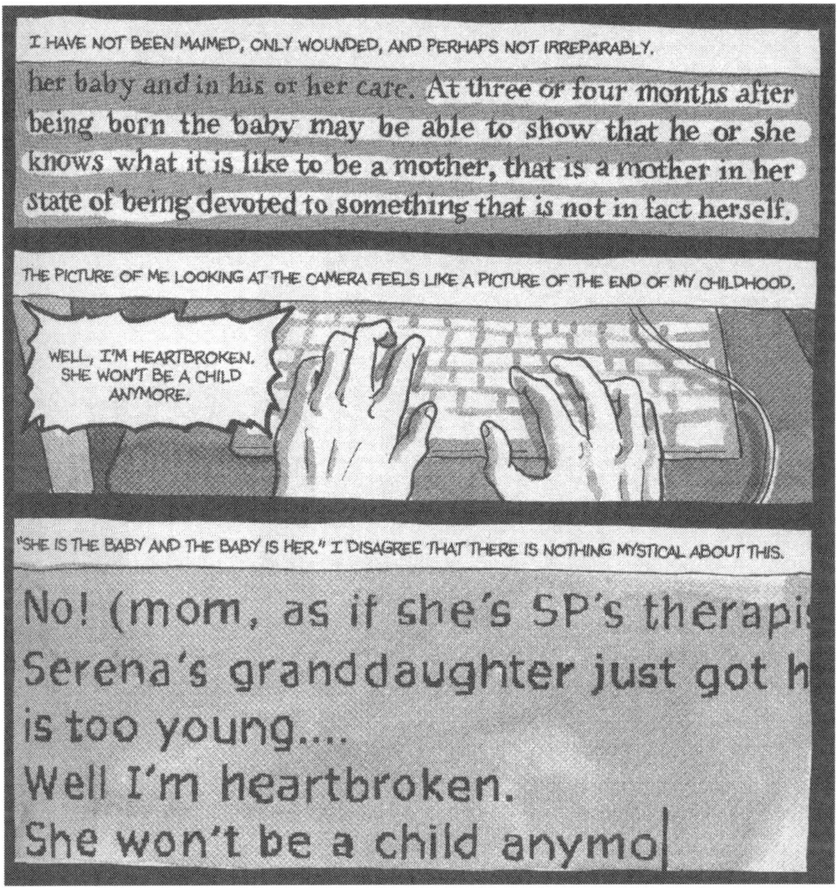

Figure 6.1 Two panels from page 35 of *Are You My Mother?* by Alison Bechdel 2012.

process as involving 'posing for all the characters in the book' (Bechdel, as quoted in Terzian 2012, n.p.). This means that the comics artist re-stages all her memories, takes a photo of the re-enacted memory via self-timer, and then uses this photography as a model for her drawing of the scene" (260). Bechdel has commented on this at length in interviews with Hillary Chute and others, and it's important to note how open she is about this process, so much that the public knows how much work she puts into capturing these real moments. More than that, though, Ruggemeier suggests that this meticulous process of posing also ties into visibility and is necessary for Bechdel to accurately present her story and her self on the page; whereas historically, comics and even graphic memoir have been seen through the lens of Horsman's "veneer of truth," or, further, as a fiction, Bechdel's process of creating her memoirs places an emphasis on recreation and accuracy.

> Even though 'fictionality' has been described as 'inherent to the medium of comics' (Pedri 2013, 129), because the act of drawing itself strongly evokes the impression that everything represented in graphic narratives is not a given fact but man-made fiction, Bechdel's foregrounding of the multiple acts of mediation that underlie her representation of past experiences further highlights the act of writing an autobiography as a process of 'making selves' (see Eakin 1999). While both the act of performance and media-based strategies of representing an autobiographical self have long been associated with deception, illusion, or fakery (see Moser 2008, 7), the characteristics of Bechdel's production process suggest thinking about the staging of an autobiographical self as a necessary process to gain visibility; and to gain visibility in graphic novels means to come into existence. (Ruggemeier 2016, 261)

In other words, Bechdel's complicated process of posing, recreating archival artifacts from her past, and recreating the past on the page through this multimodal process is anything but fictional and seeks to avoid, as much as possible, "deception" or "fakery."

This unique technique of posing for most or all of the panels in her memoirs is especially telling of Bechdel's impulse to be as truthful as possible; even amid moments of obvious subjectivity of memory, Bechdel posed for the characters included in the panels (her past self, her mother, her father, her brothers, others) in an attempt to recapture those moments, even imagined ones, as of Bruce Bechdel about to be hit by a Sunbeam truck in *Fun Home*. Because of these processes, both books are cloaked in a layer of truth that sets them apart from other memoirs, graphic or otherwise. This additional layer of truth is embodied, material, and gendered. Robyn Warhol (2011), in her article "The Space Between: A Narrative Approach to Alison Bechdel's *Fun Home*," discusses Bechdel's posing technique at length, and what it adds to the overall effect:

> If the purpose of this is, as Bechdel has explained, to get every bodily gesture, every wrinkle in the clothing, every angle just right, it also serves to give the drawings an almost palpable physicality, interestingly gendered in that Bechdel poses herself, appropriately costumed, for both male and female characters… these manifestations of the body in *Fun Home* add a material dimension to comics. (7–8)

Warhol is concerned with layers of meaning in the text, but her observations also reveal that Bechdel's posing techniques add a complex, gendered, and material truth to her memoirs. For example, in the bottom-left panel on page 197 of *Fun Home*, Bechdel (2006) depicts Bruce wearing a suit and looking "malevolent," as Bechdel says in a word balloon (197). In her article, Warhol provides that panel along with the photograph Bechdel took of herself to pose from, as Figures 4 and 5, pairing them side-by-side. In the photograph, Bechdel performs as male, wearing a blazer, tie, trousers, and belt, face held in an ominous scowl, reenacting a look and gait she remembers her father to have possessed. She could have posed wearing her own clothes, but wearing men's clothes and performing as male, then drawing from that image, creates an air of gendered authenticity that would have been absent otherwise. This, combined with the fact that Bechdel and her father share many physical similarities, lends itself to capturing the highest possible level of truth on the page, short of reproducing an actual photograph. However, due to the performative nature of this posing, Bechdel herself experienced these moments, performed them, and that material level of truth is captured on the page as well

Something Bechdel depicts in *AYMM?*, absent from *Fun Home*, is this process of posing in action, depicted on the page. On page 229, the page is composed of two small panels above a much larger third panel, all of which depict a moment when Alison hangs up on her mother, who had been expressing her discomfort with Alison's writing *Fun Home*. The top two panels on page 229 show Alison actually hanging her phone up while sitting at her desk, and the third, larger panel shows her crying, hand on the just-slammed phone, a look of anguish on her face (Figure 6.2). These panels depict an important look back at a crucial moment during the writing of *Fun Home* when she could have just quit; her mother didn't approve, and financial support from her mother while focusing on the book was an issue. Four pages later, on pages 233 and 234, Bechdel shows this moment again, though she adds the level of the Canon camera set up to take her photograph during this pose. What's different is that with the version of Alison posing, she's wearing different clothes, a purposeful indicator that these are two different levels of depiction: Alison Bechdel the artist has depicted a past version of herself on the page, who is posing in order to draw yet another version of herself on the page. A later panel on page 233 shows the camera with three beeps drawn in red to indicate the camera's timer going off. The panel on page 234 shows Allison examining the photograph the camera took, checking her work (Figure 6.3). A textbox in that panel compares her own career to her mother's acting career, and she says the difference is, "It's just that instead of playing a character, I'm playing myself" (Bechdel 2012, 234). Bechdel's metacommentary here reveals exactly what this posing process accomplishes: Bechdel acting out different versions of her past self, and that of others, and what is acting but embodying a character and making it real? The difference is that the "characters" here are her past selves, and beyond simply remembering her past, she's making it real. In posing for these shots, then drawing from them, and then depicting this process in *AYMM?*, Bechdel illustrates multiple levels of

Figure 6.2 A panel from page 229 of *Are You My Mother?* by Alison Bechdel 2012.

embodiment. As with the gendered posing for Bruce in *Fun Home*, here she poses as herself twice, performing as female, embodying past versions of herself as truthfully as is possible.

The initial hanging-up moment itself on page 229 is a metacommentary not only because she's referring to writing her bestselling first memoir within the sequel to it but also because that meta level is expanded further three pages later when Bechdel purposely shows the posing process of those panels in action, on the page. It is somewhat common knowledge among scholars that Bechdel posed for most of the panels in both memoirs, so this isn't a major revelation. What's important, though, is the fact that she depicted this process not in an interview or on her website but in the actual text of *AYMM?*, thereby adding it to the record of the book and adding it to the story she's telling. Much like her transcribed conversations with her mother that she's included within the text of *AYMM?*, these panels showing

Figure 6.3 Two panels from page 234 of *Are You My Mother?* by Alison Bechdel, 2012

the posing and photographing process are further evidence of record-keeping and working toward an accuracy of storytelling within the memoir, as well as a moment of further self-disclosure. Being a "metabook," as her mother calls it on page 285, *AYMM?* contains within it many of these self-references or depictions of creating the memoir within the memoir, serving as evidence of the meticulous process through which Bechdel has presented her truth on the page. Additionally, these self-referential moments serve as commentary on how graphic memoir functions, her graphic memoirs specifically. These can be seen as being on the same plane as the recreated photographs and other archival artifacts in both books: a means of achieving various levels of truth on the page—truth of fact, truth of experience, truth of embodiment, truth of self, truth of her creative process, and others which I may not have considered. Further, even with the pictorialized archival letters, journal entries, and other reproduced, written documents in the texts of both books, the act is performative and embodied. In the text of *AYMM?*, Bechdel (2012) provides important commentary on reproducing letters her father had written her mother that was absent in *Fun Home*:

> It was very strange to read my father's letters to my mother. … I brought the letters home with me and began typing up one or two first

> thing every morning. ... This was a peculiar performance in which I played both my mother the reader ... and my father the writer. (127–128).

Here, Bechdel again provides metacommentary on the performative nature of introducing the archive to her narrative and reproducing it on the page. The level of authenticity in both books arrives in part, then, from the embodied, gendered act of playing the parts of all the people involved, placing herself in their shoes, and encoding those accurate performances on the page for the reader.

In addition to Bechdel's purposes of exploring her past in these book to so diligently interrogate the truth about her father's suicide, her own sexuality, and her connections to both her parents, I would like to offer another explanation for Bechdel's obsession, and compulsion, for being as truthful as possible. Both memoirs demonstrate an overt awareness of authenticity and veracity (the archive, posing), going to metacommentary levels, particularly in *AYMM?*, and in both books it is clear that this openness is connected to her parents. In *Fun Home*, the audience witnesses Bechdel exploring her father's closeting—a lack of openness—as well as her mother's staunch denial of it, despite her awareness of Roy and other gay affairs. Alison herself doesn't become aware that her father is gay until she's in college, when her mother tells her over the phone, after sending both her parents her coming-out letter (Bechdel 2006, 79). Prior to that, her parents had been hiding that fact, acting as if her nuclear family was functional in all the traditional ways. In *AYMM?*, where Bechdel focuses on recording information even more than in *Fun Home*, certain moments reveal that same staunch denial Helen exhibits in the text of *Fun Home*. For example, after Alison first sends her mother a rough draft of the "dad book," her mother writes a less-than-optimistic email back, which Alison recounts for her girlfriend. Alison says, "[My mother] said she felt the dread she used to feel with Dad, of exposure and scandal" (Bechdel 2012, 165). The five panels on that page depict Alison depressed, lying on the ground, a look of anguish on her face after hearing that response from her mother. Similarly, later in the book, Bechdel depicts Alison speaking on the phone with her mother, explaining the potential of publishing a book of lesbian comics, and her mother says, "You're not going to use your real name, are you?" and Bechdel (2012) writes in a textbox after, "I understood that she was upset more about my father's homosexuality than mine" (182). Her mother feels the same need to protect information, to protect herself and the family from being scandalized, much like Bruce had exposed her to in the text of *Fun Home*. Her instinct is to deny. All of this seem to have shaped Bechdel's need to openly disclose the truth—both objective and subjective fact—and help explain why these memoirs go to such technical lengths to achieve authenticity. Given this, the focus on Alison's journal entries in *Fun Home*, with the "I think" statements and circumflex shorthand, also serves as metacommentary on her need to be as truthful as possible—the inclusion of those journal entries and the extended discussion of them is purposeful and suggests to the reader that even at that age, living with her denial-ridden parents, she was aware that she didn't know what the truth was. In composing her memoirs, though, she seeks to forcibly push back against any denial of truth.

As one last explanation for why Bechdel focuses so heavily on archival evidence and other techniques that lend themselves to authenticity, I would like to turn to Marianne Hirsch and Valerie Smith's article "Feminism and Cultural Memory: An Introduction," which introduces the idea of "cultural memory" and its associations with power and the disenfranchised. Hirsch and Smith (2002) write that "feminist and memory studies presuppose that the present is defined by a past that is constructed and contested," that we don't study the past strictly for its own sake but rather to "meet the needs of the present" (12). Further, they argue that

> Both fields emphasize the situatedness of the individual in his or her social or historical context and are thus suspicious of universal categories of experience. Beyond these broad points of convergence, development in feminism and work on cultural memory demonstrate that the content, sources, and experiences that are recalled, forgotten, or suppressed are of profound political significance. (12)

This argument speaks to the power of cultural memory, what a people remembers of the past and claim as important as time goes on. In this remembering, power is demonstrated in what is remembered and how it is remembered. This is particularly revealing of Bechdel's archive, of interrogating the past so closely, particularly the archived and remembered past of Bruce. Additionally, Hirsch and Smith state:

> To find the testimonies of the disenfranchised, we have turned to alternate archives such as visual images, music, ritual and performance, material and popular culture, oral history, and silence. We have recovered forgotten texts and have learned alternate reading strategies from them. From feminist literary and cultural criticism we have learned to be what Judith Fetterley (1978) has called 'resisting readers' who interrogate the ideological assumptions that structure and legitimate coherent linear narratives and who can decode narrative repetition, indirection, signifying, and figuration. We have learned to question claims to narrative reliability, seeking instead to understand alternate ways in which truthfulness might be assessed and used. (12)

In many ways, then, Bechdel is a "resisting reader" who, throughout both books, works to interrogate the past and the ways it has been documented, to place them into a narrative, arranged in such a way that attempts to both objectively present the past, the facts, and also give her subjective truth regarding the past, as she sees it. In *Fun Home*, the "disenfranchised" Bechdel gives testimony to is multifaceted: Bruce Bechdel, a closeted gay man living during the AIDS crisis and yet living beneath a traditional masculine façade in the Midwest; Alison's own lesbian sexuality and the ties to her father, ties she only discovers after she knows herself to be gay; her mother who staunchly denies Bruce's homosexuality and affairs with teenage boys despite knowing these things to be true. She goes to such lengths to reveal the truth, partly, then, to give power to these previously undisclosed truths. As discussed previously, Bechdel purposely includes in *AYMM?* her mother's email and phone conversation, which reveal her shame and negative feelings toward the future publication of *Fun Home* because of what it reveals. In both memoirs, Bechdel also heavily focuses on her own homosexuality, her various friends and lovers, her acts of reading and researching in college and beyond to give language to the lesbian feelings she was having, and even goes as far as to visually depict lesbian sex. In many ways, the gay and lesbian community in general are the disenfranchised to whom Bechdel grants voice and power throughout these memoirs. Bechdel achieves this by utilizing a careful attention to the archive, evidence, fact, posing, and memory to create an overtly authentic narrative and experience for the audience. Specifically with memory, Lisa M. Diamond gives a psychological perspective that helps explain why Bechdel focuses so heavily on the archive and authenticity.

Lisa M. Diamond's (2006) article "Careful What You Ask For: Reconsidering Feminist Epistemology and Autobiographical Narrative in Research on Sexual Identity Development," as the title suggests, provides an important feminist lens through which to analyze Alison Bechdel's depictions of the past, particularly with her emphasis on authenticity. *Fun Home* is especially centered on Bechdel's coming-of-age story with a heavy focus on coming to terms with both her father's and her own homosexuality. Diamond's article gives a revisionist methodology for how sexual-minority individuals (and particularly, psychologists studying them) might view their sexual history over time, especially in regard to determining "fact" or authenticity. Diamond explains how longitudinal interview studies, or observations, have typically functioned and that they may be asking the wrong questions when looking at the data of sexual-minority interviews over time. One dilemma of these interviews, Diamond explains, "concerns the problem of discerning which version of events should be considered more accurate when women's self-reported autobiographical narratives show divergence and self-contradiction over time (which I call the *authenticity problem*)" (475). Later, Diamond states that

> … findings from psychological research on autobiographical memory suggest problems with using consistency as an implicit marker for authenticity. Although it might seem straightforward enough to assume

> that accurate memory for a particular event facilitates consistency in its telling and retelling, this assumption sidesteps the more basic dilemma of defining and identifying 'accurate memories' to begin with. All memories are dynamic and situationally influenced. (477)

Diamond's research and argument about memory and authenticity as it pertains to sexual-minority individuals clearly shows that memory is fallible and, since memory is particularly important in considering sexual history and maturity, tracking these things authentically based on memory alone may be impossible. Diamond suggests that the question psychologists and individuals should be asking of the past is "What is it about this particular scenario or memory that has given it such prominence as a core feature of this individual's narrative sense of self?" (478). This lens Diamond provides can be useful when applied to Bechdel and her authenticity-focused memoirs.

Fun Home, and *AYMM?* even more so, as I've shown, rely heavily on archival evidence, gendered and performative posing for accuracy, record-keeping, and other techniques for achieving authenticity. These techniques are uniquely important in a visual medium like comics because Bechdel is able to achieve authenticity and truth on multiple levels. The memories Bechdel does provide in each are spread out through the books, punctuated by archival documents, quotes, and even with the memories comes Bechdel's posing techniques to visually get the details, angles, and genders right on the page. Bechdel relies not on memory but on evidence to narrate her family, psychological, and sexual histories to the reader. However, in considering Bechdel's sexual history in *Fun Home*, and her father's, Diamond's question of specific memories as core features of an individual's "narrative sense of self," Bechdel depicts many memories that connect to her father's death. In life they weren't all that connected, but after his death, which came shortly after learning of his closeted homosexuality, Bechdel is able to compose her narrative in such a way that is built around that single event. The book argues that her own coming-out gave motive for Bruce to commit suicide, and also pairs her own sexual feelings along an archival and remembered exploration of her father's own homosexuality, and thus makes her father central in her sexual autobiographical history. However, memory alone, as Diamond argues, can't capture the authenticity, and therefore Bechdel heavily relies on other forms of evidence to truthfully capture this story and grant it power.

Archived artifacts and Bechdel's posing—extratextual, multimodal tools and objects, brought in from the outside—play an important role in constructing truth and reality in both *Fun Home* and *Are You My Mother?*. When Bechdel illustrates a photograph, Roy half-naked for instance, the reader doesn't doubt the factuality or veracity of it because of her attention to detail. Through this technique, Bechdel truthfully captures her past on the page. In reference to *Fun Home*, Bechdel herself, in an interview with Hillary Chute (2006), says

> I also like the way [the photos] anchor the story in real life—the book is drawn in my regular cartoony style, but the photos are drawn much more realistically. It's a way to keep reminding readers, these are real people. This stuff really happened. (1009)

Similarly, in *AYMM?*, Bechdel's transcribed conversations with her mother, which she purposely pictorializes on the page, serve as evidence that these conversations really happened, and these pictorials and the information therein *become* part of the story. Additionally, this act of posing is specifically gendered and performative, which adds an extra level of embodiment as Bechdel the artist acts out all the players of the memoirs, including past version of herself. Ruggemeier (2016) claims that "Bechdel's multimodal practices of production thus demonstrate that autobiographical meaning making heavily relies on archival material and practices of embodiment not only to access individual pasts but also to open up intersubjective perspectives on past events" (265). In writing the book this way, using these graphic techniques, Bechdel opens up further avenues to achieving truth and perspective which are inaccessible to other forms of memoir. As I've posited, then, the photographs and other realistically rendered artifacts from Bechdel's past, as well as her embodiment of the past through her posing techniques, serve as a real-to-life, meticulous means of achieving truth and authenticity. This attention to detail is part of the story; Bechdel's crisis of sexuality and coming to terms with her father's death and closeted homosexuality, as well as her journey to understand her complicated relationship with her mother and the ways in which therapy has affected her life, isn't just given through the details. The details—the photographs, her handwriting, the letters, maps—*are* a part of the story. Through her composition of *Fun Home*, Bechdel also challenges these artifacts along the way, positing her own reflections on the past. This process doesn't nullify the archival evidence she renders, but rather juxtaposes it with an equally important truth: Bechdel's subjective memory and interpretation. Taken together, along with the process of closure they must already undergo between panels and pages, the reader must decide what to make of the information and pictorials Bechdel leaves for them. Similar to the final panels of *Fun Home*, the reader is caught midair, caught in a vulnerable state, infinitely unable to reach Bechdel's arms, unable to receive all the answers. Of this final moment of suspension in *Fun Home*, David Ball (2013) states "The reader is allowed to experience ... closure while also sensing an invisible 'I think' hovering over the text as a whole" (32). In both books, Bechdel leaves the question of what to make of her story and her "truth" up to the reader, which is in itself, yet another subjective version of the truth.

References

Ball, David M. 2013. "Allusive Confessions: The Literary Lives of Alison Bechdel's *Fun Home.*" In *Drawing from Life: Memory and Subjectivity in Comic Art*, edited by Jane Tolmie, 3–25. Jackson: University Press of Mississippi.

Bechdel, Alison. 2006. *Fun Home: A Family Tragicomic.* Boston: Mariner.

Bechdel, Alison. 2012. *Are You My Mother?: A Comic Drama.* Boston: Mariner.

Chute, Hillary. 2006. "An Interview with Alison Bechdel." *Modern Fiction Studies* 52 (4): 1004–13. doi:10.1353/mfs.2007.0003.

Diamond, Lisa M. 2006. "Careful What You Ask For: Reconsidering Feminist Epistemology and Autobiographical Narrative in Research on Sexual Identity Development." *Signs* 31 (2): 471–91. doi:10.1086/491684.

Hirsch, Marianne and Valerie Smith. 2002. "Feminism and Cultural Memory: An Introduction." *Signs* 28 (1): 1–19. https://www.jstor.org/stable/10.1086/340890. Accessed 25 March 2020.

Horsman, Ian. 2018. "*Imagine Wanting Only This* and the Subjectivity of Memoir." *Ploughshares*, Emerson College, February 4. http://blog.pshares.org/index.php/imagine-wanting-only-this-and-the-subjectivity-of-memoir/.

McCloud, Scott. 1994. *Understanding Comics: The Invisible Art.* New York: Harper Perennial.

Rüggemeier, Anne. 2016. "'Posing for all the characters in the book': The Multimodal Processes of Production in Alison Bechdel's Relational Autobiography *Are You My Mother?.*" *Journal of Graphic Novels and Comics* 7 (3): 254–67. doi:10.1080/21504857.2016.1199466.

Tison, Hélène. 2015. "Loss, Revision, Translation: Re-Membering the Father's Fragmented Self in Alison Bechdel's Graphic Memoir *Fun Home: A Family Tragicomic.*" *Studies in the Novel* 47 (3): 346–64. doi:10.1353/sdn.2015.0043.

Warhol, Robyn. 2011. "The Space Between: A Narrative Approach to Alison Bechdel's *Fun Home.*" *College Literature* 38 (3): 1–20. doi:10.1353/lit.2011.0025.

Watson, Julia. 2008. "Autographic Disclosures and Genealogies of Desire in Alison Bechdel's *Fun Home.*" *Biography: An Interdisciplinary Quarterly* 31 (1): 27–58. doi:10.1353/bio.0.0006.

7 Love, lust, and lucre in Leela Corman's *Unterzakhn*

Alex Link

Leela Corman's *Unterzakhn* (2012b)[1] presents a sophisticated exploration of the ways in which elements of popular culture can play a role in both identity formation and identity formatting. This graphic novel, first partially serialized in *The Jewish Daily Forward* in 2008 (Corman 2015), tells the story of twin sisters Fanya and Esther Feinberg, two first-generation working class Jewish American girls growing up with their parents, Isaac and Minna, in lower east side Manhattan in the years 1909–1923. Under the guidance of her mentor Bronia, Fanya becomes active in the marginally legal practice of promoting women's sexual health, working in a clinic modeled on the one opened by Margaret Sanger in New York in 1916, while refusing even to consider marriage or motherhood. Under the guidance of her mentor Lucille, Esther becomes a prostitute and then a wealthy celebrity of stage and screen. Fourteen years later, Fanya, destitute and living on the charity of her sister, dies in childbirth. The story of the sisters is paralleled with an interlude in the middle of the narrative describing their father Isaac's flight from persecution in Russia when he was a young man.

Critical examinations of *Unterzakhn* have been limited primarily to its representation of the Jewish immigrant and first-generation experience in the Lower East Side at the turn of the twentieth century. In particular, critics tend to return to the way in which Minna's depiction breaks with the convention of "the suffocating, overly-protective Jewish mother" (Valent 2015, 53; see also Mihăilescu 2015) or reinforces stereotypes of "fat, greedy, cold Jewish women" (Scherr 2015, 227). Rebecca Scherr's insightful analysis of relative silences and visibilities in *Unterzakhn*, and its relation to the Jewish body, takes the convention of the signaling of trauma in comics through the silent image, as described by Harriet Earle (2017, 52–3), and extends it to explore the many ways in which Jewish female embodiment is itself depicted as traumatic (Scherr 2015, 216). The scope of Scherr's examination of power differentials at work in *Unterzakhn* does not extend to a full examination of their ubiquity and the role popular culture plays in their promulgation. Likewise, while Tahneer Oksman (2016) has asserted that *Unterzakhn* "stresses the relational nature of each and every seemingly individual trajectory" (30), the power relations at work in them

DOI: 10.4324/9781003146520-7

has been left largely unexamined. These power differentials, supported by popular cultural production, found the Feinbergs' cultural milieu, shaping the opportunities and limitations of lives lived within it. Perhaps this is why Corman (2016) has replaced the *vesh* of the Yiddish word *untervesh* to create what Oksman identifies as a neologism, in "*unterzakhn*" (38 n.7), in that it more readily allows the word to expand beyond underclothes to, literally, the "things" that lie beneath life for the Feinbergs.

The conflation of underclothes with other "things" beneath the surface finds correlation in Corman's own autobiography. Writing about the sudden death of her toddler daughter in 2011 in "The Wound that Never Heals," Corman depicts herself being constrained and manipulated by the invisible silhouette of her trauma as she undertakes the "normal" actions of shopping and dancing, captioned with the words "They will think you're normal, because you will appear normal." At a cutting board, she juxtaposes the mundane task of slicing an onion with memories, in washed out colors, of discovering her child has died. Here, she remarks "I don't lose touch with consensual reality. It's more like two movies are playing at once: Where I am in time and space right now, and the moment of trauma" (Corman 2016d). The disjunction of surface and depth finds an irreverent correlation with underpants in "Irreducibles," a short comic about "those things you find inside yourself that can't be boiled away, no matter how assimilated you might be," as a Jew. Writing again about her grief at the death of her "then-only child" she flags the irreduciblity of her "black humor," citing by way of example, that in the week after her child's death she buys a three packs of underwear at Walmart that includes an exuberantly frilly white pair covered in hearts, which she comes to call "The Underwear of Affliction," adding "I'm probably a terrible person" (Corman 2016b).

At first glance, one might expect *Unterzakhn* to be a conventional *Bildungsroman* complete with parent–child friction stemming from old-world sexual and religious conservatism colliding with new-world American secular individualist agency, in which the showgirl and prostitute might be expected to come to some kind of tragic end while the family planner is revealed to be politicized, agentive, and ultimately triumphant in some hard-won and imperfect way. In fact, Minna, the girls' mother, tells her daughters just such a story about a showgirl, hammering the point home that such stories end not only in simple death but full degradation: "Everybody's bizness, she was. And how do you think she ended? Dead, in a ditch, covered in flies like a rotting dog!" (44). *Unterzakhn*, however, might be read as a revision of and rejoinder to popular cautionary and aspirational tales, doing so on their own terms, through a popular format: comics. Indeed, *Unterzakhn*'s interest in popular culture is such that its own promotion, through humorous tumblr posts and giveaways of novelty underpants (Corman, 2012a), only enhances its authenticity by fully exploiting the deep relationship between comics history, low humor, and commerce.

While Fanya grows up anxious to help women take control of their sexuality, to the point of refusing marriage outright for herself, Esther grows up fascinated with the appeal of being an object of beauty that, as an adult, she realizes is erotic beauty in the eye of the heteronormative beholder. The narrative begins with an instructive moment that seems to determine the trajectory of the girls' lives. A neighbor, Mrs. Gold, collapses in the street after attempting a home abortion. Bronia, the "lady doctor," is summoned to help her but is too late. The event highlights the many silences and pressures that surround the girls about adult sexuality and femininity, and it emphasizes the ignorance and disempowerment they experience as children on matters for which, as adults, they nevertheless will be held responsible. Fanya is sent in search of the "lady doctor," without knowing what that is (12). She sees the stain around the woman's "down there" (19) but cannot even say what "down there" is. She sees women accused of being *pritzes* or whores but does not know what that means. She catches Bronia trying to shield her from the knowledge that Mrs. Gold has died (15), making death itself yet another secret in a childhood awash in mysteries and unspeakable adult realities. What strikes Fanya is that she is being asked to deny her eyes as adults try to shield her from things she has already seen. This moment, which underscores the degree to which her world seems built upon adult fictions and silences, is perhaps her first step toward a life focused upon unromantic material fact. It is also only *Unterzakhn*'s first step in that, while a more conventional narrative might simply have mined the girls' lives as parallel trajectories that begin to diverge in this moment, this story branches out to establish other, comparable lives beyond the easy binary offered by a mere fictional biography of twins.

One might go so far as to suggest that the stain on Mrs. Gold's dress literalizes the Lacanian stain in Fanya's world—the ineradicable inconsistency upon which the coherence of her world depends and which it seeks to disavow. The stain is "the trace of what had to be precluded from the field of reality in order that this field can acquire its consistency" (Salecl 1992, 192). At its core, the stain is that which throws one's sense of reality into question by drawing attention to its provisional nature, its constructedness, its architecture of what Lacan calls the Symbolic, covering up or standing in for the Real that lies beyond representation. The stain foregrounds the "problem of convention, of a nature that is false—or, if you like, of façade" (Bonitzer 1992, 21), and that is precisely what Fanya encounters in this moment: the discovery that her everyday reality is a façade. Now that it is troubled by a stain, by a hole in its consistency, the rest of her reality is thrown into doubt. Everyday, lower-case, symbolically articulated "'[r]eality'"

> is the field of symbolically structured representations, the outcome of a symbolic 'gentrification' of the Real; yet a surplus of the Real always eludes the symbolic grasp and persists as a non-symbolized stain, a hole

> in reality which designates the ultimate limit where 'the word fails' (Žižek 1992, 239)

Fanya attempts to reconcile the memory of Mrs. Gold bleeding on the street with the fragments of cryptic explanation she has received throughout the day. Doing so, however, only produces absurd images, visualizing the challenge of resealing this rupture in her reality.

Some explanations, like that provided by the pickle lady, attempt to bring Fanya into the know with respect to abortion, to fold Mrs. Gold's death into an understanding of the world "as it is" for adults. They attempt to bring her into a reality shared by adults which is, to Fanya, as the Real is to them. The pickle lady is so at ease in this world that horrifies and mystifies Fanya that she can treat it like a joke: "A lady's got a problem with the babies, she goes to Bronia. She kills the baby, no more problem." Even she has her limits, though, refusing to initiate Fanya into the mysteries of the word "pritze." Fanya rejects the pickle lady's partial explanation as "crazy" (22).

Bronia is silent (15), while other explanations are acts of displacement. Minna provides a vague explanation and a simile that, rather than fold the rupture into the girls' reality, only covers it over. She declares that Mrs. Gold's decision to "put a wire inside her, to take out from her the baby" is "like a knife in God's eye." The analogy is vivid but explains nothing. Minna expects this non-explanation — underscoring penetration in the comparison while obscuring what, precisely is penetrated — to cover over what is, for Fanya, otherwise unknowable. Minna's words occupy the paradoxical place of the "signifier of the lack" which comes to stand in for the "lack of the signifier"(Figures 7.1 and 7.2). If Fanya encounters something for which there are no words, the very absence of any available words comes to be signified by the enigmatic simile, one strategy by which

> the stain ... is replaced by an empty signifier, a signifier which does not signify any reality—that is to say: a stand-in for a representation which is constitutively excluded from reality, which must fall out if 'reality' is to retain its consistency (Žižek 1992, 239).

As a displacement for truths that might disrupt an otherwise stable reality, the scene of Minna's non-explanation bears a striking resemblance to a similar one Corman explores in her 2016 short comic "The Book of the Dead." In *Unterzakhn*, Minna stands over a dead fish, preparing it for dinner, as she declares sexual license akin to a "knife in God's eye." In "The Book of the Dead," we are told a story in which a carp is kept in the family bathtub until it is ready to be prepared and eaten at Passover by Corman's grandmother. When her mother and aunt—whose own stories seem to have informed many elements of Fanya and Esther's—later see the carp on the kitchen cutting board, the two children are told a lie: "Oh this is a different

Figure 7.1 Three panels from *Unterzakhn* by Leela Corman, 2012.

fish. Your fish had to go away." Replicating the scene in *Unterzakhn* very closely, however, Corman adds the following commentary, again evocative of the way in which the stain—here, again, a literal bloodstain—throws reality off balance, and displaces another problem altogether. In this case, it is not sexuality but unspoken family trauma, particularly with respect to the Holocaust:

> Of course a carp is just a carp, waiting to become either your pet, or gefilte fish. But am I wrong to also see this body lying in a pool of blood, being fibbed about in plain sight, as a metaphor for all the corpses and blood never discussed? (Corman 2016a)

It seems, however, that most characters have some sort of stain with which they must contend. For example, it is difficult not to notice how much of life in the Feinbergs' world is based upon contradictions, inconsistencies, and double standards. The girls are to be ignorant of but responsible for their own sexuality. Esther is a celebrated agent of the hegemonic machine that

Figure 7.2 Three panels from "The Book of the Dead" by LeelaCorman, 2016.

perpetuates this contradiction. Bronia is an oppressive instrument of women's emancipation. Minna—and by implication others—upholds a disciplinary regime policing feminine sexuality that she does not live. Women are consistently presented as responsible for male sexuality. Isaac has erased his entire personal history, covering it over with silence and deflection.

Contrasting with these compromised positions stands Feigl, alone, a little girl representing the not-yet-socialized, who momentarily exists outside this network of double binds. Perhaps she, too, as an unrealistic possibility for the reader, is the narrative's own "stain," allowing one to believe that such a position outside of culture can actually exist. Corman herself reduces Feigl to "more of a device than a character" (Corman 2015). Nevertheless, Feigl's association with pure physicality, of the pre-adolescent body yet to be subjected to the impossible demands of policed sexuality, is explicit. In fact, she is spared those demands by her death, allowing her to retain the status of a device and making her an example of "the icon of *everychild* on the path of becoming enculturated" (Glasner 2015, 188).

Her brief appearances in the story underscore her physicality and putative pre-cultural animality, first running naked through the apartment declaring herself as belonging to no one but herself (28) and then in an image of her belching that takes up a third of a page (48). Contrast this animal body, engaged in the simple acts of eating and, on the following page, running and snorting, with Isaac's description, to the twins, of Circe's transformation of men into animals. Bronia can only deride the masculine animal as a predacious Darwinian throwback bent on treating women as "breed cows" (60). Her characterization of men as animals is consistent with the myth as Isaac tells it. The myth doubtless rings true, for Isaac, given his own experience with Cassock "dogs" (95) who drive him from his home such that he too, with Meyer, has to bed down in straw with barn animals (92). Unlike either of these uses of the animal metaphor, Esther reimagines Circe as a "happy hostess," seeming, in the promotional poster, to rule animals (194). It is a figuration as absurd, and therefore as open to imagining new possibilities, as Meyer's own ridiculous song, sung to entertain the Cassock "dogs," about interspecies sex (99). Both Esther and Meyer, in other words, demonstrate their like-mindedness in the narrative, long before they meet, through their willingness to play with convention. As happens so often in *Unterzakhn*, we balance the quotidian with the fantastical and the material with the allegorical, mapping out through word and image the territory the girls will have to navigate as idealized figures and as the objects of the patriarchal horse trade in women by turns.

Unlike Feigl, the narrative's adults live in the coded space of the Symbolic, and perhaps it is with respect to their position *vis-à-vis* the stain that one can more clearly understand what makes *Unterzakhn* different from other graphic narratives that follow doubled pairs of characters through their adolescent rites of passage. *Ghost World*, by Daniel Clowes, for example; R. Kikuo Johnson's *Night Fisher;* and—in a more complicated manner—Nate Powell's *Any Empire* features pairs of adolescents graduating high school. In each, one teenager, like Fanya, rejects the myth of simple conformist success. The other seeks to excel at conformity. Esther, however, is not quite like *Ghost World*'s Becky or *Night Fisher*'s Shane in that rather than conform to the "façade" the stain interrupts, she becomes a part of the façade itself, first serving as its alibi and then as a deity in its mythical, screen star pantheon.

In some respects, *Unterzakhn* is an ambivalent defense of Romance—that mode of narrative found at the opposite end of the spectrum from Realism—as a response to, alibi for, and aspirational impetus in spite of material fact. Put simply, Realist narrative is structured by one's assumptions about what is possible and plausible within the lived everyday, whereas Romantic narrative is freed from these structures so as to foreground wish-fulfillment and fear-fulfillment. While the precise relationship between Realism and Romance has long been a subject of debate, their relative proximity to myth (Frye 1957, 139-40) or to Greek "adventure-time" (Bakhtin 1981, 86–110) remains constant.

Romance and Realism are relative quantities, and in any narrative one finds them "mixed, like racial strains in human beings" (Frye 1957, 305). Both, too, are subject to history, in that what constitutes a "realistic" representation of experience is not constant but changes its parameters according to time, place, and focus. One can imagine narratives that are psychologically or materially or historically realistic, for example. Likewise, one could argue that Romance offers an emotional realism. However, for our purposes, Realism and Romance occupy positions at opposite ends of a range that measures plausibility and particularity from a viewer's perspective. If "Aristotle urged that literature should portray not the possible but the probable," Romance departs from the Aristotelian foundations of a realist aesthetic (Maude 2004, 427) in its tendency toward the "mythic 'abolition' of time and history" (McKeon 1987, 32), use of "traditional plots and figurative eloquence," and resistance to "the particularization of character and background, of naming, temporality, causation, and physical environment" (McKeon 1997, 2).

Romance has long had a particular, though certainly not exclusive, appeal to women; not coincidentally, the modern literary canon has historically favored Realism, with attendant, inherent, often elided biases privileging middle class white masculinity. The association of Romance with femininity is precisely why alternative knowledges cast as fantasy—such as superstition, astrology, and intuition—are conventionally feminized (Fiske 1993, 192). At the same time, Romantic "'[a]dventure' literally denotes events that come to one from without, and therefore the lives of the unempowered are full of it" (Ross 1991, 4). It is no coincidence that those novels typically found on shelves where women are conventionally expected to shop—drug stores and supermarkets—are Romances.

> Like the Freudian uncanny, the conventions of romance reinstate primitive, pre-Symbolic modes of significance. They place us in a world where coincidence is no accident, where magic substitutes for causality, and where ... the very boundaries between mind and nature become doubtful ... The conventions of romance are thus literally 'unrealistic,' because they ignore the principles that constitute 'reality'. (Williams 1995, 82)

Romance, as a feminized narrative that nevertheless reinforces patriarchal norms can, from one perspective, be regarded as an instrument of discipline, hegemonic in nature, or what Anne Williams calls, punningly, "The opiate of the misses" (138). Hence, the ambivalence of Esther's narrative trajectory, which shows her promoting romance, actively rewriting it, and to a certain extent even living it. *Unterzakhn* as a whole, too, is ambivalent in its treatment of the modes of Realism and Romance. Meyer, for example, purchases Esther from the brothel as a vulgar business investment without ever suggesting that he is some sort of white knight, but the fact that they meet at all is a romantic "coincidence [that] is no accident." Neither he nor Esther ever recognize one another as, respectively, Isaac's best friend and Isaac's daughter, miraculously brought together. Only the reader sees this wondrous *zakhn unter* the tawdry daily struggle, whereas the mundane *zakhn unter* the production of wondrous fantasies on stage and screen is an open secret.

Where else does one find Romance, or fantastic narratives of wish-fulfillment and fear-fulfillment, but in popular culture, in the fantasies of broad appeal and wide distribution played out in, among other things, myth, the music hall, the cinema, and the brothel, all of which are present in *Unterzakhn*? Emphasizing the tension between these two modes, time and again we see Romance counterbalanced by the Realistic material conditions of its production; we see it simultaneously promote and mystify the obligations of everyday life while compensating for its disappointments; we see it obscure the economic foundations of marriage in the production of fantasies of love, and we see immersion in Romance itself as a route to self-fashioning self-empowerment that might also be a self-betraying self-abasement.

The complexity of popular culture's relationship to its audience—and perhaps more accurately, the complexity of the array of subject positions with which the audience approaches popular entertainment—comes through in the representation of the girls' visit to the music hall (Figure 7.3).

On this page, as well as those preceding and following, *Unterzakhn* demonstrates the way in which popular culture presents itself as both a means of teaching the audience about itself while also allowing that audience to see itself represented. It precedes the scene devoted to the making and consumption of "pierogn" that ends in Feigl's majestic belch: a scene of simple, domestic, physical pleasure. This outing, by contrast, emphasizes the female body in public. The exterior of the hall signifies the entertainment to be expected inside through "all these lights, an' pictures of pretty ladies outside!" (44). One might see it as occupying a middle ground between the selling of female bodies at the Horse and Rider brothel and the glamour of bodily ornamentation by businesses such as Minna's, which also advertises with pictures of "pretty ladies" (23). Minna herself seems aware of this middle ground, as she remarks that while women who join "the show" end up "dead in a ditch," and even she has to admit that "the rouge and fine dresses were all right" (44).

The girls' means of entry into the music hall is also via the occupation of the visual field by female bodies, here in a literalized, material, and perhaps ironic way, as the girls "squish between two fat ladies" to sneak in, breasts and bottoms emphasized in the third panel. The certainty with which Esther assumes the women in the audience have matronly bodies points to the distance between audience member and idealized female representation on stage, as the women we see in performance and poster are slender, sexually mature, and desirable, with the exception of the caricature of the Jewish mother crying "Vey iz mir." Framing this single moment are emphases on the female body, with dancers flashing "their panties," a woman flirting with two men, and a contortionist showing off her body to the audience.

Figure 7.3 Seven panels from *Unterzakhn* by Leela Corman, 2012.

The variety of the variety show offers assorted opportunities for identification with and against possible images of self-conception, self-construction, and aspiration. Regardless of the specific content of the show, what is always shown playing out on stage is desire: who one is or is not, should be or should not be, could or could not possess.

This ambivalence between identification and disavowability is a common feature of popular entertainment with mass appeal. Such entertainment tells stories flexible enough for the viewer or reader to occupy several possible positions with respect to what they see, allowing for a range of identification with or against the material presented. This is one reason why so many narratives meant for popular consumption, from the early British gothic novel to those drugstore Romances, feature stories set in exotic times and places, yet offer points of identification for their readership.

By way of illustration, consider "Li Hung Chang Visits Hogan's Alley," a *Yellow Kid* single-panel cartoon by R.F. Outcault appearing in the *New York World* on 6 September 1896. The cartoon shows the denizens of Hogan's Alley, a motley group of immigrant tenement dwellers drawn, as usual, with caricatural racial and ethnic features. Here, admittedly, the caricatures gesture primarily to East Asian identities, with Yellow Kid Mickey Dugan's stereotypically Irish "begee" drawn in *faux* hanzi calligraphy. They are holding a parade for Li Hung Chang, a Chinese general who has come to America partly to argue against the Chinese Exclusion Act, renewed in 1892. He may be riding a tiny, goat-drawn cart, but his face and body, notably, are a faithful portrait and not at all caricatural. The contrast signifies the way in which, more generally, *The Yellow Kid* puts readers—who may or may not be literate, and who may or may not be immigrants—in a position in which they can choose to laugh at or with the Yellow Kid and to see themselves or their cultural and class others represented.

To return to the music hall scene, the caricatural representation of the Jewish family leaves open the possibility of pleasure in seeing oneself represented and pleasure in seeing the Jewish other represented for gentile audience members. It does, in a public context for the vaudeville audience, what the subsequent "pierogn" scene does for the reading audience in its representation of a private moment. The difference between these scenes lies in whether the pleasure, for a gentile audience being given some kind of touristic glimpse into the life of the Jewish other, comes at the expense of the represented figures.

This visit to the theater is Esther's point of entry into the fantastic world seemingly contained in the compact she clutches as she goes to sleep (41). It offers erotic thrill, but at something of a safe distance. It offers caricatural representation of her ethnic background that, while reductive, is not inconsistent with the ways in which we see figures in her neighborhood, such as the pickle lady, represented on the street. It offers access to a forbidden world—the girls have to sneak in, after all—that is both familiar and a window into a different way of living. Hence, the gentle irony with which *Unterzakhn* shows Esther, after having enjoyed this classic form of low entertainment, patronizing Fanya: "you just don't understand art!" (46). Meanwhile, we are reminded of the naïveté of Esther's sudden elitism with the image of a collapsed drunk on the sidewalk behind her. Even so, it is the circuitous path between theater and brothel that leads to Esther's dramatic elevation in status and class, to her becoming a modern-day goddess herself.

Emphasizing the intensity and significance of the moment, note that this is one of only two pages in *Unterzakhn* to feature emanata, or traditional cartooning icons that typically appear as "sweat beads, dust clouds, speed lines, and many other symbols" (Witek 2012, 29). In a narrative seemingly devoid of romantic love, this is the one moment at which we see Esther's head surrounded by floating hearts, as she reflects on her experience in the hall, counterbalanced by bubbles floating above the drunk man. The other moment, perhaps in telling counterpoint, shows stars floating about the head of a man who tries to rape Esther after he is hit in the head with a whiskey bottle (64). As if bringing the two men together as the shadowy backdrop to Esther's ambitions, and as reminders of her position as a poor and Jewish woman in the world, both are undone by bottles of alcohol and demonstrate passive and active dangers troubling her fantasies of glamor.

The hegemonic role of popular culture, particularly in its deployment of Romance, is perhaps obvious. However, popular culture in *Unterzakhn* is not the instrument of some shadowy power intentionally deploying such entertainments as a disciplinary instrument of hegemony by white and moneyed classes. It is true that popular culture traffics in the reinforcement of normative roles in America in *Unterzakhn*. However, its producers are as often as not from those very classes whose relative disempowerment in American culture is being reproduced through the technology of Romantic storytelling. In other words, we are shown a complex array of people both fashioning and being fashioned by popular cultural narratives in ways that are variably active or passive, critical or uncritical, conservative or challenging. The roles depicted by popular cultural Romance, in *Unterzakhn*, are often gendered, but the narrative is clear that this disciplinary vector is but one in a broader cultural complex of power relations managed and influenced by popular culture that extends to include class, race, religion, region, sexuality, family composition, and beyond.

Hence, the insistence upon differences among subject positions that, on the surface, one might expect to be uncritical and uncomplicated allies in a more conventional, arguably simplistic feminist narrative. While one might want to be sympathetic to Bronia's pioneering effort at family planning and the promotion of women's sexual health and agency, for example, it is constantly undermined by Bronia's own inability to recognize and respect difference among women. She is unable to see her feminism as a white, middle class, heteronormative American feminism regardless of her own ethnic background and that her feminist conviction carries with it an assimilationist demand. She insists that Fanya learn to read, which seems well-intentioned at first, but, in the context of early twentieth-century tenement life, it is difficult not to read this moment as invoking the history of American settlement workers promoting middle-class values that threatened to erode immigrant cultural identity (American Social History Project 2000, 214–15). Minna, the girls' mother, insists that the girls need practical training, not "the goyim's books" (33). Also, Bronia makes her services conditional on the assumption that a woman not have sex for pleasure, refusing to encourage "reckless behavior" (166) and dismissing prostitutes, paternalistically, as not "worth the risk" since helping them only contributes "to their oppression" (178). For Bronia, contraception is a form of protection from the slavery of motherhood and the assumption of responsibility for male sexuality, having nothing whatsoever to do with sexual empowerment or pleasure. Given that pleasure is precisely that territory claimed by Romance as a mode of wish-fulfillment, Bronia's inability to believe in female sexual pleasure is consistent with Judeo-Christian culture's history of treating pleasure with suspicion. In that respect, her attitude toward sexuality is part of the same unease caused by forms of popular culture when they are confused with content that is typically Romantic in nature, such as comics. It is an idea that underlies the *Ladies Home Journal*'s accusation, in 1909 that comics are "an influence for repulsive and ... depraving vulgarity" (Lambert 2008, 45)—in other words pleasure. Bronia offers emancipation, but it is emancipation into merely a different, assimilationist disciplinary regime that constructs difference as the tragic victimhood of ignorance, backwardness, or oppression.

Bronia's attitude demonstrates how Fanya's apparently non-conformist path of entering into the illegal-but-tolerated practice of family planning is, in practice, simply another instrument of a broad disciplinary regime. Bronia's attitude is unambiguously one that continues to hold women entirely responsible for both male and female sexual activity, the only difference being that Bronia is dedicated to teaching that responsibility clearly rather than having it persist as the mystery that so troubles Fanya in *Unterzakhn*'s opening pages. The clarity with which Bronia demonstrates the tricky cooption of apparent resistance into the deeper regulation of female bodies allows Fanya to double down on her resistance, as she rejects the very ideas of marriage and motherhood. Meanwhile, Esther's apparently non-conformist path of entering into the illegal-but-tolerated practice of prostitution is, through Meyer, the path through which she becomes a rewarded and powerful instrument of the perpetuation of this disciplinary regime.

If there is a point of bifurcation in the otherwise comparable trajectories that Fanya and Esther follow—since both operate on the edges of the law in professions that encourage female embodied agency—it is in their attitude toward popular culture and its promotion of Romance. Fanya rejects it utterly and completely. Esther does not embrace it, as perhaps one might expect in a simple opposition—that is more her father's tack—but becomes a producer of it. In other words, the narrative offers a third option beyond passive consumption and seemingly untenable outright rejection of Romance, which, arguably, would be equally as passive. Whether uncritical consumption or absolute abjuration, both positions are ultimately interpellated by a static relationship to a monolithic entity called popular culture; one is simply the inverse of the other, leaving that to which they are responding unchallenged and unchanged.

Unterzakhn is very clear that disempowerment is not absolutely intrinsic to a type or a class, given that sex, gender, class, ethnicity, and so on are not separable categories but always impact upon one another. Thus, power is the function of a position within a social system understood intersectionally. To this end, we see relationships in the story break down into power imbalances not only between men and women, or white Americans and immigrant Jews, but also middle class and poor, adult and child, Cossack and Russian Jew. Even the differential between American northerner and southerner is flagged as Esther advises her assistant to conceal her southern drawl so as not to be taken for a "half-wit" (170). The most powerful of many examples that drives home the way in which these relations are homologous is when we follow the adventures of Isaac and his friend Meyer in Russia. More specifically, their encounters with Cossack soldiers are cast in terms of rape. After the rape and murder of Isaac's mother and sister, soldiers speculate on taking these Jewish men to the barracks to "play with" (100). While bathing, Meyer is carried off naked by a soldier and out of Isaac's life, like any number of virgins and nymphs from popular narrative subjected to a Romantic adventure (105). Put simply, disempowerment is de-essentialized and cast as a position in a set of relations that draws parallels across groups whose power dynamics are often taken to be distinct. One way of demonstrating this comparability is by framing extreme physical and violent domination in erotic terms, as it is in this moment.

I agree that it is "no mistake that Esther is raped by a 'Mr Vanderhof,' a name signifying the white elite of old New York" which, while "not exactly the same as the Cossacks coming ... is based on similar cultural and social discourses of gender, religion and ethnicity" (Scherr 2015, 221), but I would argue that the "power differential" Scherr cites actually extends much further in the narrative, to structure the uneven power relations undergirding all cultural experience, in relation to which popular culture serves as both a disciplinary mechanism and alibi. While the sweeping generalization gives pause, Corman's own remark, when discussing *Unterzakhn*, that there is "no human behavior that is different now than it was a thousand years ago or five thousand years ago, anywhere," does encourage this expanded scope of inquiry (Corman 2015). At the same time, one must draw a firm line between the use of erotic violence, or *symplegma*, in *Unterzakhn* as a symbolic mechanism that can draw together different forms of structural violence and the history of rape as a violence that has played out, historically and specifically, on the female body. To acknowledge points of parallel commonality between kinds of violence ought not to elide the specific elements of each. Once again, *Unterzakhn* stresses difference *amongst* groups, as it seeks points of commonality between groups that, in an essentialist paradigm, might not always consider intersectionality's pressures and tensions and that might cast them as different, locating violence then in individuals rather than in disciplinary regimes. As Sara Ahmed succinctly states, "racism should not be seen as about individuals with bad attitudes ... not because such individuals do not exist (they do) but because such a way of thinking underestimates the scope and scale of racism" as systemic (Ahmed 2012, 44).

In *Unterzakhn*, Romance, as a narrative mode that speaks to desire in its consumer, is not inconsistent with the more broadly romantic as, for example, one might engage in romanticizing objects or people. That is, along with a number of popular cultural forms that provide opportunities for the ritual enjoyment of desires fulfilled, fears exorcised, and uncomfortable realities held at bay, we are presented with objects that serve a similar purpose. As receptacles that hold an unarticulated hope, promise, or memory, these objects might, at least in the context of this story, be best described as romanticized. It is true that there is nothing special about romanticized objects, when considered materially, in and of themselves. Fanya, Esther, and Isaac are all shown sleeping with objects special only to them: a lump of mother of pearl (37), a compact (41), and a braid of hair (92), respectively. The visual parallel of these moments emphasizes a deeper commonality despite the apparent differences between these individuals, their lives, and their desires. Each is shown on the cusp of dream and waking, living a reality that, like Winsor McCay's Little Nemo, is drab at best but held by the power of a wish held in, or *unter*, everyday *zakhn*.

Considered separately, each in the context in which it is a cherished possession, the three objects map out different relationships to temporality and desire. The mother of pearl is a token from Sal, an imperfectly realized pearl for an imperfectly realized love, precious matter drawn from a living body and remaining always potential as a tempting future possibility. It is dreamy but ambivalent, conflating love with sex, given that it "smell[s] like old fish" (37). The compact holds not makeup, exactly, so much as Esther's promise to herself to become precious and desired, through making her body desirable in future days. The braid is a trace of a lost, precious body, a marker of an absence, a relic Isaac unwinds and scatters on the ocean playing out the ritual of leaving it, and Europe, behind (118). He does so in silence, leaving us to guess whether this gesture is a futile attempt to sever from the past or the recognition that such relics are redundant when their traumatic significance resides in the observer, rendering forgetting impossible (Figures 7.4, 7.5, and 7.6).

The same distinction between material and content might be said about the narrative's constant exposure of the machinery of Romance—that the material nature of the object is quite separate from its romanticized social role. In rehearsal, Lucille demands that her dancing girls, who are also prostitutes in her brothel, dance "Dreamier! You're supposed to be fairies, for fuck's sake, not washerwomen" (67), contrasting vulgar everyday reality with the lightness of fairy tales, and we spend a lot of time backstage watching drab petty in-fighting that contrasts with the fantasies presented onstage, at the music hall, at the brothel, and later in the movie theater too.

Figures 7.4 A panel from *Unterzakhn* by Leela Corman, 2012.

In other words, Esther's immersion in Romance is not deluded but a working with and within the material realities of everyday life, including the material fact of the promulgation of fantasy. The form—whether film, comic, seduction, compact, myth, or song—is merely a vessel that may or may not be used to deliver and reinforce romantic messages of cultural conventionality. Indeed, it is only recently that comics themselves have come to be widely understood in mainstream North America as separate from the conservative romantic narratives with which they were almost exclusively associated—with notable exceptions such as underground comix—in popular consciousness for much of the twentieth century.

Note, too, the way in which *Unterzakhn* suggests the interchangeability of romantic vehicle by blurring the lines between a brothel and a conventional stage show. Despite her meticulous historical research, Corman herself is unsure whether an establishment such as Miss Lucille's Horse and Rider would have existed at the turn of the century (Corman 2015), even though in other comics she has since completed, such as "Luna of Cairo" in collaboration with the eponymous belly dancer, it is a given that in Egypt,

Figures 7.5 A panel from *Unterzakhn* by Leela Corman, 2012.

at least, belly dancing stardom and sex work go hand in hand; "You have to pay to play" applies equally to clients who pay in cash and dancers who pay in sex work (Corman and Luna 2016). Interestingly, such establishments were fairly common in the Feinbergs' New York, with many prostitutes working part-time and even hailing, like the Feinbergs, from the garment industry (Gilfoyle 1992, 287). With a "daily clientele for New York's prostitutes" surpassing 150,000 by a 1917 estimate (Gilfoyle 1992, 238), many businesses, from cigar stores to butcher shops, offered prostitutes, and on the Lower East Side "saloons almost had to have prostitutes in order to stay in business," with only sporadic law enforcement of anti-prostitution laws thanks to a healthy culture of protection payments made to police and politicians. By the turn of the twentieth century, many saloons

Figures 7.6 A panel from *Unterzakhn* by Leela Corman, 2012.

became cabarets patronized by "respectable" people where prostitutes nevertheless boarded and plied their trade. Intentional or not, Miss Lucille's establishment accurately echoes the 1886 remark made by Police Captain Thomas Byrnes, that "'traffic in female virtues is as much a regular business, systematically carried on for gain, in the city of New York, as is the trade in boots and shoes, dry goods and groceries'" (Gilfoyle 1992, 244-48), and for many, "commercial sex [was] a routine part of city life." Shocking as it might be to the contemporary reader, at 13, even Esther's age would have been unremarkable (Gilfoyle 1992, 284).

If the objects themselves matter less than what they signify to the bearers, and if Romance is not intrinsic to its medium, then sometimes the medium fails to be or to be used as an adequate bearer of significance. More to the point, *Unterzakhn* explores uses to which Romance might be put, making it clear that the storytelling mode, despite its utility for disciplinary regimes, is in and of itself neutral and therefore available for revision and redeployment. For example, Isaac's commitment to Homer's *Odyssey* and myth is like a dead end. He carries the book everywhere because he bought it for his sister, Chane, the day she died and the day he lost his home. He treats it as an object of mourning, a relic, reading it to anyone who will listen, and he dies a broken man. The Romance does not offer a path to transformation, either in its lessons or in passive, grieving use of it. In describing himself as having been "hatched from a witch's egg" to avoid having to discuss his family's murder, he uses Romance only to conceal the brutal facts of his life, perhaps in a way not so different from Minna's "knife in God's eye" remark after all, rather than to change how he might understand or historicize them or how the Feinbergs might see their lives now (110).

Isaac does manage to pass on a love of Romance to his daughters. He tells them nothing of his own past but raises them on myth in its place. Like her father, Fanya passively retains and recites these stories and also dies disappointed and destitute. In this respect, while Fanya has a surrogate mother in Bronia, she remains her father's daughter. By contrast, *Unterzakhn* ends with Esther living in a provisional family, with surrogate parents Lucille and Meyer, and caring for her sister's newborn. Esther, like Meyer, and like *Unterzakhn* itself, takes these inherited tales in and rewrites them. Fanya might call the rape and marriage of Persephone a "creepy story" (192), but Esther revises the tale of Circe for the stage to make her a "happy hostess," which Fanya also rejects as "ridiculous" (194). These revisions of myth are just one aspect of the way in which life in the brothel—and by co-extension, on stage and screen and within the mechanisms of popular fantasy—seems to facilitate fluid subjectivities. It is in becoming a part of the mechanism that writes and re-creates popular fantasy, rather than simply living as its consumer or custodian, that self-transformation seems possible. Visually, this fluidity is apparent in that the narrative's only androgynous character, the "little queen," is only ever seen at the Horse and Rider (144–145). We watch as Esther, born into the world of the Gibson Girl, transitions through stage roles and whorehouse aliases as Aphrodite, Circe, Salome, and especially Delilah to emerge as a member of this pantheon in her own right: "It" girl and celebrity Esther Fine. From emulating fantasy, she becomes minimally different from fantasy in celebrity culture, secular contemporary America's nascent answer to pagan myth.

Esther's success is qualified, then, by her having been born into the context of a feminine ideal, that of the Gibson girl, whom Dana Mihăilescu (2015) describes as

> trying to make a passage from the Victorian Cult of True Womanhood … toward a New Woman look in which social outreach and a self-centered interest in forging a tempting, fashionable appearance became

equally important. In the early twentieth century this progressivist Gibson woman especially highlighted the importance of bodily forms and beauty as commodities, and forms of consumption underlying dignified American women.

This Gibson girl, "tall, with a clear and fearless gaze, her nose slightly uplifted, and a slim waist" (Mihăilescu 2015, 217) is a complicated body in Esther's world. Physically, she is distant from the stereotypical Jewish female body, and Esther's nose is, as Scherr notes, an irrefutable marker of Esther's difference from it. At the same time, this body is precisely the one to which we are introduced as part of Minna's storefront, as an ideal she sells even if she cannot emulate it herself. In a way, Esther, who immerses herself in the consumption of bodily forms, first with a crude literalness as a prostitute and then more in keeping with the Gibson girl ideal by replacing it as the ideal image to be emulated, has not traveled very far from where she began, other than to inhabit and transform a mythic narrative of womanhood into which she otherwise did not fit. Esther becomes an icon of a new feminine ideal at a transitional moment American popular history, emphasized in the full-page illustration of Esther as the twenties "It" girl in an advertisement (159), that mirrors and replaces that of the full-page Gibson girl advertising Mina's business (23) (Figures 7.7 and 7.8).

Perhaps it is true that "America clearly offers opportunities for success to those like Esther who can seize them" (Tabachnik 2014, 155), but what constitutes success, and at what cost, is an especially fraught and insoluble question in *Unterzakhn*. Esther's immersion in Romance comes with a price, one greater than the alteration of her Jewish name, as so many other Jews in the history of popular entertainment, including comics, have done. Esther's celebrity success requires a kind of absolute complicity with the systems of power into which she was born that, *within* the terms of these systems, is empowering. If the world regards a woman's body as capital—and after all, as a youth, Isaac does compare dating to horse trading (97) while the brothel, too, is called "Horse and Rider" (39)—then Esther takes to heart Lucille's remark that "a pretty girl is a very valuable thing" (65) and invests it. She makes her mother's words come true in a literal sense, making herself "Everybody's bizness." Hence, the disparity between the sisters: when Sal confesses love and steals a kiss from Fanya, she reacts with rage (75). But when Esther is raped in the brothel, her only response is to ask if her face—which is to say her market value—was bruised (72), while Lucille the madam merely regrets having lost the opportunity to sell Esther's virginity. By the end of her story, Esther has a powerful man who calls her empress literally under her heel (163). Whether, in the context of erotic play, such domination is meaningful is open to debate. Nevertheless, in the world of *Unterzakhn*, if one's body is capital, then one can be traded in an arranged marriage, invest oneself like Esther, or like Fanya try to keep oneself off the market altogether.

Figure 7.7 An image from *Unterzakhn* by Leela Corman, 2012.

After all, the equation of the body with capital is an open secret to Esther. If objects can be infused with romantic value, then, bearing in mind the braid Isaac cherishes, so too can the body be infused with capital value. Nowhere is this more explicit than in the body of the prostitute, obviously, but it is also apparent in the child's body as a source of labor and clearly in body of the Jew. From the very fact that the woman bleeding out on the street is named Mrs. Gold to the Cossack feeling Meyer's body in search of gold with his hand suggestively obscured by a speech balloon (100), the relationship of the Jewish body and capital is insistent, making plain once more, as with Meyer's abduction, the possibility of a bridge between it and constructions of the female body. The two are brought together most

Figure 7.8 An image from *Unterzakhn* by Leela Corman, 2012.

forcibly when Isaac overhears soldiers joking that, when they raped his sister, they "should have cut that redhead all the way open to find" some of the gold the "damned Jews must have swallowed" (88).

Esther's choice to invest (in) her body coincides with the dissolution of what remains of her family as her father and younger sister die and as her twin Fanya disowns her. It is a moment that marks her departure from her father's nineteenth century world of close family cohesion into American twentieth century marked by individualist competition. This individualism is underscored further, at this moment, by Esther's own induced miscarriage (134). Having disowned her sister, Fanya nevertheless helps Esther abort this last impending family tie, which demonstrates that Fanya is at least a somewhat "more egalitarian reformer" than Bronia (Mihăilescu 2015, 222), though I would argue she remains as inflexible as Bronia, merely depending on different constants. The miscarriage is a moment of ironic rebirth, as Esther rises from the deathbed of the maternal destiny she has been told to dread since childhood and begins her rise in popular culture, returning to prostitution with newly awakened ambition.

Referring to Esther, Corman herself observes that Esther "survives. Now the question is, is survival worth it?" (Corman 2015). In working within the rules of a game she cannot control, whether Esther's compromise is "worth it" is a tricky question, in that it is a question also modeled on exchange, and one that perhaps measures integrity according to the terms of the system in which virtually everyone in *Unterzakhn* has been set up to fail. The clearest demonstration of this rigged system comes in the form of the circulation of *pritze*, as a term. Time and again *Unterzakhn* shows us the way in which the prostitute, or pritze, is a social category that works as marriage's other, perhaps in support of its own Lacanian stain. That is, so long as one has prostitutes, one can pretend that marriage is for love and that, indeed, love exists. One could go so far as to say that prostitution functions, in some respects, as marriage's popular cultural alibi, or other. Prostitution is convenient in the same way that, as mentioned above, the individual racist can serve as a convenient alibi that elides systemic disenfranchisement. One might reasonably ask that if "the Sunday comics supplement [is indeed] 'an influence for repulsive and often depraving vulgarity'" whether such moral anxiety about them and other popular entertainments also places them as mechanisms for the concealment of other such stains.

Arranged marriages—love matches based on commerce—are always in *Unterzakhn*'s background. Fanya is unable to see marriage as anything other than a surrender of power and independence, and reasonably so, given the inequality seemingly built structurally into marriage in this story. This inequality is facilitated by the circulation of the term *pritze* or whore, against which it is impossible for any woman to defend herself: she cannot prove that she is unblemished. It is a test one can only fail, a term circulated through the same informal channels of gossip that whisper about Minna's licentiousness behind her back (80) and that speak admiringly about Esther-the-ex-prostitute's celebrity. In the tradition of Eve Sedgwick's work on the terroristic structure of homophobia (1985, 88–89), one literally cannot *not* be a *pritze* if the community decides one is—behavior having nothing to do with it—and it is the very ambiguity of that ever-present threat that gives the aspersion its power to format subjectivity and social relations. Even

Bronia invokes the threat of the term as leverage to persuade Minna to allow her to teach Fanya to read. Regardless of whether she knows about Minna's extramarital liaisons, her claim that Minna is incapable of teaching Fanya to be a "decent lady" may have contributed to Minna's acquiescence, her silent reflection before doing so leaving open the possibility that she is weighing the consequences of public exposure. The threat of accusation forms a part of the matrix of conversations in which it may not even be an explicit part.

The term's primary purpose is the reproduction of social control. The promotional material that complemented the publication of *Unterzakhn* makes this purpose plain. The Pantheon Books "Yiddish Word of the Day" series includes a definition penned by Corman's editor:

> Pritze (**pritz**'eh): Whore.
>
> Or any young woman who lingered too long on the tenement stoop with her date for the evening, in full view of all the busybodies hanging out of the windows eagerly searching for any such couple,

a definition Corman calls better than anything she herself could have written (2012a). Call the availability of the term an example of price fixing in the trade of women, turning every marriage into the rescue of a fallen woman: Isaac's of Minna, Joe-the-john's attempted rescue of Esther whom he calls "not just another whore" (129), and Sal's attempted rescue of Fanya, who should consider herself lucky someone wants her, he says (142). Against this backdrop, Esther's repeated stage roles as harem girls and, tellingly, the lead in a play called *Hostage of Presumption* (160) is apt. After all, women in particular in *Unterzakhn* are hostages of presumption with respect to the price of their marriageability. In other words, popular culture and celebrity culture are charged with the task of insisting on a difference between marriage and prostitution or captivity, a difference that, in *Unterzakhn*, is minimal at best. How much of Esther's success is the result of her canny agency, and how much the blind luck of holding an Adorno-esque winning lottery ticket in a culture industry looking for its next big alibi is an open question. If Esther ends the narrative by announcing Fanya's death, ironically, with the words "Fanya doesn't live here anymore" (200), then it is also possible that Fanya's use of the exact same words to describe Esther (160) might, retroactively, be read to suggest that in a certain sense Esther, too, is no longer exactly alive.

There are no loving marriages in *Unterzakhn*. With the possible exception of the relationship between the sisters, and especially as Esther takes in Fanya and ultimately Fanya's newborn, it is difficult to see any sign of love at all. Both Isaac and Esther are tricked into believing a Romantic fantasy of running off with their lover, and both are stood up (116, 130). Their disappointment reinforces the sense that theirs is a world devoid of miraculous rescue, governed exclusively and coldly by relations of power and exchange. After this disappointment, Isaac marries Minna, exchanging free passage to America for taking yet another "pritze" off a respectable family's hands (117). Joe stands Esther up, and Esther's expression, hand to forehead, is of a woman who knows she has been a fool (132). But at a moment that coincides with Minna's death (149), Esther—to her immense gratitude—is literally purchased from the brothel. As crass as the moment is, it is reliable. In this world of manufactured fairies contriving to be ever "dreamier" for the audience, it offers some relief from Romance and is the closest one gets to authenticity. This fact is underscored in that, while Joe only ever knew her as Delilah, Esther tells Meyer her real name upon her purchase. On one hand, we are left asking just how different this openly commercial transaction is from everyday life, when love seems only to exist in the popular cultural fantasy Esther sells, as something to be longed for, but not actually realized. On the other hand, the fact that her purchaser is Meyer Birnbaum complicates matters, causing the narrative to prevent this moment from being a full rejection of Romance.

Unterzakhn seems to maintain that popular culture formats its uncritical consumers but can also open new possibilities for the active rewriting of identity, albeit in limited and compromised ways. In the process, it can create new, newly functional, provisional families in place of ones that seem unworkable and that we see dissolved in this new world. Our story ends with Esther having cared for her surrogate mother, the madam Lucille; holding her dead sister's baby; facing the child's father who may or may not know the child is his; and maintaining a close relationship with theater agent who purchased her. The agent is a kind of surrogate father but in more ways than one. Unbeknownst to everyone in the narrative, he is Meyer Birnbaum, Isaac's friend from Russia, who was carried off naked long ago, himself repeatedly dismissed, in that part of the story, over his own penchant for melodramatic Romance in a world of hardscrabble survival. While Isaac used Romance to cover over the past, Meyer—like Esther—produces and transforms it. He emerges from that past with all the dramatic irony of being intimately related to Esther's past, while they meet as strangers through wild chance: the very stuff of Romance. It is the kind of fairy tale our characters would know better than to believe they were in anyway. And yet, all this time, Meyer and Esther have survived, and even risen to power, by entertaining their various captors with silly songs and stories, like the kind one might find in vaudeville, or the movies, or the funny pages.

Note

1 All subsequent references to *Unterzakhn* are to this edition, with page numbers cited parenthetically in the text.

References

Ahmed, Sara. 2012. *On Being Included: Racism and Diversity in Institutional Life*. Durham: Duke University Press.

American Social History Project. 2000. *Who Built America? Working People and the Nation's Economy, Politics, Culture, and Society* Vol. 2, *1877 to the Present*. Boston: Bedford/St. Martin's.

Bakhtin, M.M. 1981. *The Dialogic Imagination*. Edited by Michael Holquist. Translated by Caryl Emerson and Michael Holquist. Austin: University of Texas Press.

Bonitzer, Pascal. 1992. "Hitchcockian Suspense." In Žižek, *Everything You Always Wanted to Know*, 15–30.

Clowes, Daniel. 1998. *Ghost World*. Seattle: Fantagraphic Books.

Corman, Leela. 2012a. "Leela Corman Talks about her 'Unterzakhn'." Interview by Alex Dueben. *CBR.com*, 24 April. www.cbr.com/leela-corman-talks-about-her-unterzakhn/.

Corman, Leela. 2012b. *Unterzakhn*. New York: Schocken Books.

Corman, Leela. 2015. "*Unterzakhn*, Dirty Laundry, and the Map of Lost New York: An Interview with Leela Corman." Interview by Jaime Cleland. *European Journal of American Studies* 10 (2). doi:10.4000/ejas.10879.

Corman, Leela. 2016a. "The Book of the Dead." In Corman, *We All Wish*.

Corman, Leela. 2016b. "Irreducibles." In Corman, *We All Wish*, np.

Corman, Leela. 2016c. *We All Wish for Deadly Force*. Washington DC: Retrofit and Big Planet Comics.

Corman, Leela. 2016d. "The Wound that Never Heals." In Corman, *We All Wish*.

Corman, Leela, and Luna of Cairo. 2016 "Luna of Cairo." In Corman, *We All Wish*.

Earle, Harriet E. 2017. *Comics, Trauma, and the new Art of War*. Jackson: University Press of Mississippi.

Fiske, John. 1993. *Power Plays, Power Works*. New York: Verso.

Frye, Northrop. 1957. *Anatomy of Criticism*. Princeton: Princeton University Press.

Gilfoyle, Timothy J. 1992. *City of Eros: New York City, Prostitution, and the Commercialization of Sex, 1790-1920*. New York: WW Norton and Company.

Glasner, Lily. 2015. "Embracing Childish Perspective: Rutu Modan's *A Royal Banquet with the Queen*." In *Representing Multiculturalism in Comics and Graphic Novels*, edited by Ian Hague and Carolene Ayaka, 177–93. London: Routledge.

Johnson, R. Kikuo. 2005. *Night Fisher*. Seattle: Fantagraphic Books.

Lambert, Josh. 2008. "'Wanna watch the grown-ups doin' *dirty* things?': Jewish Sexuality and the Early Graphic Novel." In *The Jewish Graphic Novel*, edited by Samantha Baskind and Ranen Omer-Sherman, 43–63. New Brunswick: Rutgers University Press.

Maude, Ulrika. 2004. "American Romance." In *A Companion to Romance from Classical to Contemporary*, edited by Corinne Saunders, 424–37. Hoboken: Blackwell Publishing.

McKeon, Michael. 1987. *The Origins of the English Novel 1600-1740*. Baltimore: Johns Hopkins University Press.

Mihăilescu, Dana. 2015. "The Lower East Side as Mishmash of Jewish Women's Multicultural Images in Leela Corman's *Unterzakhn*." In *Representing Multiculturalism in Comics and Graphic Novels*, edited by Ian Hague and Carolene Ayaka, 212–27. London: Routledge.

Oksman, Tahneer. 2016. "'Not a Word for Little Girls!': Knowledge, Word, and Image in Leela Corman's *Unterzakhn*." In *Visualizing Jewish Narrative: Jewish Comics and Graphic Novels*, edited by Derek Parker Royal, 29–39. London: Bloomsbury Academic.

Outcault, R.F. 1896. "Li Hung Chang Visits Hogan's Alley." *New York World*, September 6. *The Yellow Kid*. San Francisco Academy of Comic Art Collection, Ohio State University Cartoon Research Library. cartoons.osu.edu/digital_albums/yellowkid/index.htm.

Pantheon Books. "Pritze." March 29, 2012. pantheonbooks.tumblr.com/post/20121096012/unterzakhn-yiddish-pritze.

Powell, Nate. 2011. *Any Empire*. Marietta: Top Shelf.

Ross, Deborah. 1991. *The Excellence of Falsehood: Romance, Realism, and Women's Contribution to the Novel*. Lexington: University Press of Kentucky.

Salecl, Renata. 1992. "The Right Man and the Wrong Woman." In Žižek, *Everything You Always Wanted to Know*, 185–94.

Scherr, Rebecca. 2015. "Bleeding through, drawing out: The circumscribing of Jewish women's bodies in Leela Corman's *Unterzakhn*." *Studies in Comics* 6 (2): 213–29. doi:10.1386/stic.6.2.213_1

Sedgwick, Eve Kosofsky. 1985. *Between Men: English Literature and Male Homosocial Desire*. New York: Columbia University Press.

Tabachnik, Stephen. 2014. *The Quest for Jewish Belief and Identity in the Graphic Novel*. Tuscaloosa: University of Alabama Press.

Valent, Cosmina-Iulia. 2015. "Representations of Immigrant Life on New York's Lower East Side in Leela Corman's *Unterzakhn*." *[Inter]sections* 18: 45–56. www.intersections-journal.com/wp-content/uploads/2016/03/Valent-Cosmina-article-1.pdf.

Williams, Anne. 1995. *Art of Darkness: A Poetics of Gothic*. Chicago: University of Chicago Press.

Witek, Joseph. 2012. "Comics Modes: Caricature and Illustration in the Crumb Family's *Dirty Laundry*." In *Critical Approaches to Comics: Theories and Methods*, edited by Matthew J. Smith and Randy Duncan, 27–42. London: Routledge.

Žižek, Slavoj, ed. 1992. *Everything You Always Wanted to Know about Lacan (But Were Afraid to Ask Hitchcock)*. New York: Verso.

Žižek, Slavoj. 1992. "'In His Bold Gaze My Ruin Is Writ Large'." In Žižek, *Everything You Always Wanted to Know*, 211–72.

Index